Juggling

JUGGLING

◆

*The Unexpected Advantages
of Balancing Career and Home for
Women and Their Families*

◆

Faye J. Crosby

THE FREE PRESS
A Division of Macmillan, Inc.
NEW YORK

Maxwell Macmillan Canada
TORONTO

Maxwell Macmillan International
NEW YORK   OXFORD   SINGAPORE   SYDNEY

The Free Press
A Division of Macmillan, Inc.
866 Third Avenue, New York, N.Y. 10022

Maxwell Macmillan Canada, Inc.
1200 Eglinton Avenue East
Suite 200
Don Mills, Ontario M3C 3N1

Macmillan, Inc. is part of the Maxwell Communication
Group of Companies.

Printed in the United States of America

printing number
1   2   3   4   5   6   7   8   9   10

Library of Congress Cataloging-in-Publication Data

Crosby, Faye J.
    Juggling: the unexpected advantages of balancing career and home
for women and their families / Faye J. Crosby.
        p.   cm.
    Includes bibliographical references and index.
    ISBN 0-02-906705-7
    1. Working mothers—United States.   2. Work and family—United
States.   3. Sex role—United States.   4. Sex discrimination in
employment—United States.   I. Title.
HQ759.48.C76   1991
306.87—dc20   91-19534
                                                          CIP

To my students, past and present,
with love and gratitude for all that they have taught me.

✦ CONTENTS ✦

✦ ACKNOWLEDGMENTS ✦

Here is the beginning, written at the end. As I plonk out the words on my word processor, I think myself the luckiest woman alive. I feel fortunate, in the first instance, for the many friends who have helped me with the manuscript. I list below in alphabetical order people to whom I owe a special debt of gratitude. Each knows what she or he has done to help the project and each has given me more help than I would have thought possible.

Lea Ayers
Rosalind Barnett
Kathy Bartus
Linda Batchelor
Angela Brega
Eric Brewer
Jaqueline Magnant Brugin
Devika Choudhuri
Travis Crosby
Sidonia Dalby
Julie Dennis
Francine Deutsch
Karen Dwyer
Alice Eagly
Mary Faucette
Edith Flagg
Sue Fournier
Lisa Fox
Gail Fries
Ellen Galinsky

Barbara Gutek
Helen Horowitz
Heide Lange
Bergen Langlois
Marilyn Machlowitz
Maureen Mahoney
Kathy McCartney
Susan Milmoe
Susan Nolen-Hoeksema
Joseph Pleck
Harry Reis
Rena Repetti
Jill St. Coeur
Jill Saltzman
Christina Smith
Lisa Silberstein
Janice Steil
Roberta Sigel
Abby Stewart
Bonnie Strickland

Carol Tavris   Judy Worell
Gladys Topkis   Camille Wortman
Emily Weir   Clare Wulker
Robert Weiss   Sue Yi

Smith College also deserves my thanks. The institution, through its Committee on Faculty Compensation and Development, has supported the research and writing in a generous fashion.

I think myself fortunate, furthermore, for having the kind of life—the juggling life—that has enabled me to keep at the project for more years than I would like to admit. The creation of this book has involved some heartache—times when there was no progress, when discouragements followed each other in rapid succession, when rejection seemed the operative word of the day. Alongside the negative moments, there has been much joy and laughter. Certainly, there has been struggle and growth. If I had not had friends and a family—my Tim, Matt, and Travis as well as Andree, Bob, Jim, Carole, Tom, David, and Abbie—I might not have kept plugging away during the bad moments. And if I had not had my other work, the teaching and the more technically oriented research, this work might have overwhelmed me. But there was balance in my life, and for this I am grateful.

It is my hope that the reader of this book will benefit from it even a fraction as much as the writer has.

NOTE TO THE
READER

◆   ◆

The conclusions I reach in this book are based on empirical findings. Thousands of women and men have participated in numerous surveys, conducted mostly by social and behavioral scientists other than myself. My task has been to synthesize what is now a voluminous research literature.

The published studies do not address all the pertinent issues. To supplement them, I interviewed approximately 50 people especially for this book. The interviews varied—many were brief; some lasted four or five hours. Most were tape recorded and analyzed numerous times, as I went over and over them listening for patterns.

I have changed the names of those quoted or described. Usually, to preserve anonymity, I have also changed identifying details—for example, making a lawyer into a doctor or the mother of two boys into the mother of two girls. Whenever possible, I have checked all quotations with my interview participants. Everyone who participated in my study of juggling deserves a hearty thank you.

· 1 ·

The Issues and the Metaphors

We three arrive as the lunch crowd has begun to drift contentedly away from China Gardens. A thin young man seats us and hovers around until we order. Then comes the long wait for food. Never mind. We have our beers and our high spirits. The school term is ending for us before it ends for our assorted children, and we three women—two research assistants and I—are free of family and work responsibilities for the next hour and a half. We have just discovered our common liberation by accident and have decided to celebrate by eating lunch. Eating lunch is not something that any of us does every day, and eating lunch at a downtown restaurant is something we do only at times of celebration or sorrow.

The food arrives, and conversation slows. Anne and Naomi use chopsticks—pince, pince, pause; pince, pince—while I resort to my fork. Still, a slippery noodle constitutes no mean challenge, even with a fork. So focused am I on the mission of transporting sesame noodles to my mouth without spattering my dress that it takes me more than a minute to notice that Naomi has stopped eating and started crying.

What had happened? Naomi, Anne, and I had all been so light-hearted only a moment ago. Besides, Naomi is a scrapper. If year-books had a category, "Least Likely to Cry in Chinese Restaurant,"

Naomi would have been the titleholder. Hers has not been an easy life, but she seems equal to any challenge. The woman has spunk; she has vitality; and she has a sense of humor like Lily Tomlin's.

A few years ago Naomi sold her house; left an abusive marriage; moved herself, her toddler, and her infant from one state to another; and resumed her education. Her college called her a mature student. Along with other mature students Naomi worked hard to make a life for herself and her children. She graduated with honors. And now it seems as if the struggles are over, and the good life has begun. Naomi's job doesn't pay very well, but it offers good hours, good company, and lots of intellectual stimulation. Her second grader, Ian, is doing well in school, and Jesse, the little one, loves preschool. She has been seeing a man named Jim Day. Naomi and Jim have begun to consider marriage.

"Naomi." Anne puts down her chopsticks and speaks gently. "Naomi, are you okay?"

"I'm sorry, you guys. Geeze. You can't take me anywhere. Here we go out to celebrate, and I start sniffling." Naomi breathes in little hiccups of air between her words. "But I'm exhausted and I just can't keep it all going."

"You don't have to keep it *all* going," I say. "The term's over, remember? That's why we're celebrating."

"Our terms are over," explains Anne. "But Naomi's isn't. She let the project slide, and she now has two weeks to code and compile everything. I mean, it's really a lot of work. Mega amounts."

As she resumes eating, Naomi paints for us the picture of herself as a juggler. Like a circus performer, she keeps everything in motion. But it is life's responsibilities, not Indian clubs, that she maneuvers. Up goes each responsibility. Up goes Ian, the seven year old. While Ian is flying through the air, launch Jesse into preschool. Rush, pant, catch. Catch Ian. Catch Jesse. What about work? Launch a research project. Oops. Here comes Ian. Toss the project a little higher. Quick, catch Jesse before he crashes. Phew. Close call. Get Jesse. Oh, the boss needs some data analyzed. Up. Up you go again, kids. Up you go to school. Damn! The computer center is closing for repairs. And—oh, drat— the muffler just blew. Quick, toss in a little moonlighting on the side to pay for the car.

I can see it. Can you? I can see Naomi heaving each responsibility in the air, again and again. There's a sense of excitement and fun, but as the force of her movements increases, the act takes on a frenetic quality. The more vigorous the toss, the longer things stay aloft. But vigor buys only a little time; the harder the toss, the less control she has. In my mind's eye, it is only a matter of minutes until Naomi is running wildly about, more and more frantic, more and more exhausted, covering greater distances as everything begins to tumble and threatens to crash all at once.

Naomi cries because she, too, imagines this and more. She visualizes the imminent heap—Ian, Jesse, the mufflerless car, the data sheets, the women friends, Jim—all parts of the new life she has created. And who is at fault when the juggling act leads to such disaster? Who is to blame? The culprit, she thinks, is surely the person who let things slip; the person who lost control; the person who lost her balance—the juggler.

"What's wrong with me?" asks Naomi. "Why can't I do it all? Why can't I juggle? Others seem to manage. Why can't I?"

Lives Without Margins

Naomi is not unique. At every turn women seem to be asking why they find it so difficult to combine the different aspects of their lives. The insecurity of jugglers has become increasingly noticeable to me over the last few years as I have read volumes of research on gender and role combination, introspected about my own juggling life, spoken with hundreds of women about their lives and their life-styles, and formally interviewed dozens more.

Always for the juggler, there is a curious mix of emotions. Interwoven with her *joie de vivre* and her well-deserved pride in her accomplishments are her feelings of guilt and self-doubt. Most jugglers feel happy and fulfilled by their busy, active, and varied lives; at the same time they are overwhelmed. Mixed in with the exhilaration is the fear of proving unequal to life's tasks.

"Our time," comments Yale University psychologist William Kessen, "is one in which we all lead lives without margins." There are no margins, no room for mistakes. The tight schedules, the detailed plans, the carefully organized sequence of opportunities and obligations do not easily accommodate modifications, revision, or corrections. The excitement is palpable, but the stress can be enormous.

While it is totally contemporary, Naomi's plight—the plight of the juggler with no time for rehearsals, the plight of the person who lives life without margins—is not new. Outside of paradise, people have always had to work to subsist. To provide for themselves and their families, able-bodied adults need time and energy. The dependent young (and the dependent old) also require their attention. The demands of nurturing and maintaining one's family necessarily place restrictions on the time and energy available for work. The basic conflict between work and nurturing is not a recent one.

The conflict between productive work and nurturing has taken different forms for women and men over the centuries. In colonial America, fathers were thought to have much more responsibility for, and influence on, their children than were mothers. Guidelines for parenting were directed toward fathers, while the responsibilities of mothers were rarely mentioned.[1]

While fathers have sometimes had executive responsibility for children, mothers have always managed the day-to-day tasks. Even in colonial America, men were not biologically equipped to carry within their bodies the unborn or to suckle the very young. Partially because they cannot breast-feed, grown men have played a much smaller role in the care of infants and children than have grown women. The care and feeding of children has interfered relatively little with men's productive labor, but women—to paraphrase sociologist Cynthia Fuchs Epstein—have always raised the children as well as the chickens.[2]

Chickens can be raised at home—right alongside the children. Prior to the industrial revolution, much productive work took place within the family setting. Before there were factories and offices, many women could engage in the production of goods and services and still be accessible to their children.

Then came the industrial revolution, and many women (and, of course, many men) went to work outside the home. To survive and to help their families survive, many women had to work at some distance from their children. During and after the industrial revolution, no doubt it was primarily the poor and destitute women who were removed from and unavailable to their children. The factory poor of yesteryear did not have a choice.

Today many women have choices. Working-class women are better off now than 100 years ago. Contemporary middle-class and especially professional women have even more options. To be sure, the options are not unlimited; many women are economically able to decrease or forgo paid labor entirely while their children are young. Precise figures would be hard to calculate, but we can safely estimate that at least one-third of the women who currently juggle career and family do not see themselves as working because of finances.[3]

Women and men also have new options about the size and form of their families. Only in the twentieth century have recreational and procreational sex become separable for the majority of people. Women have more control than ever before about whether and when to have children.

Current realities have, thus, changed some timeless questions. How to provide for everyone's material and emotional needs is not a new question. The late twentieth century is not the first time in history that women and men must ask how to combine private, domestic responsibilities with public responsibilities. Every generation has had to grapple with the issues of work and love. Now, as more and more women of childbearing and child rearing ages are employed outside the home, more and more families find themselves facing new challenges.

The challenges that confront families are seen and felt as special challenges for women. Some women wonder whether they ought to decrease their commitment to paid jobs. For others—especially, it seems, for young women who are currently graduating from high school or college or starting their careers—the question is reversed. Bright-eyed young women today seem to be asking themselves if they should jeopardize their careers by having family lives.[4]

Predictably, given that the issues are both timely and enduring, questions about how women are to be engaged in productive labor outside the family while nurturing those within it command attention. The inaugural issue of the feminist *Ms. Magazine* in 1972 depicted a woman with eight arms juggling all her responsibilities. Since then stories about jugglers have appeared regularly in newspapers and magazines and on radio and television. When a catchy phrase such as *the mommy track* is used at a professional meeting, the general media give it instant and wide currency.[5] Such metaphors influence the way we conceive the problems.

Juggling—while hardly ever labeled as such—has also held a fascination for scholars. Over the last few decades, increasing numbers of social scientists have been conducting systematic investigations of the pressures and pleasures of the different manners in which women and men love and work. By and large, they use the vocabulary and assume the basic concepts of role theory. To play a life role, say the theorists, means more than simply performing unrelated actions. When a person enacts a given role, he or she typically performs an identifiable set of actions with a distinct cast of characters. Different life roles require, at a minimum, a change of script. They often also involve a change of scenery and wholly or partially new casts of characters. And they always involve expectations, about others and about the self as well.[6]

Consider Naomi. Her life roles include mother, friend, daughter, fiancée, worker, community activist, and ex-wife as well as paid employee. The cast of characters in Naomi's world when she is in her mother role overlaps considerably with those in some, but not all, of her other roles. Naomi's mother helps out with the children as do her friends and, on occasion, her coworkers. Jim and his family are increasingly involved in raising Naomi's children.

The cast of characters in Naomi's professional world, when she is in her role as research assistant, does not generally overlap much with people from other parts of Naomi's life. Some coworkers know her friend Jim; but although pleasant, the interactions tend to occur in a rather limited and predictable way—as, for example, at the annual office picnic. The people with whom Naomi works do not typically know her as a mother; but here, too, some exceptions occur. Naomi's boss, for example, is a woman named Gertrude. Gertrude's younger child is a friend of Naomi's son Ian. When Naomi interacts with Gertrude at work, only some topics are typically discussed. Other topics are reserved for interactions outside the office.

It is not simply a matter of topics. The structure of interactions also influences role behavior. For example: Gertrude (in the role of supervisor) is more likely to interrupt Naomi (in the role of subordinate) than vice versa. When Naomi and Gertrude interact as mothers, however, they are social equals. Both the topics and the unstated rules of conversation change.

A large number of significant life roles have become available to many contemporary American women. They commonly include, but are not limited to, all those described for Naomi; the roles of granddaughter, niece, sister, cousin, aunt, grandmother, wife, widow, and employer are other possibilities. Every role involves role partners. Every change in role partners entails a change in rules of interaction.

The need to interact differently with the same person as roles change is one of the challenges of combining different life roles. It is a relatively gentle challenge. Much more difficult are the challenges of limited time and energy. For many women, it is hard to find the resources to meet all the demands of any one role, and it is very hard to find the resources to meet the demands of many roles. Even when the roles do not make mutually exclusive demands on a person, the sheer addition of task on task can make a woman doubt her ability to do all she wants or all she feels she needs to do.

Risks and Doubts

Juggling is a special form of role combination. As the metaphor implies, juggling entails risks. Objects have weights and sizes of their own, and the juggler must contend with these and with the forces of gravity. Time is of the essence. A responsibility that is not caught in time can end in trouble, suddenly and dramatically.

The risks of juggling are one reason why the process holds the attention of onlookers. When the stakes are high, we watch any dangerous enterprise with almost horrified fascination. The higher the stakes, the greater the dramatic suspense. And what stakes could be higher than the long-term mental and physical health of our children?

Mothers of young children who work outside the home, for example, often express concern over their inability to respond easily and quickly to unexpected illnesses in the family. The evidence is concrete. One survey conducted in 1984 by John Fernandez, for instance, polled 1,200 women at five large, technically oriented companies. Over three-quarters of the female managers with very young children at home had missed at least one day of work during the previous year due to the illness of a child; presumably many women had missed much more than one day of work. Sixty-two percent of the female managers with preschool children and 20 percent of the women with children aged fifteen to eighteen said that caring for a sick child was a problem. Many women felt concerned about the relative inflexibility of their work schedules. Indeed, over half of the women with children aged two or under claimed that they would leave their current job for one with better child care benefits.[7]

While the image of a routine emergency such as chicken pox can make almost any working mother anticipate guilty feelings, more diffuse fears plague quite a number of jugglers. Many mothers worry that any interruption in giving full attention to their young children could result in harm to the children, either now or in the years to come. The fears, apparent to me in the women whom I have known, have now been documented by a number of researchers. Lisa Silberstein, a psychologist at Yale University, interviewed both halves of twenty dual-career couples. One businesswoman in her early forties captured the sense of many mothers:

> The children will probably be at college before I feel comfortable being out of the house all day Monday to Friday. If I could find a job that was

rewarding both vocationally and financially and had a wonderful career path that would go 9 A.M. to 3 in the afternoon—well, there would probably be a zillion other women ahead of me. I don't think I'll ever resolve what must be inborn guilt to be there and be here, too.[8]

Similar sentiments were voiced to Kathleen McCartney and Deborah Phillips, two developmental psychologists. They have conducted a series of case studies of women who combine paid work and new motherhood. "Most women," say McCartney and Phillips, "fear the unknown consequences" of early child care outside the home.

McCartney and Phillips go on to describe Doreen, "a thirty-year-old speech and language pathologist who admits that her concern drove her to read everything she could get her hands on about child care and its effects. Her son, Patrick, just celebrated his first birthday. Doreen started working a couple of days a week when he was two months old and yet recalls:

> When people would inquire whether I was working or not, I would reply: 'No, I stay home with my baby.' I wonder why I said that when in fact I was working . . . I still keep wondering about when he is 16—if there is some sort of incident that will emerge during a more stressful time in our relationship. Intellectually, I say probably not. On the other hand, I really sort of do believe that deep down it might."[9]

Since the dawn of parenthood, mothers and fathers have surely worried about how to do the best by their children. While the concern is ancient, the worry of Doreen and other working parents today takes a new form. Doreen cannot rid herself of guilt. Like Naomi, and like many other women, Doreen blames herself when difficulties arise. She mistrusts the good times, fearing that they might be only temporary. She stands ready to blame herself for the bad times, today or in the future.

The central importance of good child care arrangements for the peace of mind of jugglers is well known to every working mother. It has also been demonstrated in a small study of female graduates of a midwestern college. Among the sample were 45 women who employed other people to take care of their children while they worked. The researchers asked the women about role strain and about coping mechanisms. The data from the questionnaire clearly revealed that adequate child care was the single factor most relieving of role strain. Feelings about their child care arrangements affected perceived role strain in the women more than did their husbands' attitudes, their husbands' incomes, marital satisfaction, feelings of accomplishment, personal health, the number of children in the household, the age of the children, or a host of other variables.[10]

We want to do right by our children and other people in our lives, but we are not always certain about the proper course of action. Given the rapid change in sex roles, many women and men today find themselves confronted with situations for which they are ill prepared or about which they worry. Ironically, our mothers and grandmothers with their circumscribed lives may have felt more certain of themselves than we do. Contemporary jugglers often question whether they are doing what they ought and whether they are doing as well as they ought.

"I don't know how well I'm doing," confesses a young architect with a newborn baby. "I'm trying to juggle it all. But I doubt my capabilities."

"Some days I feel pretty good, you know, about having the kids and a job," says a mother of two teenagers who works part time as a set designer, "but other days I'm just overwhelmed."

Observes another woman, Marion: "A lot of people are convinced that it's the kids who get harmed when the mother works. And sometimes I think those people are right." When asked if her own commitment to a career has harmed her children, this mother, personnel manager, and feminist laughs and says that her own children have been glad to have her out of the house. "But," she admits, "I wonder. I really do."

"Oh me?" mumbles artist and family woman, Jane, as I interview her on the subject of juggling. "I don't think it's my upbringing that makes me feel so small and uncertain. I believe it is just in the genes. When I think about career women with children, women in demand with their calendars all filled up, I think of myself as inadequate. [There's] this thing about self-esteem."

This Book

This book is first and foremost for any woman who has felt the curious mix of self-doubt and exhilaration as she tries to combine life outside the house with love inside the home. It is for the juggler who collapses into bed at the end of the day happy and exhausted—or just exhausted—and wonders why her "to do" list is no shorter than it was when she had arisen in the morning. It is for the woman, not in poverty's grasp, who recognizes her options and privileges and who has as a consequence been tempted in the fashion of Naomi to blame herself for not juggling better.

The book is also for anyone—juggler or not—who wishes to find out about current research on gender, health, and the combination of various life roles. It is for the person who suspects that women, men, and children might all benefit from changes in society that would make it easier for able-bodied adults simultaneously to care for dependent others and to provide for them. It speaks to those who think that surely juggling could be made easier and no less satisfying.

Guidelines, Not Formulae

The book offers little by way of concrete advice or generic formulae for happiness. Those who want ten easy steps to stress-free juggling will find it disappointing. I believe that lives are complex and varied and that information, analyses, and even speculation better serve readers than a one-size-fits-all set of specific recommendations. I suggest no rules about the month and day that an infant can best tolerate her mother's return to work outside the home, about the most effective way to manage a boss who thinks that a mother ought to be home with her children (or ought to be on the job seventy hours a week), about how a woman can schedule sex with her husband, or about a number of other very real but very specific life problems.

The book does, however, articulate a general three-part prescription, which derives from systematic and thoughtful observation and especially from the findings of social and behavioral scientists. It is new. It may surprise jugglers. It may also help them.

The first part is this: Jugglers should not blame themselves when they experience difficulty combining work outside the home with family responsibilities. The problems they experience are not the result of personal inadequacies. If the difficulties of role combination came from personal inadequacies within individual jugglers, most women would find it simple to combine paid employment with the care and tending of a family. In fact, even as they enjoy the process and reap the benefits of role combination, most women admit the stress and arduousness of the effort. The prevalence of role strain leads almost inescapably to the conclusion: the problem lies not in the juggler but rather in the situation.

Does the difficulty of juggling mean that effort ought to be abandoned? Numerous commentators and columnists advise women to simplify life, to eliminate excess responsibilities, to prioritize goals. Mothers who do not need to work for pay have been told directly or indirectly to keep themselves and their families healthy by remaining out of the work force. Mothers who do need the income have been counseled to stop trying to be superwomen.[11]

The advice to cut back, to scale down, or to give up the hope of combining productive labor with family work is neither useful nor appropriate for many women. For women who have the financial option to forgo paid labor, the advice contributes to a sense of guilt or maternal irresponsibility. For most women, the option to stay out of the labor force occurs only if they are willing to make sacrifices in their standard of living. For some women, there is no option: The sacrifices may concern the essentials as well as the luxuries. Given the cost of living today, a family of four with one income provider earning the minimum wage is currently $2,000 under the poverty line established by the federal government. When the husband in a family with two children earns a low income, the wife's employment is a necessity, not a luxury. And when the family includes no husband, the need for women to participate in the paid labor force is even greater. Between 1979 and 1984, the number of female-headed families in America grew from 5.5 million to 9.9 million. To advise less labor force participation on the part of the mother in these nearly 10 million families is patently ridiculous.[12] Even for those who have more options in life than do women living at the poverty line, the days when women could rise above financial concerns have become quaint memories.

The second part of the prescription, then, is that jugglers should not let the stresses of juggling deflect them from combining different life roles. The woman who tries to minimize the stresses of juggling by eliminating significant roles or by reducing her commitments is chasing an illusion. Women today have a hard time juggling not simply because of the strains of playing multiple roles; women also have difficulty juggling because there are still great barriers in the path of a woman who wants to play any important adult role in this society—even if she plays it in isolation and to the exclusion of other roles. Sexism has cast a long shadow. So too has the American ethos of individualism. The next chapters describe how society makes life unnecessarily depressing and stressful for wives and mothers, no matter what their participation in the paid labor force, and unjustifiably difficult for employed women, no matter what their domestic situations. Because stresses exist as potently for women *within* each role as be-

tween roles, the hope of escaping harm by restricting one's involvement either to the labor market or to the family is misguided.

Nor would a woman benefit her family by decreasing her role commitments. Women are accustomed to making sacrifices for the sake of
other people. As John Fernandez's study (see note 7) illustrates, many
mothers would gladly make adjustments in their careers if they believed that the adjustments would benefit their children. With our
heritage of sexist thinking, it is easy to imagine that children suffer
from maternal employment. Only a short leap of logic is then required
to conclude that children are nurtured and aided by keeping mothers
out of the work force. In fact, accumulated data now show that forcing a woman to stay at home when she does not wish to be there does
little to foster growth in children. Children need happy mothers, not
captive mothers. Under the right circumstances, children of jugglers
can thrive.

To say that children can thrive is, of course, not the same as saying
that they do thrive. A world of possibilities often separates what can
be from what is. We could make life easier and better for our children,
our spouses, our colleagues, and employers, and even ourselves if we
changed some of the structural conditions that now make it difficult to
combine family life and work outside the home.

Thus, we come to the third part of the prescription: Given the
mismatch between contemporary social conditions and human needs,
jugglers might reflect on ways to change the conditions before they
think about ways to change themselves, to rid themselves of their
needs. Before concluding that the attempt to combine paid labor and
family life is too arduous or risky, women should entertain strategies
to make the attempt less arduous and less risky.

The necessary changes are not easily effected. They take time. Many
depend on the cooperation of colleagues and friends. Some require
collective action or modifications in policy by organizations over
which women have little control. Take, for example, corporate child
care policies. A survey by the Bureau of National Affairs showed that
in 1984 only one-third of the nongovernmental employees with fifty
or more employees used flextime. Yet flexible working hours can help
to ease the strain on working parents.[13] Similarly, employed mothers
and fathers express happiness with companies that offer corporate
child-care programs, whether through on-site care, reimbursement
schemes, or even informational programs. Yet, the number of organizations that offer corporate child care is tiny. An early survey of
Fortune 1,300 corporations, conducted by the advocacy organization
Catalyst, showed that only one-fourth of the executives favored such

policies and only 1 percent of the organizations provided on-site care.[14] More recently, despite the general willingness of small businesses to accommodate the family responsibilities of their employees, delegates to a White House Conference on Small Business overwhelmingly opposed government-mandated employee benefits such as parental leave.[15]

Even harder to budge than corporations has been government. The United States is surprisingly backward in developing parental leave policies. As recently as the summer of 1990, the House of Representatives sustained President George Bush's veto of the Family and Medical Leave Act, a bill that would have required employers to grant workers time off without pay for births, adoptions, or emergencies in the family. Many people know that Sweden anchors the opposite end of the continuum. There, both men and women are allowed nine months of parental leave at 90 percent of their earnings and an additional nine months at reduced pay. Sweden is not the only country to regulate parental leave. Every industrial country in the world, save the United States, legally provides for parental leave from employment. According to respected policy analysts, including Edward Zigler, the Sterling professor of psychology at Yale University: "the United States stands alone among industrialized nations in its lack of a formal policy recognizing a social responsibility toward the well-being of the family."[16]

Many Third World countries could serve as models for us in this regard. Eighty-one developing nations already have family leave laws.[17] Women in Mozambique, and India, for example, receive six to eight weeks paid leave after giving birth. Turkish labor laws stipulate that a woman may have between six weeks and six months of maternity leave without risk of losing her job. In Chile, eighteen weeks of maternity leave is mandatory.[18] As part of the struggle toward economic health, Irish industry has joined its more prosperous European partners in providing paid leaves to new mothers.[19] Soviet women are allowed to stay at home until their children reach eighteen months, receiving partial pay. And once they return to work, Soviet women are assured on-site child care, often of very high quality.[20]

Why have American parents not demanded child care systems, including parental leave policies, as good as those of other countries? Part of the problem may have to do with ambivalence. We are confused about how much we have a right to expect from the government for our children. We seem to believe that the only way to be responsible parents is to retain sole and isolated responsibility for our children.

To begin the work of needed change in society, we must first recognize the changes to be made within our own lives. Some of the changes challenge prevalent cultural myths about gender and life roles and about individual and community responsibility. Confronting the myths is not easy but unless we do so it will be hard, perhaps impossible, to decrease the stresses of role combination without jeopardizing its benefits.

We all have assumptions about what constitutes psychological maturity. We may rarely be called on to list what distinguishes the healthy from the unhealthy person, the happy from the unhappy person, the good person from the bad. Although usually unexamined, the lists are there, pounded in through socialization. Our preconceptions and assumptions about maturity in men and women serve to organize our perceptions of people and we then take the perceptions as confirmation of our biases.

It may seem an adolescent exercise, but much can be learned by asking yourself: Who is the mature person? What psychological attributes distinguish a woman from a girl? A woman from a man? Who is the emotionally healthy woman? She who has it all? She who does it all (complaining or not)? The one who never asks for help? If you are like many people, you may unconsciously equate maturity with self sufficiency and femininity with the ability to please others. You may believe, at some level of consciousness, that the mature, adult female is a person who manages to give pleasure while asking for no help.

Finding ways to decrease the stress of juggling depends on recognizing the tangle of assumptions and preconceptions about psychological health and growth that constitute part of our cultural heritage. Some of these may be hindering efforts to decrease stress while retaining *joie de vivre*. To question and release our deeply held assumptions may not transpire without costs but these costs surely constitute part of what Judith Viorst calls necessary losses.[21]

Research

My unconventional prescription, recommendations, and reflections are based primarily on the findings of researchers who have been investigating the issues of gender and life roles.

Ten years ago, and perhaps even five years ago, there was simply insufficient evidence from which to draw confident conclusions. By now, however, a small army has undertaken a great many studies of the consequences for women, men, and children of different role combinations. Today an impressive amount of data warrants social action.

My goal is to compile, analyze, and present the evidence on gender and life roles in a way that is relevant to women who combine paid labor outside the home with the nurturance of life within it. At a minimum, the evidence ought to make the despairing juggler disparage herself less, and give to the exhausted juggler hope for better days. It should also validate the woman who knows how much satisfaction she derives from role combination.

In and of themselves, research findings provide no guide for improvement. To be useful, the findings must be seen in context. The book describes the participants in various studies in enough detail for jugglers to envision the similarities and differences between those studied and themselves. It also describes methodology in enough detail to make clear to what extent the researchers' findings are predetermined by their questions. Perhaps no science is value free; certainly investigations that involve gender issues are always colored by the values and assumptions of the investigators.[22]

Organizing the Research Findings

The majority of the women with whom I have spoken imagine themselves to be the only ones who have difficulty coping. The research, summarized in chapter 2, suggests otherwise. It shows that most women who combine different life roles complain of time pressures and of feeling unable to accomplish all they wish to achieve.

Analysis of the findings also shows that the stress women suffer does not necessarily arise from juggling. We have misidentified the source of difficulties. The problems that appear to result from combining employment and motherhood, for example, probably result from either employment or motherhood in isolation. Contemporary American motherhood places virtually impossible demands on women. While we are accustomed to assuming that role combination is the source of stress, the fact is that motherhood—as currently conceived in America—is the real culprit.

If the stresses of juggling are more apparent than real, what of the benefits? The evidence, put forward in detail in chapter 3, is that women who combine significant life roles are better off emotionally than are women with fewer roles. Even as they acknowledge stress and time pressure, jugglers demonstrate less depression, higher self-esteem, and greater satisfaction with life generally and with different aspects of life than do women who play fewer roles. There is also some indication that juggling enhances physical as well as psychological health.

Chapter 4 examines in detail the many reasons why people derive benefits from role combination. The reasons for which role combination benefits women are distinct from the reasons for which it causes stress. This means that a person can reduce stress without automatically jeopardizing the health-producing aspects of juggling. Taken together, chapters 2, 3, and 4 lead to this conclusion: the woman who abandons paid labor, matrimony, or maternity may pay a high price psychologically to do so.

Women have, of course, others than themselves to consider. If we can emotionally benefit from juggling and yet avoid paying a high price in stress, will someone else have to pick up the tab? The most pressing anxiety of many jugglers is the fear that they are risking emotional harm to their children. The fear is a realistic one.

Certainly the negative image of maternal employment has been communicated by many authorities on child development. Take T. Berry Brazelton, chief of the Division of Child Development at Boston's Children Hospital, professor of pediatrics at Harvard Medical School, and former president of the Society for Research on Child Development. He is a man of responsibility and influence. Until recently, Brazelton frequently and publicly said he missed the days when mothers stayed home with their young children. Strongly implying that a mother's place was in the home, Brazelton's publications have bewailed the negative consequences for babies and for mothers when infants are put in what he has called substitute care.

Detachment, projection, and denial are three responses, according to Brazelton, among mothers who leave their young children in child care. "Not because she doesn't care," he has written, "but because it is painful to care and to be separated, the mother will tend to distance her feelings of responsibility and of intense attachment." For the baby, the results of such maternal detachment could be quite serious indeed. Brazelton had little doubt that the infant and young child needs the exclusive attention of his or her mother, who herself needs to "feel herself free of competing demands of the work place" to engage in positive interactions with the child.[23]

Not long ago Brazelton changed his mind. In a lead article for a recent issue of *Newsweek* magazine, he openly admitted a new view and avowed a new understanding.

> In our culture, we live with a deep-seated view that a woman's role is in the home. She should be there for her children, so the theory goes, and both she and they will suffer if she's not. I felt that way for a long

time myself, and it took constant badgering from my three militant daughters, who all work, as well as from a whole succession of working parents in my practice, to disabuse me of my set of mind.[24]

We need not rely on badgering to change attitudes. We now possess an armamentarium of solid facts about the children of working mothers. We know a great deal about the effects of child care outside the home.

The actual facts, and our collective resistance to them, comprise the gist of the fifth chapter. As is demonstrated in chapter 5, there is little evidence to support the old assumption. Indeed, a growing number of studies give credence to the counterposition. An in-depth look at the systematically collected data may dispel the fear that it is the offspring of those who benefit from multiple roles that suffer.

While many people have been concerned about whether the worker and the mother roles combine well, few have worried about the combination of matrimony and employment and even fewer have fretted about the mix of matrimony and motherhood. Once again, our preconceptions have blinded us: husbands, not children, constitute the major issue for many women who seek to juggle. The research shows that men, especially traditional men, have been more disturbed by women's involvement in the paid labor market than have children. In chapter 6 we see how women's successful juggling has unsettled many husbands and husband surrogates. Whenever women really show their power and challenge traditional sex roles, they inconvenience many men and even frighten some.

How do women react when they recognize the gender inequities that can make it so hard to combine marriage with other life roles? Many women react with anger at men. In the words of one woman whom I know: "My big question is still: What do you do with the anger?" Some even argue that women ought to dispense with men to the extent possible.[25] But such a point of view is not congenial to many women. Besides, traditional marriage—with its confinements and unhealthy expectations—is to blame for the problems; not men. Blaming men cannot solve the problem; modifying the conventions of marriage can.

Revising marriage and revamping motherhood are major strategies for reducing the stress that has been incorrectly attributed to juggling. Such strategies involve massive efforts and ultimately require collective action. To expect any woman to effect lasting improvements on her own would be inappropriate and unhelpful. As I propose in the final chapter, almost every woman can take the first steps toward change herself.

One step that can be taken by every woman is to examine her own beliefs about the American ideal of individualism. "The sin of dependency" is the label that British social historian Rupert Wilkinson applies to what he identifies as a basic American fear.[26] Because we Americans are convinced that dependency is bad, we deprive ourselves and our families of the benefits of mutual interdependence.

Even many feminists in America have retained the belief that each family should function as a separate unit in the raising of children. Perhaps one reason that many working parents do not agitate for collective reform, such as more governmental or corporate child care, is that the parents fear, deep down, that to share responsibility for child rearing is to abdicate it. I believe that society ought to bear a responsibility for children. Thus, rather than ducking their responsibilities, individual parents are acting on behalf of their children when they demand that society fulfill its duties toward the nation's young.

Another helpful step is to clarify beliefs about femininity. The last twenty or thirty years have been a time of extraordinary change, but the residues of sex discrimination and of stereotyped thinking are difficult to wash away.[27] Quite a few women, even women who have careers rather than jobs, still carry the feeling that they are in the paid labor force by permission and not by right.[28]

A recent study of dual-earner families revealed unconscious sex-role stereotyping among women. The working women in the study rated "a typical working woman," "a typical wife" and "a typical mother" on a number of different dimensions, such as assertiveness, warmth, and health. The ratings of the mother and of the wife resembled each other; but the typical working woman was seen as very different from the mother. When questioned in a subtle way that reduced the tendency to present a socially or politically correct image, the women gave a strong indication that at some level, they perceived working women as nonmaternal and, indeed, unfeminine. And yet, the women in the sample were married mothers who worked at least thirty-five hours a week for pay.[29]

Clearly, we are in a time of transition; widespread ambivalence about gender roles is hardly surprising. It is difficult for any of us to feel certain about what a woman should give to her family, her employer, or her community and what she has a right to expect from each. Clarifying her own views makes it easier for a juggler to ask for and work for those goods and services to which she may be entitled.

Clarifying our own views will not solve all our problems. But it will be a start. Without clarity, we can too easily become discouraged and critical of ourselves. Aspiring to juggle well, we watch, with a mixture of awe and envy, those mythical characters who dance across the glossy magazine page or across the television screen and do it all. On the screen people can do it all alone with no apparent props or help. But in real life, we can't. In real life, there are problems; and these problems require cooperative solutions.

We all imagine that the joys and the problems we individually experience are unique and wholly personal. They are not, and the image serves no end. Comparative information yields knowledge of the conditions that foster healthy role combinations. Anyone who wishes to combine domestic responsibilities and paid employment with the least stress and most enjoyment might start by pondering this paradox: the first step to better functioning is to stop blaming herself for not functioning well enough.

· 2 ·

Costs

Have you ever attempted to carry on a serious conversation over the telephone while trying to put on your underwear? I have, and in such situations, there always comes an impasse. Either I cannot manage to hoist myself into my slip or brassiere without taking my ear from the receiver or I cannot quite stretch far enough to reach the dresser for my pantyhose. Or I knock over the potted plant as my feet grope for my shoes. Or I do remove my ear, ever so hastily, from the telephone to hoist, yank, or pull, only to find when I resume contact with the instrument, that I have missed the crucial sentence of what the other person was saying.

And have you, like me, ever reached into your briefcase or your bag for the notes and statistics that you need for an important business meeting to discover that the folder marked "meeting notes" contains yesterday's shopping list and nothing else? Or have you ever, left hand on shopping cart, reached with your right hand into your sack for the grocery list and found instead some memo from the boss?

Do you ever vacuum at midnight? Forget your partner's birthday gift at the store? Phone your children from work to find out if they've made it safely home? And then again later to make sure they're still safely at home?

If so, you're not the only one. If you wish you had a clone for the office and a clone for the house, think you need a thirty-hour day, or find yourself lusting after a nap or a good night's sleep, you are not alone. I feel the same. Women across the country are looking for those

20

moments of repose when nothing is expected of us or needed from us; and we are not finding them.

The lack of free minutes leaves us feeling stressed and unequal to life's tasks. Like Naomi whom we met in chapter 1, we are overwhelmed and ready to blame ourselves for the lost bits of conversation, the rush, the mislaid notes and memos. We feel inadequate or undisciplined for having housework to attend to in the middle of the night because as little girls we had learned that housework was to be done in the morning. Fatigued and irritable, we question our priorities.

Evidence of distress is accumulating in numerous academic studies and countless popular articles. Reports of current life patterns seem to leave little doubt that today's juggler experiences more stress than is healthy. Glancing at the findings of contemporary studies, many of them carefully conducted by reputable social scientists, anyone might conclude that women today are typically overcommitted and need to learn how to cut back on their obligations.

Quick impressions can, however, deceive. When the evidence is amassed, systematically arranged, and carefully scrutinized—as in this chapter—there are surprises. The problems are real but the sources of the problems are not what we have assumed them to be. Juggling, the apparent source of much stress, is in fact a potentially important way of alleviating stress.

Hours in the Day

When psychologist Lisa Silberstein asked people, "What aspects of your dual-career marriage would you most like to change or improve?" the question elicited long and thoughtful responses from people who sought to combine professional careers with family life.

"What I would like is to have a few more hours in the day," said a woman in her thirties. "What would you do with a few more hours?" Silberstein pursued. "I'd love to relax after work before I start cooking dinner, or go to the gym and swim. When I went to pick up the kids yesterday, I had a cake in the oven. Heaven forbid that I get stuck in traffic! I'd love not to have to be somewhere at a certain time." Another woman in Silberstein's study, a professional in her early forties, framed her frustrations similarly: "Everything is structured. You're constantly structuring: the house, like making sure the cupboards are

stocked and the kids are set, and the job, taking care of the office, etc."
Said another: "The thing I keep coming back to is the need for time."[1]
Silberstein's jugglers identified the unrelenting pace of life as a persistent problem. They spoke of lacking time to relax. They spoke of pressured schedules. They spoke of cramming weeks of work into the hours of the day.

That they should speak so is not at all surprising in one sense. These people typified the new upwardly striving young professional. Silberstein's sample included twenty couples in which both the husband and the wife considered themselves to have not just jobs but careers. Also, they all lived in the urban Northeast, mostly in New York City or New Haven. And all of the couples had at least one child—sometimes an infant or a toddler. In one sense, then, it seems natural that people with such busy lives should feel rushed. Perhaps time pressure is simply the price of life in the fast lane.

The frantic nature of fast-track urban life was impressed on me again recently during a conversation with my friend Constance. Constance divides her time between her professional work as a researcher and her personal life as a New York society woman. Married to a financial genius, Constance moves among her laboratory, her apartment in Manhattan, her house-in-progress on Nantucket, and the schools and summer camps of her two children.

A few days prior to a recent conversation, Constance had been slightly detained by a minor personnel crisis at the lab. She had then hurried home, jumped into the shower, pulled on an evening dress, and rushed out to a waiting cab. She instructed the driver to proceed at breakneck speed to the club where she was meeting her husband for a gala arts benefit. As soon as the taxi turned to go cross town, it stopped short, totally blocked by post-rush-hour traffic.

Frustrated, Constance reached into her purse and found her date book. She opened it to recheck the time that she was supposed to be at the club. Only then did she discover that she had confused two events in her mind. The Arts Gala was one week hence. The event toward which Constance was rushing, also to take place at the club at 6:30, was a potluck dinner for parents of boy scouts. Everyone else would be casually dressed and, in their midst, Constance in a strapless gown.

Women throughout the United States also have acknowledged the time pressures described by the women in Silberstein's study and, more vehemently, by my friend Constance. In 1984, David Chambers mailed a twelve-page questionnaire to most women and some men who had graduated from The University of Michigan Law School between 1976 and 1979. In one question to the women, he asked: "Do you believe that, for reasons that relate to your being a woman, you balance your career and private life differently than most men you know doing comparable work?" Three-quarters of all the women in the sample—and 89 percent of them mothers—said yes.

A great number of women went on to explain their answers. No other question in the survey elicited such a strong and consistent response. Typically the women said:

> I "balance" by losing myself—my free time. I have no hobbies, little free time to assess who I am and where I want to go. I "balance" by forgoing social opportunities and chit-chat with peers.

> I value my marriage and my friends, I have a two year old and am expecting another. I am half crazy because I put in fewer hours at work than my colleagues and I feel I am falling behind.

> I am a mother with two small children and expecting a third. No further explanation necessary.

> I am so tired of being tired.[2]

While it seems appropriate in one sense for the high achieving, high pressure women in Chambers's or Silberstein's studies to bemoan their lack of time, on reflection their distress seems surprising. All of the couples in Silberstein's study were in their thirties or forties and were in good health. All were highly educated, and some were quite affluent. All of the women in Chambers's sample had graduated from one of the top law schools in the nation. They typically earned very large salaries and married men with even larger salaries. One-third of the married women in Chambers's study enjoyed family incomes in excess of $100,000 annually.

So why should these highly accomplished mothers have such a poor quality of life? If someone as accomplished and affluent as Constance finds herself making embarrassing mistakes for lack of time to organize herself, how am I to function? If intelligent, resourceful, healthy, and wealthy women are experiencing pressure, what about those less privileged? If women who can, for instance, afford to purchase the domestic services of others feel tired and harassed, how must everyone else feel?

In Short Supply

The answer is that around the country, and in all strata of society, women who juggle home and work are finding time in very short supply. The feeling of being chronically rushed is a familiar one. If jugglers were to ask their friends (should they have time to have any), their neighbors (should their packed schedules ever overlap enough to encounter any), or their colleagues (should the pressures of work permit them to chat with any), they would no doubt discover that these people, too, suffer from a sense that there are not enough hours in the day to accomplish what they feel they ought to accomplish.

Systematic research confirms the conclusion. Study after study has shown that contemporary women, so rich in opportunities, are impoverished in time. Findings such as these are representative:

One researcher in Oklahoma asked people about the conflicts they experienced between home life and work. Forty-four percent of the conflicts involved time and especially the shortage thereof.[3]

Another study included 100 mothers with children in a local elementary school, 44 of whom worked outside the home for at least thirty hours a week. Among the working mothers, 61 percent agreed that they were "pressured by a hectic schedule."[4]

Still other working mothers were contacted through child care centers in Ohio and asked if they had time for various life activities. Eighty-seven percent of the women had no time for community involvement; 80 percent had no time for hobbies; and 69 percent had no time for travel. Over half of the women had no time to attend to their wardrobes, and about a quarter lacked time for personal health care.[5]

Sixty-one married mothers who were on the faculty at Northwestern University were asked about their lives. On average each spent 48.5 hours per week on her professional work, 35.1 hours on child care, 24.6 hours on housework, and 56 hours on sleep. That left her with only 3.8 hours per week to devote to everything else in life.[6]

Over several years, sociologist Arlie Hochschild and her colleague Anne Machung interviewed in depth fifty dual-earner couples with children who lived in the San Francisco area. Hochschild characterized the women as exhausted and found that, no matter what their social class or ethnic group, working mothers put in a second shift of work at home. The additional hours that women put in during the second shift would amount to an extra month of work each year.[7]

Recently, 35,000 readers of Family Circle responded to that magazine's survey. One question asked: "Are there enough hours in the day?" One-third of the women said sometimes; and half said never. Most readers reported that they had two or three hours a week to themselves as personal time; and one in five women reported that she had no personal time at all.[8]

Even more recently, the *New York Times* conducted telephone interviews with more than 1,000 women and 500 men. In dual-earner families with children, 49 percent of the husbands and 84 percent of the wives said that they did not get enough time for themselves.[9]

The evidence could not be more straightforward. Week on week, month on month, today's juggler inscribes each day of her life right out to the edge. Life is lived, to paraphrase William Kessen, without margins. Women today are experiencing role expansion, not role redefinition. At home and at work, new responsibilities are added to the old ones, none of which are dropped.

Crunches

Sometimes, too, the condition flares, and a woman suffers an acute attack. A time crunch exists whenever two or more activities demand her immediate and full attention.[10] Time crunches always feel stressful.

Time crunches can occur within any major life role. In many jobs, for example, people experience time crunches. Consider the true story of a professor named Jacqueline. Last year, she was working on two separate books of collected chapters by different authors. The work entailed much editing, checking, and cross-referencing, as well as some rewriting and some mediating between warring authors. Despite careful planning, the schedules on the two books became yoked. When page proofs were due for one, page proofs were due for the other. When irate authors had to be soothed with long telephone calls (made at times convenient to the irate authors) for one, irate authors had to be soothed for the other. When references had to be checked for one, references had to be checked for the other. Jacqueline found herself scrambling to complete all the tasks required by her profession.

Jacqueline is not the only professional or worker to have experienced such a time crunch on the job. Telephone operators, high school guidance counselors, physicians, mail clerks, company presidents, secretaries, nurses, tax accountants, ticket sellers, and lawyers all know how competing tasks can collide within one role. Virtually every occupation has its own unique time crunches that equally afflict women with or without other roles.

And those who have more than one child know how difficult it can be to juggle everyone's schedule to anyone's satisfaction. Elise, community activist and mother of three, advises newlyweds to have no more children than they have hands. When the children are young, keeping them fed, clean, and engaged in some activity (other than watching television) can seem a nearly impossible task. As children approach the teenage years, tending everyone simultaneously becomes less challenging than before; but the need to chauffeur them all to their different locations creates new time crunches.

While each life role contains its own crises, the different life roles can also collide to produce more crises: A juggler is in the middle of an important business meeting, and the sitter calls to say that the baby has developed a high fever. Crunch. Another juggler is on the verge of persuading her aging parents to sign up for a retirement home (listening sensitively to their hopes and fears while muffling her own) when the four year old starts screaming upstairs. Crunch. Just as she is dashing to him, the front door bell rings; a colleague has decided, very kindly, to drop a memo by her house. Double crunch.

Some time crunches last more than a minute or a morning. Around age thirty-five, many of today's career women begin to experience what author Molly McKaughan calls *baby lust*. At least, it seems, the assertive, competent career women who are likely to respond to a personal questionnaire in *Working Woman* magazine do. Women who are happy to put off the job of having babies at age thirty or thirty-one suddenly find themselves hungering for infants.[11] Yet, as counselor Carole Wilk reports, many women early in their careers fear "they would be unable to return to work after having a child without having to start all over again."[12]

If career women do opt for children, time pressures proliferate. And they can hit working mothers at any job level or stratum of society. A female assembly line worker moaned to one investigator in Pennsylvania: "It's a hassle to worry about babysitters. Also, it's hard when a kid gets sick. I worry and don't get work done as well. I get in a bad mood at work, preoccupied with worrying."[13] Said another woman, an upper-middle-class owner of two businesses, to one of my associates, Ann Cameron: "My girl went through a stage that was psychologically induced. She became ill every day before school. If I stayed home with her, she got better. If not, I'd be called later in the day by the school to come get her. She hated me to leave her, so working was definitely a conflict."

Even when they are well, small children take up vast quantities of time and energy.[14] Typically the bearing of babies and the rearing of infants and small children occur when a woman is in her twenties and thirties. Generally, then, the years of most intense family involvement collide with the early years of occupational involvement. The young woman must find a toehold in her work and try to creep or leap toward secure footing while attending, every minute, to the children at home.

Certain periods of the year, too, produce an abundance of problems. What do you do when your child is on vacation and you are not? "Vacation acrobatics," exclaimed one friend, "that's what it is." "Vacation acrobatics nothing," snorted another, "it's vacation murder." Vacation-time crunches can last an entire summer.

Young children are not the only people for whom women care. The population of this country is aging. Currently more than 5 million citizens over age sixty-five need some type of long-term care. Families usually provide that care. An estimated 70 to 80 percent of the care of the elderly is performed by family members. Almost invariably, the job falls most heavily on women. Trying to help and care for aged relatives while caring for family and holding down a job exacerbate time management problems—acute as well as chronic.[15]

Time management has certainly become a major issue for Julie Allen of Weston, Massachusetts, aged thirty-five. Julie is a warm and friendly administrator who, when asked, characterizes herself as "mother, wife, professional, volunteer worker, friend, and daughter." Her children are young, and her mother is old. Several years ago Julie and her husband acquired their house at a very friendly price from her mother, who continues to live close by, and now she and her husband have amassed the funds to start fixing it up. Julie's already full life became instantly fuller as she and her family negotiated with the contractors. Said Julie: "There's not enough of me. Everybody needs so much of me. I constantly feel as if one person or one group of people has one of my arms, and another group has the other arm, and they are pulling in different directions. And then two other groups have my feet. And then the phone rings."

Inflexible Schedules

Jugglers, chronically short of time, find it especially hard to meet acute demands. In and of itself, a minor crisis need not assume major proportions. When the babysitter phones in ill, the executive mother can (in theory) reschedule her meetings; the physician mother can (in theory) shift her patients' appointments; and the professor mother can (in theory again) rearrange the day's classes. In practice, life usually proceeds otherwise. Colleagues, patients, and students rarely have the temperament or the freedom to recast their own timetables. Even when the situation permits the juggler to reschedule her appointments and obligations, her own rigid time boundaries makes flexibility unlikely. Shuffling appointments to accommodate acute but small emergencies becomes a task of vast magnitude because daily life includes no margin for errors, no room for modifications.

Because of the chronic shortage of time, a small upset can provoke a large reaction, even when it does not provoke massive rescheduling. The account of Debbie, a thirty-three-year-old nurse, given to author Anita Shreve, describes a situation that many jugglers will recognize. As Debbie said:

> It was my day off. But I had to get up at 7 A.M. with my son. I put him in the high chair. As I reached into the fridge to get him some juice, I knocked over a cup of milk on the shelf, and it spilled over everything. It was the last straw. I threw the cup into the sink and slammed the refrigerator door. I started crying. I felt incredibly angry—my day off, and I had to clean the fridge. I picked up a chair and threw it. My husband came in to see what was going on. He'd never seen me this upset. By that time I was on my knees, taking everything off the bottom shelf and throwing it into the sink.[16]

Time pressures that women feel become obvious to their children. Even in the absence of the kind of drama that Debbie provided for her son, most children are aware of the fact that their mothers feel short of time. Reported Emily, a successful corporate consultant, whom I interviewed: "One day we were talking about hard work and my [adolescent] children told me that they were surprised I had written a book "cause Mommy [Emily's voice takes on a higher pitch] your vocabulary is much too small to write a book. 'We're late' is the only phrase we've heard you say in the last four years."

Mistaken Impressions

The frantic pace and the chronic shortage of time—apparent consequences of the urgent quest to have it all and do it all—must surely take a physical toll. Everyone knows that stress results in poor health and premature death. The effects seem to occur both directly, by causing physiological deterioration, and indirectly by leading to behaviors such as smoking and alcohol consumption that injure health.[17]

Given the sense of time pressure that women admit when they combine paid labor and domestic responsibilities, it would hardly be surprising to find that as more and more women juggle, more and more women suffer ill health.

Medical researchers have seen, or imagined, associations between women's occupational successes and their health failures. Illustrative of the medical mind-set is this quotation from a recent book on cocaine addiction: "[I]n recent years . . . women have sought career opportunities and gained other rights and privileges similar to those of men. Along the way they have unavoidably acquired additional sources of stress as well, a factor that may be contributing to the increasing rates of substance abuse among today's women."[18]

Even the most liberal people link changing sex roles with possible health hazards. One feminist, cartoonist Garry Trudeau, cautioned the 1987 graduating class of a leading women's college:

> For women, in particular, there has never been more room, more opportunity in the professional realm. It may surprise some of you to learn that of the nearly 8 million jobs created since 1979, an astonishing 88 percent of them were filled by women.
>
> And yet the sensation of vulnerability, that need for control over one's life, persists. For women, the price is only now being measured. In 1966, the ratio of male to female ulcer patients in the United States was twenty to one. Today it is two to one. More distressingly, in that same time period, the rate of infertility in women your age has nearly tripled, from 4 percent to 11 percent. Explanations vary, but what is clear is that as women come to terms with what it means to have power . . . the pressure to embrace certainties, to pursue concrete goals unquestioningly has become unrelenting."[19]

Such presentations of statistics mistakenly create the impression that there is solid documentation of the health consequences for women of their participation in the paid labor force.

In the face of substantial evidence that role combination threatens a woman's physical well-being, it would be irresponsible for women to juggle home and work. If it were, in fact, true that the juggler runs a risk of death or disease, women who juggle may be jeopardizing the long-term future of themselves and their families. The seriousness of the issues is the main reason why we cannot be satisfied with impressions, why we need evidence.

Evidence exists in abundance. At the most elementary level are many statistics on the comparative rates of death and of illness in women and men. Such statistics, moreover, have been compiled for a long time, enabling longitudinal analyses.

The figures lead almost immediately to a conclusion quite at odds with the impression created by Trudeau's speech. The fact is that women in America live longer than men.[20] In every decade since 1900, and for both whites and nonwhites, the average female life span has lengthened more than the average male life span.[21] You can see the trend in Figure 2–1. In 1900, the average life expectancy for men was forty-six years; for women, it was forty-eight years.[22] At the turn of the century, in other words, females lived, on average, two years longer than males. By 1980, the average life expectancy was seventy years for males and seventy-seven and a half years for females.[23] The gap between males and females had increased by five and a half years! For those who attain a century of life, only one man is alive for every five women. Such figures are certainly not consistent with the idea that changing sex roles have had a negative impact on women's health.

Gender, Stress, and Mortality

Of course, life expectancy figures tell only part of the story. Skeptics may wonder how much such general figures hide as well as how much they reveal. Life expectancy figures do not, for example, reveal the cause of death. Cause of death is crucial. Female life span, but not male life span, has been dramatically affected since 1900 by improvements in obstetrical technology. Perhaps the major cause of the increase in women's longevity has been the sizable decrease during the last seventy-five years of the number of women who die because of child-birth. Perhaps obstetrical advances mask other types of deterioration.

Could it be that women are dying more frequently than they used to from stress killers such as heart attacks? In 1900, diseases of the heart accounted for less than 10 percent of all deaths in the United States; by 1976, for more than 20 percent, mostly by heart attacks.[24]

Traditionally, the heart attack has been a male medical event.[25] Is it not the case that women—in sharing power with men—have come to share the diseases of power? The suggestions of Garry Trudeau and of some other thoughtful feminists would certainly make it seem so.

And so would some facts. Figure 2–2 shows the gap between male and female deaths from heart disease. Note that the gap has narrowed since 1960. Fewer men have died from heart attacks, but the number of women has remained roughly constant. Fewer men have been dy-

FIGURE 2–1
Life Expectancy by Sex and Color, 1900–77

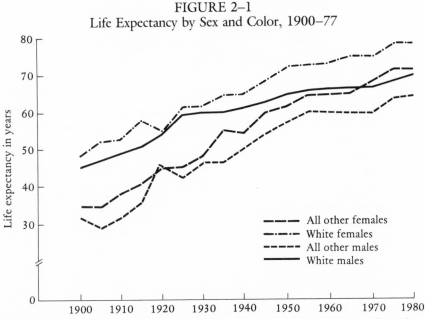

Reprinted from Dorothy P. Rice and Anne S. Cugliani (1980), "Health Status of American Women," *Women and Health 5,* fig. 2, p. 8.

ing from heart attacks because of advances in medical technology and changes in life-style. Why then have the advances not benefited women? Possibly, the advantages of improved health care for women have been offset by a steady deterioration in women's health habits. Professional women give up smoking less frequently than do professional men, for example,[26] and working women exercise less than other people.[27] Maybe the ambitions and hopes of contemporary women, and most particularly of those who juggle home and career, are killing them.

Charts such as Figure 2–2 tempt us all to conclude that women are literally dying to be equal to men. It seems that women are paying a hefty price for the new life-styles. The numbers seem to say that all modern women, and perhaps especially jugglers, have bought the new freedoms and satisfactions with an increase in heart disease and possibly all stress diseases.

If I consider the possible connections between female accomplishments, on the one hand, and mortality on the other, a rush of names and faces immediately present themselves. I think of my dissertation advisor, Clara Mayo, blond and round faced, who had kept her ill health a secret and then died suddenly one evening from pneumonia.

FIGURE 2–2
Death from Heart Attacks

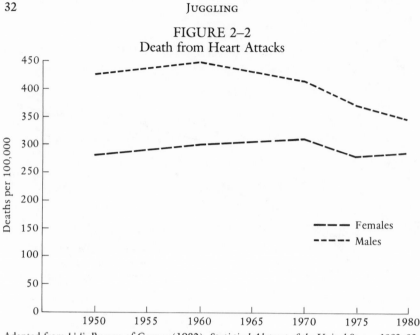

Adapted from U.S. Bureau of Census (1982), *Statistical Abstract of the United States: 1982–93*, 103d ed. (Washington, D.C.: U.S. Printing Office).

Clara died well before her fiftieth birthday, leaving a shocked community of colleagues and students. I think of Marcia Guttentag, one of the few women on the faculty at Harvard in the 1970s, who suffered a heart attack while traveling on business. I think of the energetic Barbara Wallston, who broke her ankle while away from home. Impatient at having to stay in a New York hospital, Barbara arranged to be transferred to Nashville, only to die at home from an allergic reaction to her medication. I think of Nancy Datan, a brilliant researcher, mother, and wife whose studies of life-span development ended when cancer overtook her. From her hospital bed, Nancy wrote fierce essays about physical and mental health. And most of all I think of the late Grace Baruch, whose research on women's life roles informs so much of what I say on these pages.

No doubt you, too, can call to mind the images of women who died out of season, midcourse, leaving unfinished work and partners, children, parents, colleagues, and friends. And perhaps in conjuring up such images, we worry about the implication of statistics such as those in Figure 2–2. The proofs begin to seem self-evident.

But even as we think of specific women whose cases appear to substantiate the grim trends, it is important to question the seemingly self-evident proofs that juggling harms women's health. Appearances are not the same as truth. Consider, as did psychologist Bonnie Strickland, what else might account for the narrowing gender gap in heart attacks. Investigating plausible alternative explanations of the health data, Strickland discovered that the major reason why women still die from heart attacks despite medical advances is that they are living longer and longer.[28] Old people have worse health than young people.

In other words, the narrowing gender gap in death from heart disease does not indicate the stressfulness of women's current lifestyles. Rather, it reflects two facts: a decreased number of deaths from heart attacks among young and middle-aged women and a statistically offsetting increased number of old and very old women in the population. The trend is not apparent in men because, as we saw earlier, men's life expectancy is currently seven and a half years less than women's.

Again, the figures can be graphed. Figure 2–3 shows what happens when the statisticians adjust the figure to take age into account. The age-adjusted rates shows no change in the gender gap. When we disentangle the issues of age from those of gender, we can see beyond the impression to the truth. Women have retained their life-span advantage.[29]

FIGURE 2–3
Death from Heart Attacks, Adjusted for Age

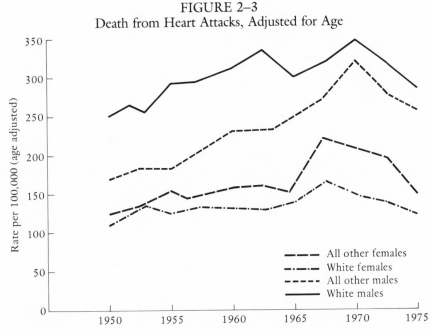

Adapted from *Chartbook for the Conference on the Decline in Coronary Heart Disease Mortality* (Hyattsville, Md.: National Center for Health Statistics, August 1978).

In Sum

The next time someone asserts that the juggler is digging herself into an early grave, we should ask what figures support that point of view. Female ambition can be difficult to accommodate. While openly misogynist views are no longer socially acceptable, many are willing to say, in essence "you do, ladies, and you die." Medical statistics can—and often do—seem to support the impression that the liberated woman has freed herself only to risk premature death by stress. When scrutinized, however, the accumulated data on gender and mortality show not even a hint of harm to women from their expanded opportunities for playing a variety of life roles. In fact, medical sociologists have recently discovered among one sample of mothers first studied in the 1950s and then recontacted thirty years later, that involvement in multiple roles predicted a longer life, not a shorter one.[30]

Gender, Stress, and Illness

Death does not exhaust the negative possibilities; there is also illness with which to reckon. Statisticians commonly distinguish between mortality (death) rates and morbidity (illness) rates. Perhaps changes in gender roles—which have not had a negative influence on how long women live—have resulted in problems for how well women live. If it is not killing women, is stress perhaps making women ill?

Looking at my own life, I recognize, or imagine that I recognize, strong evidence of how stress can make a person ill. I experienced a jolt the other day as I reviewed some correspondence with a professional friend. I needed to look at the file for some specific information and was shocked to observe the opening paragraphs of her letters to me over the last two years. They read.

9/1/87 — Dear Faye,
          Sorry to hear about your shoulder . . .
1/5/88 — Dear Faye,
          Thanks for the recommendation. Hope that everything is back to normal in terms of your health . . .
6/7/88 — Dear Faye,
          It seems as if all my women friends are having health problems. And so I was sad but not surprised to learn . . .

2/2/89 — Dear Faye,
      Greetings from Israel. Hoping that your arm is feeling better.

When I am not careful, I begin to blame my arthritis and other ailments on my long-time efforts to combine career and family life. I count the days and months of poor health and slip into the trap of thinking that my shoulder, arm, or hip would never hurt me if only I hadn't been so set on having a family and a career. But when I am careful in my thinking, I remember that as far back as junior high school and high school, long before I ever even planned to juggle work and home, my health was already spotty.

Moving beyond the personal, we need to recognize that women's health today is worse than men's. For most disease categories, there are more women than men in every age bracket. The male advantage remains strong whether the researchers use approximate and fairly unreliable techniques such as asking people how they feel or more behavioral and stringent techniques such as counting days missed from work, days in a hospital, or incidence of illness as shown in medical and insurance records.[31]

A portion of the medical data makes it seem as if women's elevated rates of illness might be due to their entry into the work force. The most frightening statistics came from a study on heart disease that the National Heart, Lung, and Blood Institute has been conducting since 1948 in Framingham, Massachusetts. In that town, 11 percent of the women who had three or more children and who also worked outside the home developed coronary heart disease while only 4.4 percent of housewives with three or more children did.[32] Things looked bad for jugglers.

Detailed analyses soon revealed, however, that the health risks occurred only among clerical workers who juggled heavy family responsibilities with commitments outside the home. Professional workers showed no such pattern. Nor were women working in clerical jobs at risk for coronary heart disease if they were married to men with white-collar jobs. Findings such as these bolster the observation that it is the absence of money, not the presence of employment, that interferes with women's physical well-being.[33]

A similar point has been made by a leading researcher of women's health, Lois Verbrugge.[34] In her massive Health in Detroit Study conducted in 1978, approximately 350 women and 250 men recorded their health status and physical symptoms each day for six weeks. Verbrugge and her associates also asked all the study participants for details about their lives and their health.

Verbrugge found, as had others, that women suffered more symptoms, took more medication, and generally experienced worse health than men. And, as in earlier samples, most of the men in Verbrugge's sample were employed and married parents, while fewer of the women juggled all three life roles.

Verbrugge's next finding was important news: the more roles, the healthier the person—woman or man! In the Detroit study, feeling burdened and tired by one's life predicted ill health, but feeling burdened was not a typical consequence of too many life roles. A person who engaged in many activities on a regular basis enjoyed better health than the person who engaged in few activities.

The implication of the research is clear: Women's burdens—not their opportunities—cause ill health. Women's ill health, relative to men's health, is not related to the fact that women have yet to "come to terms with what it means to have power" as Garry Trudeau suggested. It is rather related to the fact that women have not yet obtained power and freedom equal to that of men.

Logical Leaps

In many ways jugglers are simply trying to lead the life that traditionally has been reserved for men. Men have been expected to hold a job, marry, and have children. And men have benefited from role combination in wealth, happiness, and even health. Women have been expected to remain at home with the children. A woman who wanted an occupation outside the home was supposed to feel guilty about how she was letting down her family.

Today, the majority of women are employed, and they are not remaining single. Few people today would object overtly or directly to their participation in the labor force. Lip service is given to gender equality throughout the United States. Yet old habits of thought persist. People are still searching for proof why women should not, after all, seek to combine paid employment with domestic responsibilities. Our receptivity to the proposition that women's accomplishments interfere with their health springs from a continued ambivalence about gender equity. If a woman were to jeopardize her health simply for the immediate gratification of keeping up with Ms. Jones in the superwoman competition, she would be an irresponsible creature indeed.

Blaming the Victim

That someone like Garry Trudeau—a liberal, thoughtful man who supports women—would link ill health with women's accomplishments says worlds about the temper of our times. So, too, does the public's appetite for books that either promise women that we can have it all if we try hard enough or blame us for not having it all. One book reviewer observed that while "the suburban housewife's spiral into despair and Valium addiction was the stuff of popular memoirs and best-selling novels" in the 1970s, times have changed. Now, in "the post-feminist decade, this modern Ophelia has slipped from view—and resurfaced as a lady with a briefcase. These days, the Diary of the Mad Superwoman is the book every publishing house is after."[35]

The reviewer, Susan Faludi, goes on to recount the story lines of several books in which real-life heroines depict how all their attempts to juggle ended in heartache or heartburn. One high-flyer even suffered a prolonged coma, which she attributed to her effort to combine roles and not to her serious diabetes.

Implicit in all of these accounts, notes Faludi, is the notion that role combination is somehow to blame for women's problems. Such a notion reflects and reinforces the conviction that women ought not to aspire to have both a career and a family life. Rather than inclining us to think about ways to change society, negative views of role combination hint that the source of all difficulty is women's neurotic need to be superwomen and not—as is actually the case—unsatisfactory social conditions.

Exposing the Lapse in Logic

With misinterpreted statistical studies and misguided popular books to lead us astray, it is easy for women to *misidentify the sources of their current problems*. The problems are real enough. Most women today— and not just the one I quoted at the outset of the chapter—are strained. The research shows beyond any doubt that women who juggle feel constantly rushed. It is also undeniably true that contemporary women combine work and nurturing in ways that our foremothers did not envision. The statistics are indisputable, but the conclusion purportedly derived from them—that women's attempt to combine work and family is the major source of their physical or mental problems—is faulty.

There is an important hole in the argument. You can spot the lapse in logic most easily if you translate the popular view into a syllogism.

Major Premise: Many women today juggle home and work.
Minor Premise: Most jugglers feel stressed.
Conclusion: Juggling is the cause of the stress.

While both the major and minor premises are true, the conclusion simply does not follow from either premise. Nor is there much evidence to support the view that juggling causes stress.

What about all those harried, tired, overwhelmed, harassed women whom I quoted at the outset of the chapter? What about all the studies showing that time pressures bother jugglers across the social spectrum? Do these not provide the evidence that juggling causes stress?

No, they do not. To show that juggling causes stress would require comparative statistics. At a minimum, there would have to be studies that reveal that jugglers feel more pressured, anxious, or stressed than women who do not juggle. Without such comparative studies, it is impossible to tell whether it is life-style (i.e., juggling) or gender (i.e., femaleness) that produces the acknowledged feeling of stress and pressure.

Scholars and media writers alike have assumed that there are many studies showing that jugglers experience more stress than other women. I once shared the assumption. With high hopes, five students and I undertook very thorough searches—both computerized and manual—of publications in the social and medical sciences. We tracked down all the studies that we could find that promised to compare the emotional and mental health of jugglers and other women. We then sorted them into two piles. In the first were studies that concerned depression, self-esteem, happiness, or general well-being. In the second were those that concerned specific feelings of stress, pressure, or of anxiety. It was in the latter pile that we expected to find the documentation of elevated stress among jugglers compared to other women.

Our expectations were not confirmed, and our assumptions turned out to be wrong. There were only about a dozen studies in as many years. There were, in other words, only a few pertinent studies. Instead of the torrent of data that we had expected, we tapped into a tiny trickle. Nor did the few pertinent studies tell the story we had anticipated: Three investigations found jugglers experience more stress than other women; eight detected no difference between jugglers and others; and two actually found less stress among jugglers than among other women. Feelings of stress, pressure, and anxiety are obviously not the exclusive province of women who seek to combine major life roles.[36] Housewives can have as much stress as working mothers.

There is a lesson here. Clearly, conflict between roles is not the source of stress that everyone has thought it to be for contemporary women. As with physical symptoms, so it is with the subjective sense of stress. Role combination is not the source of our modern malaise.

Other evidence strengthens the case. Although pressed for time and overwhelmed, women who juggle work and home are not overwhelmed because their different life roles interfere with each other. If you separate the problems that arise *within* any one role from the problems that occur at the intersection *between* different roles, there are few problems at the intersections. One study, for example, focused on the inter-role conflicts of married mothers who were returning to college. The participants were requested to identify up to three situations that reflected conflict among their life roles. Less than 10 percent of the sample generated a list of three situations, and over 30 percent could not think of a single conflict between the roles.[37] Similarly, in the national survey of 1,500 workers, only 38 percent of women in dual-earner families agreed that their work life and home life sometimes interfered with each other. Sixty-two percent reported no conflict at all![38] In a beautifully designed and executed study of 153 women in business and in college teaching, conducted by Camille Wortman and her associates, three-quarters of the women reported that they experienced conflict between their work and their family responsibilities "nearly every day"; but the experience of inter-role conflict appeared to be caused by having too much to do at work.[39]

The case of Glenna, an attractive woman in her mid-thirties, illustrates these concepts. Glenna married early and soon became a mother. By the time her son had reached the sixth grade, Glenna and her first husband divorced, and Glenna soon became serious about her career. Trained as a graphic designer and working for a medium-sized corporation, Glenna eventually rose to a responsible position in the public relations department. Glenna remarried when her son was in high school and continued to work.

During an interview with Glenna, I asked her to list her "life roles," and she replied without hesitation: "mother, wife, and graphic artist." The interview continued:

F.C.: Do you ever find you have too much to do?
GLENNA: Yes, *definitely!*
F.C.: Do you ever wish that you could cut back?
GLENNA: Yeah, I've had those thoughts. If I had a choice, of course

it would be my career. Well, not cut back, but change it, alter it so that it were my own business, which may not be cutting back actually. I'd like to do the work at home more, do the same work but with more time to be with my family.

Later in the interview, Glenna elaborated on how fulfilling she finds paid employment, commenting on the good feeling of being relied on by others in the organization and also admitting: "I've tried the house-wife number, and it's not for me. I know that I have to work." But she returned to the issue of autonomy. "I wish," she said "that it could be my own business." If she had her own business, Glenna felt, she could arrange her hours to be more available to her husband and her teenage son and she could "directly reap the fruits of [her] labor."

Like Glenna, you can probably distinguish between two types of problems: those stemming from the incompatibilities between marriage, parenthood, and paid employment, and those arising from the nature of your work or the structure of your family. If you are like Glenna and like most people in the academic studies, you may have begun to realize that the second type of problem is far more pressing than the first. And yet, commentators persist in focusing on the first problem, the inherent incompatibility between life roles. I wonder why.

I also wonder why so many commentators emphasize stresses but not coping skills. Psychologists typically distinguish between stress and coping. Because some people cope well with life challenges, to admit challenges such as inter-role conflict, does not amount to an expression of distress or dissatisfaction.

Even when women do perceive conflict—between different life roles or within them—they do not necessarily feel overwhelmed by it. Such was the indisputable conclusion of a study by Janet Dreyfus Gray. She elicited information from 232 married women—physicians, lawyers, and professors—in the Philadelphia area. Seventy-seven percent of the women said that it was a strain to fulfill both professional and domestic roles. Yet, less than one in five of the women felt dissatisfied with how she coped with the strain. Half of the women were "mildly satisfied" with how well they managed to combine the roles, and a third were "extremely satisfied."[40]

A complicated and detailed survey of school teachers in Michigan reinforced the findings of the Philadelphia study. School teachers in Michigan, most of whom are women, experience more overload if they are married than if they are single. They also experience more overload if they have children than if they do not. But single women suffer the consequences of role overload more than married women do. Single women become worn down and ill if they feel short of time. The same is less true of married women and least true of mothers. In other words, for school teachers in Michigan—like professors in Philadelphia— those expressing the greatest stress also show the greatest coping.[41] And coping with stress is associated with good mental health among jugglers.[42]

While it is certainly not the case that employed mothers suffer more distress than nonemployed mothers, it may be the case that employed mothers suffer more distress than employed fathers.[43] Why? The reasons is that women, more than men, are expected to be available to other people. The (female) secretary is expected to take dictation, type a report, make a phone call, or run an errand at times convenient to the (male) boss. Mothers, more than fathers, are expected to be at the beck and call of their children. Wives, more than husbands, are expected to provide a listening ear, a helping hand, a comforting touch at the time when the spouse needs an ear, hand, or touch.[44] When more than one of the other people to whom the woman is supposed to be available call on her time at any given moment, she experiences a time crunch. Any individual can be responsive to a number of other people. But rarely can a person be responsive to the needs of several others at the very instant that the needs are felt.

These abstractions take concrete form in many women's lives. A mother of six can find time to listen to the daily grievances of each child, but she cannot always listen at the moment most convenient for each child. When two children need her attention at one moment, she may be instantly responsive to only one of them. A secretary may type all the letters of the four law partners for whom she works. But it is physically impossible for her to type instantly the letters of two different partners who appear at her desk at the same moment.

It does not matter whether those who need and want the woman's attention are at home or at work. What matters is their number. Indeed, for some wives and mothers paid employment may ease feelings of time pressure because paid employment legitimates unavailability to the incessant demands of husbands and children.[45]

Stress within Each Role

Media and scholars alike have given an inordinate amount of attention to conflict between roles. When those in authority assert that women are jeopardizing their health simply by engaging in paid employment while raising children, the average juggler is inclined to believe them. She knows, after all, how tired she is. But believing the authorities on this particular point is a mistake. The attempt to combine life roles has not so much caused problems as it has exposed to view the problems that have existed now for quite some time.

Fixating on juggling as the source of stress is a diversionary tactic. As long as people mark juggling as the problem in the lives of contemporary women, they ignore problems that arise for women within each major life role—as mother, as wife, and as worker. While appearing to be sympathetic toward women, the assertion that inter-role conflict produces most of women's stress serves the needs of the establishment. It perpetuates the status quo. Change will not come until we focus on the problems that beset women as workers—no matter what their family status—and the problems that beset women as family members—no matter what their employment status.

Employment Discrimination

What are the problems that women face as workers, spouses, and parents? What makes conflict within each role more problematic than inter-role conflict? What are the sources of pressure?

Think about paid employment. Every job, no matter how wonderful, has its unpleasant aspects. Some jobs are dull and repetitive. Some are meaningless and lacking in challenge. Still others have too much challenge, or too many demands for the resources available. Every job, in short, can produce dissatisfaction and feelings of stress.[46]

While every job has its drawbacks, some jobs have more drawbacks than others. Some are especially difficult, hazardous, or boring. Some career paths wander or describe a downward course. Despite all the variations among women's experiences and all the variations among men's experiences, important differences remain between the work life of women, on average, and the work life of men, on average. Women are paid less than men, achieve top positions less often than men, have less interesting jobs than men, have less flexible work schedules than men, and fill service positions more often than men.

For a long while, everyone assumed that differences in men's and women's work experiences resulted from differences between the male and the female personality. Gender is a very salient personal characteristic. It is difficult not to notice if someone is male or female. Because gender is so noticeable, people naturally use gender as the explanation for all sorts of variation—often quite erroneously.[47]

We imagine, for instance, that secretaries are nice, warm hearted, rather unambitious people because they are almost always women. But this is not so. To the extent that secretaries are nice, warm hearted, and unambitious, it is the nature of the job, not the gender of the jobholder that produces and explains the behavior. When we look at people on their jobs, we see that the personalities of women and men in the same positions do not typically differ from each other. Bosses are assertive—whether they are male or female. And underlings—of either sex—are people-oriented. Good staff members know how to anticipate their bosses' needs and show respect and caring for them.

Women's supposed lack of assertiveness, in other words, is not the cause of women's lowly position in most organizations. It is the result![48] A number of studies have shown this to be so. Particularly instructive was one study of people employed in the legal profession.[49] Female lawyers, male lawyers, and female legal secretaries were interviewed about their attitudes and job aspirations. According to traditional hypothesis, the female lawyers ought to have resembled closely the legal secretaries and differed from the male lawyers in their attitudes. Consider, for example, the reasons for working outside the home. The secretaries said that one important reason that they worked was to have contact with interesting people and a major reason that they liked their jobs was that such social contact was fun. The male lawyers cared very little about social contact. They claimed to work because they liked the feeling of accomplishing useful and important tasks. What about the female lawyers? Their motivations and rewards matched exactly those of the male lawyers and differed markedly from those of the legal secretaries. Job, not gender, determined people's attitudes and feelings.[50]

If women and men are so similar, why are there still major discrepancies in their earnings and status? What is going on? Could it be that sex discrimination still operates in the American economy?[51]

Sex discrimination exists whenever women and men receive unequal rewards for equal work and whenever women and men have unequal opportunities despite equal qualifications.[52] Discrimination can arise from hostility toward women; but discrimination can also occur without any conscious or unconscious desire to harm women or to keep women down. A person or organization does not have to intend harm to do harm. (Anyone who has ever been in a minor car accident knows exactly what I mean.)

Nine times out of ten, business practices that have discriminated against women have not been established because someone wishes to harm or handicap women. Indeed, organizational leaders are often unaware of how certain practices put women at a disadvantage. Many corporations, for example, traditionally made a practice of transferring their rising managers around the country as part of the training for executive positions. The fact that women are less geographically mobile than men meant that the policy automatically put women, especially married women, at a disadvantage. Even the most radical feminist would not claim that corporations instituted the practice of transferring managers simply to exclude women from the upper ranks of power. Insensitivity, past and present, exists more often than should be expected; but malice plays less of a part than one might think.

We must recognize the unintentional aspect of sex discrimination for several reasons. First, it is actually unfair to those in positions of power to hurl blame at them when their major crime has been a lack of imagination. Second, and more importantly, recognizing the unintentional nature of sex discrimination leads us to see that good intentions do not automatically protect an organization from perpetrating in practice injustices of which it disapproves in principle.

If you have ever suggested to an employer that sex discrimination may be a feature of his or her organization, the employer has probably responded with the immediate defense: "Hey, we're liberated. We harbor no sexist attitudes here." This defense is really no defense at all. Just as bad attitudes do not produce the problems, good attitudes do not instantly solve them.

The gap between the egalitarian attitudes and sexist economic realities becomes clear as soon as the hard realities of wages and salaries are examined. Economists have gone to great lengths to assess the extent of sex discrimination. Their methods are sound, and their conclusions do not bring cheer.

A multinational study by two economists, Donald Treiman and Patricia Roos, presents a classic example of the investigations that economists have performed.[53] They documented the association between earnings and various job qualifications (e.g., education, years on the job) for male workers in nine countries between 1972 and 1977. Using statistical techniques, they determined the average cash value of each type of qualification.

Treiman and Roos then turned to the female workers. Generally, in each country they were less qualified than the male workers. No one disputed this. The question was: Did the women reap the same cash value from each of their qualifications as did the men? Knowing the dollar worth of each job qualification, and knowing how much of it each woman possessed, the economists calculated what women in each country would have earned if they were men.

Did the women earn as much as they should have? The answer, emphatically no. For all countries, the actual female earnings fell far short of what they ought to have been. In the United States, women earned $3,000 less than men with equal qualifications.

Such figures can, I realize, make the eyes glaze over. While apparently impersonal and remote from the details of daily life, the findings of scholars such as Treiman and Roos actually carry extraordinary significance for us all. They are the numbers that describe our lives.

You can see the personal relevance in the true story of a woman whom I call Lucia. Lucia married Gregory in 1970. In September of 1972, Lucia started her graduate work at a university close to home. Then, in July 1973, she gave birth to a son and continued with her studies. Three years later she obtained her Ph.D. and entered the job market. Teaching jobs were hard to come by in 1976, and Lucia's family situation (especially her husband's job) meant that she had geographic limits on her job search. After months of effort, she stumbled on a vacancy at a nearby college.

Lucia was able to schedule most of her courses in the late afternoon and to hire a babysitter for the child, then three years old. Her starting salary was $9,800. She paid about $50 per week in commuting costs and $3 per hour for child care. Her earnings, net of taxes and expenses, amounted to $2,000 for the entire year.

Lucia loved her son and her husband, and she loved teaching; but the heavy demands on her at work and at home left her with little spare time for her research. She began to scrimp on sleep to work on some research that was close to her heart. By the end of the first term, Lucia was losing steam. She attributed a minor car accident that she had at the end of the first term to fatigue.

One day during a lecture on work force statistics, a student posed a direct challenge to Lucia. Impatient with abstractions, the student asked Lucia, if she earned the same salary as the new male teacher in the department. The male teacher was still working on his Ph.D. and so was less qualified than Lucia on one of the explicitly acknowledged job characteristics. Lucia had no idea what her male colleague was earning but she felt certain that his earnings would be approximately the same as hers. At the insistence of the class, Lucia promised to ask her colleague.

When she did ask her colleague about his salary, she was astonished to discover that the young man, whom we'll call Frank, earned close to $11,000. The young man was equally surprised to learn that his female colleague with a Ph.D. earned over one thousand dollars less than he. Together they went to the chairman for an explanation.

"Ah," said the chairman, "it's easy to explain. Frank here is on a continuing appointment, while Lucia is on a replacement appointment."

"So?" pushed Frank and Lucia, uttering the same thought simultaneously.

"Well, Frank is theoretically eligible to sit on committees, and committee work takes time. Now, if we do manage to convert Lucia's job to a continuing appointment," said the chairman, "she, too, will have to sit on committees. But for the moment, she does not."

"But I don't sit on any committees," objected Frank.

"Yes. Well, that's because it's your first year here," came the reply. "And during the first year, according to union regulations, a professor is not supposed to be put on any committees."

So by virtue of her degree, according to departmental rules, Lucia ought to have been earning a thousand dollars more than Frank. In the end, then, the system had cheated her out of $2,000 or more. That $2,000 would have relieved stress for Lucia. She could have taken her family on vacation. She could have hired a housecleaner. She could have hired a research assistant. Or, she could have bought 667 additional hours of high-quality child care.[54]

Employment: Slow Improvement

Lucia's conversations with her male colleagues took place in 1977. The statistical data on which Treiman and Roos based their conclusions were collected starting in 1972. Surely, one might think, the world has changed since then.

Our country has, indeed, been undergoing astounding shifts in attitudes. In 1976, 68 percent of Americans said "yes" when George Gallup's pollsters asked: "Do you approve of a married woman earning money in business or industry if she has a husband capable of supporting her?" A decade earlier only 55 percent said yes; and in 1936, a meager 18 percent. And since 1976, the change of heart has, if anything, accelerated.[55]

The shift in attitudes has not yet produced substantial changes in how economic rewards are distributed in our country. The most recent studies by economists have confirmed the persistence of sex discrimination. In some fields, the gap between male and female earnings is now as little as two dollars in ten, but in no field are women compensated at the same rate as comparable men. The famous 59 percent figure is still all too accurate.[56] National statistics also show that a woman who is fired or laid off from any given job has a harder time than a man fired or laid off from the same job in finding new employment at the same level.[57]

Economists are not the only scholars to document gender injustices in the workplace. In a study of job and home satisfaction in Newton, Massachusetts, I uncovered some undeniable inequalities.[58] My sample included 185 employed men and 163 employed women. The two samples were matched perfectly in job prestige, years of education and training, hours on the job per week, and age. Yet the men earned, on average, $8,000 a year more than the women!

Oddly enough, the working women in Newton were not aware of their own personal disadvantage. On question after question, the answers showed that the women felt as content with their jobs as did the men—even when the questions concerned salary. Surprisingly, this lack of awareness did not extend to the general situation of the existing salary inequities between men and women in the United States. All of the people in the Newton study, and most especially the employed women, knew that sex discrimination was a serious problem for the country as a whole. Everyone, especially the employed women, felt upset and angry about sex discrimination in general. Yet very few translated their political views into an understanding of their personal situations. It was as if each woman knew that women in general are discriminated against and thought herself an exception to the rule.

The blindness of everyone, including the victimized women themselves, to the harsh realities of sex discrimination gives me pause. I believe that by concentrating attention on the supposed problems of the juggling life, we sometimes seek to avoid confronting the real problems within each role. Like the drunk who drops his car keys when he steps on the curb and then moves some yards away to look under the lamppost for his key, we are searching where the light is, but not where the key is.

Once we sober up and move away from the lamppost, we can begin to solve the real problems that cause women pain and anxiety. Certainly one excellent way to reduce the difficulties that allegedly arise at the juncture between work and home would be to correct the difficulties that persist for women at work. If employed mothers were paid what they deserved, the increased earnings would no doubt make the purchase of domestic services easier. The more one earns, the less it pinches to pay the babysitter, the housecleaner, and the takeout restaurant.[59]

Improvements needed in women's work life extend beyond monetary ones. Sexual harassment at work is a problem for many women. According to survey researchers such as Barbara Gutek, between one-quarter and one-half of employed women have been harassed at least once during their working lives. Women are two or three times as likely as men to receive unwanted sexual advances. Some men are flattered by sexual attention at work, but most women are not. They feel disgusted, angry, and vulnerable. Although unlikely to register complaints with their employers (who are, after all, sometimes the worst offenders) women who have been harassed become less satisfied with their jobs, often to the point of changing their jobs.[60]

The feelings of distress at work can spill over into a woman's home life.[61] Negative interactions with coworkers and especially with bosses can make a woman irritable. The irritable wife may say that she finds it hard to combine work and marriage when what she really feels is that it is hard to go to work. Likewise the irritable mother. Stopping work or otherwise running away from the problems brings no lasting relief. We should stop dreaming up ways of distancing women from the labor market and concentrate instead on finding the ways to make the labor market a more decent and healthy place for all workers—female as well as male.

At Home

At home, too, attention must be paid. June Cleaver and Donna Reed did well in the 1950s, but for the rest of us, family life has not always been a picnic. At home, women have had a lot of work and little power.

Until quite recently, most doctors of the body and of the soul assumed that it was woman's sacred destiny to be a wife and mother. In the late 1950s, family planner and physician Alan Guttmacher wrote that he wished it to be "emblazoned on the walls of high schools and colleges that women should start their families early."[62] Guttmacher's advice derived in part from scientific information available at the time about the health of babies born to women of various ages. In part, too, the advice grew out of his moral conviction that every woman ought to be a wife and mother.

Once she had been wed and bedded and had brought forth issue, the ideal woman of the 1950s was expected to stay home with her children. Said the revered Dr. Benjamin Spock in the first edition of *Baby and Child Care:*

> It doesn't make sense to let mothers go to work making dresses in a factory or tapping typewriters in an office, and have them pay other people to do a poorer job of bringing up their children . . . the younger the child, the more necessary it is for him to have a steady, loving person taking care of him. If a mother realizes clearly how vital this kind of care is to a small child, it may make it easier for her to decide that the extra money she might earn, or the satisfaction she might receive from an outside job, is not important after all.[63]

Obviously, times and attitudes have changed. Few people today would make blanket statements that all women ought to be mothers or that all mothers ought to stay home to provide care to their dependent young. Or, at least, few would make such a statement unselfconsciously. There are new public attitudes as well as new economic realities.

Yet old ideas linger like the stench of smoke on a garment. Can't you smell the old ideology when some husbands speak of domestic chores? Some men "help" their wives around the house. They do not wash dishes; they help with the dishes. They do not vacuum the floor; they help with the vacuuming. They do not bathe the children. They help with the children. Such men even babysit for their own children when the wife goes out to work or shop. And they are married to women who help out with the family finances or who return to school or work so that the family will be proud of them.

Another vestige of the old ideology is the continued idealization of young motherhood. Many young women and men look forward to parenthood as an idyllic time of life filled with smiles and coos and hugs. Most likely you did, too. Can you remember when you anticipated your first child? You probably dwelled on the joys of breastfeeding and longed for the moments when your baby would hold you in her gaze and wrap all her tiny fingers around just one of yours. You no doubt thought of the walks and talks and giggles. You certainly felt ready for the magical and recurrent moment when, you imagined, your child would release the day and drift contentedly and securely into sleep.

During all your tender imaginings, did you anticipate the sleepless nights, the hours of pacing, pacing, pacing as you tried to help the colicky baby find relief? And when you looked longingly into the future, did you foresee the mountains of laundry, the rashes, the temper tantrums, and the boredom? Did you understand, as you gazed into the crystal ball, that later would come the struggles over toilet training, the bickering among siblings, the din and racket, the armed combat in the aisles of the local grocery store? Did you know that there would be moments when you would experience such anger at your child that you would feel on the verge of physical violence?

Those who did foresee the problems were certainly insightful; nothing in the public media prepares women for the rigors of motherhood. Commercial advertisements feature lots of babies, but virtually nowhere can the expectant mother learn, for example, that for many months she will be devoting six to eight hours a day simply to the task of breast-feeding. When it comes to recognizing the pains and worries of parenting, the country seems to be caught in the grip of a great conspiracy of silence.

Until recently, psychologists in particular were mute about the plight of new mothers. In the words of Rosalind Barnett and the late Grace Baruch, two authorities in women's issues: "[S]ocial scientists have, along with everyone else, assumed that child rearing is a mother's natural job, [and so] we have made little effort to examine the extent and pattern of maternal participation in child rearing . . . we have assumed that caring for children promotes women's well-being."[64]

As soon as psychologists turned their attention to the question, they discovered a truth known secretly by millions of American women: *mothering is hard*. Despite the considerable joys and satisfactions of parenting, motherhood can be quite a demanding and dreary business.[65] Tending children can be a source of enormous frustration and strain, even as it is a source of joy and fulfillment.

Without a doubt, the hardest time is infancy. When taking care of an infant, the demands are enormous. Every parent knew this simple truth at some time, and then most of us suffered amnesia. It is amazing how rapidly we forget the sheer physical drain of caring for a young baby.

An interchange that I observed recently recalled for me the nature of life for mothers of babies. I had taken one child and his playmate to select a dozen doughnuts at the shop on the corner. As the children devoted exquisite attention to the choices at hand, the young woman behind the counter began to wilt visibly. I assumed she felt impatient, but neither she nor I nor the other, older woman behind the counter disciplined the children into making a decision.

Then the older woman asked: "How's the babe?"

The young woman replied sluggishly. She described how she had hired a friend to mind her baby during the previous afternoon and how the baby—who was only three months old—seemed to sense the change in caretakers and so slept all afternoon instead of staying awake as was her habit. And then, instead of sleeping as usual at night, the child stayed awake interacting with her mother until 3:30 A.M.

Finally, my son and his friend made their selections. Shutting the doughnut box, the young clerk sighed heavily. "With only three and a half hours of sleep, I feel so tired," she said, "that I think my heart is going to stop beating."

When their babies are young, women become overtaxed emotionally as well as physically. Babies present many causes for concern. Their mothers are at risk for depression; they derive less pleasure from their marriages, and their self-esteem can dip.[66] They become disillusioned, and they suffer marked feelings of loneliness.[67]

Anyone who—like the women in the statistical accounts—has experienced baby blues and thought herself unique or somehow psychologically maimed, may be consoled to learn about investigations like that of Jeannette Ickovics of George Washington University.[68] As part of a large study of Army training policies and family well-being, Ickovics collected information from 315 young Army wives, one-third of whom were employed outside the home. Approximately one-fifth of the women had a child between the ages of three and twelve months at the time of the study. All the women filled out questionnaires that asked such things as "Have you been feeling emotionally stable and sure of yourself during the last month?" A score of seventy-three or above on the questionnaire indicated well-being, and a score of sixty or less meant severe emotional distress. The average score of the women with babies was sixty-one—one point away from severe distress![69] As one psychologist has noted, no matter what the myths say, "young motherhood is not a rosy, carefree time of life."[70]

Mothering

We make mothering harder than it need be. Some of the stresses and worries of parenting are inevitable, but some are the result of specific ways of living that can be altered. We middle-class Americans could change some of our ways and make motherhood less stressful.

A problem of major proportions is that our middle-class culture overemphasizes individual responsibility and independence and thus isolates people from each other.[71] When a mother is isolated and is expected, during certain stretches of the day, to care for one or more young children entirely on her own, life becomes hard. The need for vigilance is ever present for one in sole charge of a child. When yours are the only eyes watching the toddler or the small child, you know you should never nod off. Sometimes a mother cannot even blink. Yet, constant and unrelenting years of vigilance erode a woman's physical and mental health.[72]

Recalling the pioneering years on the Great Plains, some have linked the national penchant for individualism to our history as an expanding country. Long after civilized Europe was bursting its seams, the American continent allowed for expansion. We have been a country on the go, nomadic. Perhaps the impulse toward a self-contained nuclear family is simply the heritage of a glorious past.

Perhaps, but the facts suggest not. For one thing, families in America have not always been as atomized as they are today. In the past, households were more likely to include many unrelated people and distant members of the extended family and not simply people in the immediate family. The households of yesteryear expanded and contracted as people came and went. Since World War I, the trend for middle-class households to become inhabited exclusively by people who are closely related to each other has been marked.

Even in my lifetime, there has been change. After I was born, my unmarried aunt and my maternal grandmother moved in temporarily to help my parents manage the newborn (me) and the toddler (my sister). My aunt and grandmother eventually went back to North Africa where they lived, and friends and neighbors became surrogate relatives. Our family went on vacation with other families, and during the school year and work year, there was an easy coming and going of all the children among all the houses of the neighbors. Many of my friends had grandparents living with them intermittently or constantly.

Although no one I knew took in boarders, our house had a steady flow of out-of-town guests. Guests from overseas often stayed for several weeks or months. So, occasionally, did American friends: In 1953, some out-of-town friends came for the weekend with my family and stayed for three months. The husband of the visiting couple had suffered a severe heart attack during the weekend visit, and those were the days of long recuperations.

It's hard to envision anything similar today. Think about your household. How often do you have people who are not immediately related to you live in your household for weeks or months? Chances are, hardly ever—unless of course you are lucky enough to have live-in help. Now think about your neighborhood. How many three-generation families live in it? Probably precious few. Among the middle class, even two generational families are becoming scarcer!

Demographers like Mary Jo Bane of Harvard University have studied changes in the composition of American households since the days of the Pilgrims.[73] Her analyses compellingly demonstrate that the American family is, on the whole, becoming less and less fluid, and more and more isolated. The atomic family (one mother plus one father plus a couple of children) that we take for granted as traditionally American has—without a question—not always been the norm.

Some have suggested that the current American drive toward tiny segments of families is the inevitable result of our nomadic life-style. Yes, Americans are nomadic. We move around a lot. But not all nomadic people are intensely individualistic and segmented.

Among the Efe people of Northeastern Zaire, for example, movement and a strong sense of community seem to go together. The Efe are a seminomadic people who seem to require little privacy. They stress cooperation, group identification, and sharing to such a large extent that they even make the care of a newborn a group effort. A baby born among the Efe is immediately taken from the mother. For the mother to hold the child right after birth is considered potentially harmful. The newborn is passed among the group of women who attended the birth and is nursed by all of the women who are lactating. Only after several hours do the mother and her baby have their first contact. The practice of communal caretaking continues throughout the infant's first months. Efe infants do not seem particularly stressed by this pattern of child care, and they develop into socially adept and gregarious children.[74]

If the Efe customs seem extreme, think how extreme our practices must seem to them and to others. Ours is one of the few societies that thinks it normal and natural for an individual adult to spend more than three hours a day solely in charge of young children.[75] In many African and Pacific cultures, and in some parts of Europe, children are in the care of groups of women, not individual and isolated women.

In middle-class America, we have made a totem, it seems, of the nuclear family. Keeping friends and neighbors at a distance, we do not even encourage extended families. More often than not, grandparents are nowhere close to hand. And where are the aunts and uncles? They are off somewhere, in some distant city or suburb or on a farm, providing for and nurturing their own, small, separate broods.

In between the two extremes—the Efe on the one hand and the

Americans on the other—exist some attractive compromise solutions to the problem of families and children. One of them has been described by Urie Bronfenbrenner in his classic *Two Worlds of Childhood.* Bronfenbrenner contrasts the individualistic American style with the more communal style of the Soviet Union.[76] It is quite common in Moscow for an adult who has a seat on a crowded bus to pull a standing child onto his or her lap, even if the child is a total stranger. Children, in the Soviet ethic, belong to everyone, and every adult has a responsibility for the care of the young. Contrast this with what would happen if a stranger tried to hoist a five-year-old on her (or his!) lap in a crowded New York city bus.

How much easier, safer, and saner life would be if we could trust other adults to help in the care and tending of our offspring! Wouldn't it be nice to let the child climb on the lap of some friend or stranger as we struggle with our parcels? Many hands make light work.

Children, as well as harried parents, would benefit from a community-minded approach to child rearing. Think how much children have benefited from a communal approach to education. Although many people understandably lament the state of public schools, virtually no one questions whether or not we ought to have a public education system in this country. We take it for granted that the nation has the right and the obligation to educate the young. Most parents have no problem delegating the education of their children to schools, public or private. Today across all strata and in all locations, the parent who insists on educating a child at home is regarded as well meaning, yet aberrant.

Yet in some levels of society, it used to be a mark of parental love and concern to supervise the education of one's child at home. People of substance did not automatically entrust the education of their young to schools. Indeed, only 150 years have passed since the first state instituted compulsory education. Many did not compel school attendance until some years after World War I.[77] What seems evident today—that loving parents should delegate the academic instruction of their child to some authority outside the family—did not appear self-evident even four generations ago!

Next time worries intrude about having nonfamily members take care of your children, remember education. Is it irresponsible to send a child to school? Do we reject or otherwise deprive our children when we hire a piano teacher, a computer tutor, or when we sign him up for swimming lessons at the Y? Of course not. You know that delegating responsibility for education is not the same as abdicating it. So why do parents feel guilty when they hire a babysitter or send the child to a child-care center? To share responsibility for the emotional and psychological development of a child is to promote the child's welfare.

Alternatives

Middle-class attachment to the sanctity of the nuclear family produces a profound ambivalence about surrogate care. This ambivalence, in turn, immobilizes many women with guilt. Parents ought to be lobbying Washington for better child-care facilities. Instead, most stand passively by while the federal government avoids responsibility for child care and while the state governments also fall woefully short in regulating it. In 1980, for example, Washington published the Federal Interagency Day Care Requirements specifying the minimum acceptable standards for child care in staff-child ratios and so on. Several years later the requirements were withdrawn, but the Department of Health, Education, and Welfare urged the states to use them as yardsticks for programs in their jurisdictions. At the moment, Massachusetts is the only state that requires the proposed staff-child ratio for both infants and toddlers before it grants licenses to child-care providers.[79] Child-care workers are overworked and underpaid. Nor do workers in family-based centers fare better than those in child-care centers. One government study determined that 87 percent of family-based child-care providers were earning less than the minimum wage.[80]

What a vicious cycle! Because working parents do not feel entitled to demand that society provide adequate care for our young, society does not provide it. Then, knowing how scarce is excellent care, parents worry when they make arrangements for their children. Ambivalence inhibits action.

At a personal level, too, guilt can cause a woman to take actions she ought not take or to refrain from taking actions that she ought. Some of us have run out of milk for the baby or discovered, during the baby's nap, that the diaper box is empty. We have made a mad dash to the local store while the child slept. One woman whom I interviewed had on several occasions run out of diapers for her child. Claire hesitated to call the downstairs neighbor to help her out. This woman had felt that her predicament indicated a lack of planning and that the empty diaper box gave testament to her inadequacy as a mother. Rather than impose on a neighbor and expose herself to potential criticism, she drove at breakneck speed to the corner store and hoped to arrive home safely before the baby woke up.[81]

Raised on such adages as "you made your bed; now lie in it," Claire—a single, working mother—felt in some corner of her heart that any small imperfection in her planning revealed an unforgivable irresponsibility. Claire felt that to ask for help was to admit defeat. In her horror of appearing anything less than perfectly responsible, Claire behaved in ways that actually increased the probability of harm. To awake to an empty apartment would, after all, have been more frightening for her child than to awake to the familiar face of the neighbor.

Claire is not unusual. Many women wing it on their own rather than ask for help from friends and neighbors. Their reluctance to ask for help is born not only of politeness or of consideration for the neighbor. Many times, women such as Claire attempt to meet all challenges alone without complaint because they think they will otherwise be criticized for weakness. Ironically, the fear of criticism actually increases the chances that a woman will not prove adequate to the demands of the juggling life.

How women might overcome the fear of criticism and work together at the life task of raising children has been suggested in a beautiful book, *All Our Kin* by anthropologist Carol Stack. It analyzes how black households in a midwestern city in the late 1950s coped with grueling poverty.[82] Stack documents how kin and friends help a family in need by the process of "child-keeping." For shorter or longer periods of time, and always with the expectation that the help will be reciprocated, one or more of the needy family's children might live for a while away from the parent or parents.

Some commentators might condemn as selfish and irresponsible the adults who allow or require their children to live with others. Such a view, says Stack, is extremely ethnocentric. A better way to understand the trading of child-rearing responsibilities among poor urban blacks, Stack shows, is to see the practice as a highly adaptive strategy for survival against enormous odds. By refusing to be possessive about their children, the people in Stack's study maximized their slim opportunities. Fluid households are the best indication not of irresponsibility but, on the contrary, of responsibility and of caring. "Children born to the poor in The Flats," writes Stack, "are highly valued and the rights of these children belong to the networks of cooperating kinsmen."[83]

Middle-class jugglers today lack time in much the same way that the poor black people of The Flats lacked money. Shared responsibility for children and other dependents enhances the health and well-being and minimizes the stress of women in all walks of life. A sense of community provides the safety net that women need as they juggle life's responsibilities. And all children, not just the desperate poor, benefit from living in a world where many adults merit trust.

Habits of Thought

When it comes to gender arrangements, ours is an era of uneven change. In some regards, the rules appear dramatically different than they did a few decades ago. Less than 7 percent of the population today lives in the 1950s-style middle-class family—the family with an employed father, an at-home mother, and two or more dependent children. Most women who are graduating from colleges and universities today expect to have careers. Their mothers did not. Only a generation ago, the mother of young children who sought paid employment outside the home was often the object of pity, distrust, or condemnation and rarely the object of envy.

Yet, in many respects, old habits constrict our thoughts. In the long shadow of sexism, girls and women have to work harder and achieve more than boys and men to receive equal compensation. The female partner in an adult heterosexual couple is still expected to organize the home, even if the male partner is willing to do some of the drudgery. Child care remains almost exclusively the responsibility of women. And given our values of rugged individualism, which dictate that each nuclear family ought to raise its children largely in isolation from others, each mother is left to carry an intolerable burden on her own. The fear that she may not be measuring up to some unstated standard then muzzles her. The ensuing silence is both uncomfortable and misleading.

Small wonder, then, that scholars, commentators, and jugglers themselves have attributed real problems to the wrong sources. The problems that women face today—the pressures, the lack of time, the need to structure and remain ever vigilant, the inability to relax—are real. At first glance, filtered through the assumptions of the past, the problems appear to stem from the impossibility of combining work and family. It seems at first that they would all be solved if women would simply abandon some of their unhealthy ambitions and stop trying to have it all or do it all.

Methodical investigations have revealed the fallacy of appearances.

Conflict between life roles is not the major issue, though certainly it can be an issue for some women from time to time. The major source of strain is the persistent difficulties within each life role. When these strains are eased, when we rid ourselves of the vestiges of sexism and of the unhealthy aspects of individualism, we will be rewarded by decreased stress and increased energy.

· 3 ·

And Benefits

The two little knobs on the top of the tape recorder, plainly visible to Laura, turned soundlessly. She watched them as I posed the opening question of the interview: "Would you say that you ever experience difficulty combining your different life roles?"

Even before the last words had left my mouth, Laura started laughing. "Ever?" she teased. She laughed some more and said in a gently mocking voice, "oh never." And then she said: "Always? Absolutely. Always. It's always difficult to combine. They all conflict right now, but they are interesting in that respect. There's been conflicts between my role as mother and wife, between mother and worker, between wife and worker, between child and wife. Yes, absolutely, lots of conflict." For the next hour and a half I questioned, probed, and pried. Laura, with a ready smile, answered all my questions. Without embarrassment or pretense, she spoke of life's stresses—her husband's ill health, her pregnancy with a second child, her father's continued descent into alcoholism, her parents' divorce, her still-wobbly law practice, her financial worries. She did not shy from the difficulties.

Had we ended the interview after an hour and a half, I would have come away with the impression of a modern woman struggling to fulfill the obligations that came from her roles as daughter, mother, wife, and lawyer. Had I not asked further questions, I might have concluded, mistakenly, that women today are suffering from an excess of expectations. But, fortunately, I did ask: "What do you see as the advantages of juggling?" Laura answered:

59

It keeps life interesting. I think it makes you feel so much more whole to be able to do all these things. It proves to me that I am a capable individual, somebody who can handle the role of mothering and everything else, too. And even more than that, I think, is something else. My time away from my son is actually to his advantage and my advantage. Because we have this space from one another, I'm thrilled then when I see him. And he is always excited to see me. It makes our time together that much nicer and gives me a chance to feel good. There's nothing worse than being home all day, all night, in one role. Everybody needs some kind of variation, especially with mothering. It's such a constant job. You're never free of it, and so it's good to put a different hat on. Be a lawyer or whatever you want to be. You get breaks from being a wife, too. When I'm a lawyer, I feel like I'm not playing the role of being a wife. I think variation is an important part of anyone's healthy state of being. It keeps you focused. It keeps me focused as a mother to be involved in other things.

Sometimes when I'm working on a boring case, I just can't wait to go off and do something else. And so it's nice to have the excuse, if I want an excuse, to say "Oh, whoops, gotta go get junior." Jobs can get very boring. There was one case that I worked on that just did not seem to end. Constant revisions and changes. It was great to be a mother at the end of the day. Or to have to do something domestic.

"Moderation," concluded Laura with a laugh, "is the key to everything." Later in the interview, I asked Laura if she had ever thought about what life would be like if she did not play all her current roles. "Well," she replied, with a deep intake of breath:

It would certainly be different, wouldn't it? I am thrilled with the mother role. It's something I've always wanted, and I feared that I would never get to be a mother. I would hate ever to lose that role, God forbid. It has been so fulfilling for me to be a mother that I would have always felt something greatly missing if I had not had Jake [her son].

The role of wife—that's a hard one. It is important because I like the whole sense of family, the car, the dog, the children. There is something very comforting about all that. To not have that, I think, would be unpleasant. Not that I couldn't survive without it, but again, there would be something missing. I am the kind of person that needs a mate.

And my role as lawyer gives me a great sense of accomplishment. I feel like I'm finally there—or getting closer anyway—to being an independent individual. I had always felt a certain sense of inadequacy, felt not as good as most other people. Going to law school cured me of that. It made a big difference, being around so many smart people in a prestigious law school. . . . It gave me the courage and confidence to go into practice on my own.

So, my different roles all contribute to one another. And right now I feel pretty good about them all. Life feels good. It's at a point where it's coming together. . . . I know there are going to be more conflicts. There probably always will be; but I feel a great sense of accomplishment.

The woman sitting before me conformed to no media image. Although crisp, neat, and very attractive, she was not the carefree juggler who periodically strides across the pages of the women's magazines. But neither did Laura conform to the stereotype of the overwhelmed and overly ambitious woman of the '80s and '90s. She was no Ophelia with a briefcase. Although she had worries, to be sure, she was not about to drown in them. This woman, in fact, enjoyed and felt invigorated by the challenges of contemporary role combination.

Rewards Outweigh Costs

Nor was Laura alone among the women I interviewed over the years. Again and again, struggle and achievement have recurred as twin themes. So persistent and yet subtle has been the connection that I decided to study the two themes further. During the summer of 1989, I contacted twenty middle-class women between the ages of thirty and fifty who had at least one child in the local schools in my little Massachusetts town and who worked outside the home. In response to the question, "Do you ever find that you have too much to do?" all twenty women in the study replied yes. And every woman was able to identify some stresses in her life-style. Everyone also obviously enjoyed the juggling life. When asked at the conclusion of the interview, "On balance do you think that it is more stressful or more beneficial to you to juggle?" three of the twenty women felt the negatives outweighed the positives; two claimed the score was tied. For the remaining fifteen, the benefits outnumbered the stresses.[1]

Although they felt stretched by the unrelenting demands of motherhood, marriage, and career, the women to whom I spoke exuded positive feelings. Neither carefree nor totally careworn, these jugglers projected a sense of realism and hope.

Felice was a free-lance commercial artist, the mother of three young adult women and one adolescent boy, and the wife of a prominent member of the local community. She maintained a house in town and one in the country, rented out a third property, and worked more than full time at her job, on which she faced constant deadlines. About her life-style, Felice commented:

> You don't get bored. That is one of the reasons I keep doing all this. Also, I get paid. And *that* is another reason why I keep working. I like the interest and variety of the job and even the challenge of trying to fit more into a given time than you probably ought to. . . . In thinking about cutting back, I am not sure that I would want to cut back to the point where there isn't any stress. I certainly would not wish to give up so much so that I wouldn't have to do any balancing.

Felice's enthusiasm for her various activities was not unbounded. She admitted that she would "like to cut back on the noncreative office work" and that she "would be very happy if [she] never had to do another load of wash or run a vacuum cleaner again in [her] life." She joked that: "I have lists left, right, back and front, and some things never get done," and complained: "there are certain things that I am simply not doing as well as I should. There just aren't enough hours in the day to get done all the things you *should* get done, never mind the things you'd *like* to do." But Felice also confessed to feeling pleased and proud "when you somehow manage to get more done than you thought you possibly could, or even should."

Similar sentiments were expressed by Jennifer, a married college administrator. Jennifer prominently included in her list of major life roles the role of daughter because, for a number of months she had cared for an ailing parent. The day of our interview, she was also preparing her young child for minor surgery. When I asked her if she ever found that she had too much to do, Jennifer laughed: "yes, every day." She said she wished to be free of "worry about an aging parent," and identified the stress "of having to do two things at once" as a fairly regular feature of role combination. Needing to attend to several tasks at once made Jennifer feel that she was not doing any one task as well as she would like. And the need to divide her attention prevented her from relaxing while working.

Even with all its problems, the juggling life appealed to Jennifer:

> As my mother always says about old age, "it's better than the alternative." And what would you give up? You don't want to give up having a child. You don't want to give up having work. You might want to give up your marriage. [Here she laughed.] I don't know. Each role has something compelling that you wouldn't want to give up. There's nothing that's obvious that could be dropped. Having this kind of life-style

is clearly more stressful than having another kind, but it's also more beneficial. I feel like I have some choice, and this is what I've chosen to do.

One businesswoman who was active in local politics and the married mother of two young boys offered a slightly different analysis. When asked what she saw as the costs and benefits of role combination, businesswoman Jane said: "I can't imagine not doing it. I cannot imagine being one dimensional, having just one role. I know most people have at least two or three. There are those times when I feel 'ach, why do I do this? This is just too much.' But, on balance, it's more beneficial to juggle." What she found most beneficial about juggling was: "Getting to utilize all of who I am, not feeling that there is a part of me that is thwarted or that I haven't explored. I think it's a good role model for the kids. They get to see that people can do different things. It makes me feel accomplished. It gives me a sense of accomplishment."

A sense of accomplishment or fulfillment was mentioned by many women in my small sample. One labor organizer joked about "being so tired that I am constantly looking forward to retirement" and yet observed: "I feel if I were retired right now, I would look back on my life and say 'ah, this has been satisfying.' It has been satisfying to do everything."

Other Places, Other Times

My small survey is not the first to have shown that most women feel enriched as well as stressed by juggling occupational and domestic responsibilities. Indeed, nearly twenty years ago sociologist Cynthia Fuchs Epstein began to investigate the positive aspects of juggling. Throughout her distinguished research career, Epstein has shown a particular interest in one group of working women: female lawyers.

The women lawyers whom Epstein interviewed over the years did not benefit from flextime or organized child care. They were the pioneers—more the creators than the beneficiaries of programs to help people integrate their disparate life demands. The lawyers sometimes, but not always, were in a financial position to buy enough child care and household help so that they could delegate labor. But they never delegated the executive function at home: It was they who made all the decisions about how to care for the children and the home, and they supervised the arrangements. And, almost without exception, the women were subject to subtle and blatant prejudice in their professional lives. In an era when only 6 or 7 percent of law students were women, at a time when the dean of a professional school could say aloud that he rejected a well-qualified woman because she was "too pretty, too likely to get married and have babies," education in the profession was harder for women than for men. Once admitted to the bar, discrimination continued. Some women lawyers had to endure harassment from male colleagues. All had difficulties to surmount at work.[2]

> Professions, like other institutions, typically defend themselves against threats. That the legal profession defended itself against the inclusion of women in its ranks was clear from the histories of the hundreds of women I interviewed who had tried to become lawyers before the 1970s. To become lawyers, women had to be stronger, more resourceful, and, in general, more advantaged than men who wanted to enter the occupation.[3]

Yet, in spite of all the hurdles, Epstein's women lawyers by and large managed to combine professional careers and a family life and to do so with success and vigor. Wrote Epstein recently:

> Despite the absence of childcare programs or flexible work schedules, many of my respondents reported that they felt effective and full of life. . . .
> Some of the most successful women I spoke to told me that they did not feel they had any problems. When I asked one woman, who had attained partnership early in a large corporate law firm, about the problems she faced in reconciling her roles as a Wall Street partner with three children under the age of twelve, she answered, "No problems," and then qualified herself: "Well, not no problems, but none I can't deal with."[4]

Like the sociologist who studied them, the pioneering women lawyers found fulfillment and satisfaction in the very act of balancing work and home.

The same sense of purpose and satisfaction has also been visible to feminist researchers looking at the generation of women that followed the pioneers. Making careers work alongside family is, according to researcher Lisa Silberstein, a central concern for contemporary middle-class women.[5] Many of the women in Silberstein's study of dual-career marriages feel stimulated and enriched by struggling to continue their careers during their children's early childhood years. When they do not give in to a culturally sanctioned sense of guilt, they are filled with excitement and with a firm sense of self-worth. Of course, as we saw in the last chapter, the women in Silberstein's sample—like jugglers in many samples—are perpetually caught in time crunches. Virtually all of them described the need to manage time very carefully. Some complained more than others about the pressures of constant scheduling.

Given the range of responses in Silberstein's sample, it seems only fair to wonder if some women are very happy while others are unhappy with demands of role combination. For every woman in Silberstein's survey who finds juggling exhilarating, is there not one who felt depressed and beaten down by it? To find out, I contacted Lisa Silberstein and asked her about the amount of variation within her sample. Here is what she answered:

> Of course there is some variation among people. Some women had very helpful spouses and good support services. Others felt they had their hands more than full. But, really, the biggest variation was *within* people, not between people. Every woman in the study seems to have experienced times that were stressful and other, smoother times. Each woman has had many moments of clear sailing and then times when, say, a child was sick or one of the careers was floundering. On the whole, the women in my study were vitalized by what they saw as swimming upstream and succeeding at it.

Both Silberstein and Epstein studied middle-class and professional women. We must not ignore the importance of socioeconomic status. Juggling may be less fun when you are the cook, maid, chauffeur, and secretary than when you hire the cook, maid, chauffeur, and secretary. Perhaps the juggling life contains little pay-off, psychological or material, for working-class women.

Some observers have proposed that juggling might actually prove harmful to women of modest means. The observation comes partly from a recognition that life is harder when women do not have the resources to purchase domestic services and partly from a myth that working-class women subscribe to the housewife ethic. Supposedly, working-class women are so houseproud that they love to do housework.

When someone decided to test this notion, the evidence showed that working-class wives are not, in fact, enamored of housework. Like middle-class women, working-class women enjoy working outside the home, derive a sense of satisfaction and self-esteem from paid labor, and dislike housework. In the mid 1970s, sociologist Myra

Marx Ferree interviewed 135 married women living in a working-class neighborhood in Massachusetts.[6] All of the women were white and most of them were in long-term marriages. More than half of the women were employed outside the home. Ferree found that 92 percent of the part-time workers and 83 percent of the full-time workers were satisfied with their lives while only 74 percent of the housewives were. Under a quarter of the employed women felt that what they did during the day was less interesting than what their husbands did. More than half of the housewives felt that way.

Clearly, the stereotype is wrong: Working-class women are no more attached to the housewife role than are their middle-class sisters. Given this lack of attachment, it should come as no surprise that working-class women—like their middle-class sisters—function well when they combine family and occupational responsibilities. Research on working-class jugglers is less copious than on middle-class women; but the research that exists strongly suggests that the tonic value of having multiple roles is not limited to the affluent.

Typical are the findings of a large survey by psychologist Rena Repetti.[7] Repetti investigated the dynamics of good mental health among tellers and other clerical workers in an East coast and a West coast bank. On standardized, objective measures Repetti's jugglers appeared to be psychologically healthy. They were no more or less depressed or anxious than the other women in the study. The self-esteem of jugglers matched the self-esteem of women with fewer life demands. The women's own accounts of their lives also revealed strong and healthy functioning. Given that they were participating in a study about how factors at work affect life at home, the clerical workers in Repetti's study had ample opportunity to complain about the difficulties of juggling different life demands. Typically, however, they had few complaints about the juggling life-style. "There was one woman," reports Repetti, "who was having a hard time keeping everything on an even keel. But that woman was in the midst of a divorce at the time I was interviewing her. Everyone else seemed to be doing fine."

Images and Realities

In today's popular culture, two images of the juggler predominate: At one extreme is the glamorous Ms. Juggler, the woman with a perfect figure and a face untouched by age or care. At the other extreme is the bedraggled Mrs. Juggler whose supermom cape has become badly tattered.

The first image can make a perfectly normal woman feel grossly inadequate. The woman's rational mind tells her that the model is posed and paid to look so fresh and lithe. But to her irrational self the glossy image whispers doom. Like Naomi in the Chinese restaurant, a woman can conclude on the most insubstantial evidence that other women are more competent, better organized, or just simply better than she.

The second, bedraggled, image is unlikely to provoke feelings of inadequacy by comparison, but it offers a struggling woman cold comfort. It seems to say "see, this is what you, too, will become if you have not already." The image is an implicit rebuke, telling a woman that she should be ashamed of her ambitions.

Both images do real women a disservice. At a very basic level, the focus on the juggler herself—rather than on the social conditions that make her life easy or hard—fosters the tendency to scapegoat women for the problems of modern society. As I showed in chapter 2, it would be more accurate and more useful for everybody if, rather than blaming women, we considered instead the role played by our slavish adherence to an obsolete ideal of the nuclear family.

The extreme nature of the media images compounds the problem. By detaching the difficulties faced by working wives and mothers from the advantages of role combination, the media create the false impression that women either lose or gain from role combination. Actually, women both lose *and* gain from role combination. And, as we shall see, one of the gains—an inoculation against psychological depression—far outweighs the losses.

The sense of simultaneous loss and gain figured prominently in the account of Ann, a physician, mother, wife, and politically active citizen whom I interviewed in the summer of 1989. Speaking, sometimes poignantly, of the different pulls in her life, Ann admitted that she often wished that she could drop one or more of her roles or cut back her obligations. She then went on to say:

> You know, I often wish that. But the other side of that is the wish to do it all, to experience and enjoy all those things. The real problem for me is that I truly do enjoy a number of things. I cannot do them all well. But [on the other side] there is the pleasure of not losing a part of myself. I love being in the world. I love being a leader, I love being an achiever. I loved being active, before the children were born, in my professional world and in the political community. Those were very true to me, those extroverted, active roles. . . . But I could not pass up having children. Realistically, it's a very masochistic kind of role, but I've had some of the most joyful experiences of my life as a mother, the

most meaningful. So if I had my major wish, my really *major* wish, I wish I could manage it all.

As to whether the benefits of role combination outweighed the problems, Ann mused: "I think if you lose yourself, you're dead. So it's more beneficial for me to struggle, I mean juggle [she laughs at her own slip]—to struggle and juggle. To be dead is worse."

Depression

Death—at least, emotional death—has unfortunately been the fate of millions of American women whose life options have been more restricted than those of Ann or of the other women in my sample. Are women who juggle more or less prone to depression than women in the traditional generations before us? Back in the Leave-It-to-Beaver days, many thousands of women experienced depression. Following World War II, war depression became a women's problem on a grand scale. Indeed, during recent decades, depression has been known as "the female malady."[8]

"Depression," in the words of one expert, "is the common cold of psychology."[9] Like the common cold, depression covers a number of different symptoms—not all of which occur in any given bout. Among the symptoms that most textbooks list are loss of appetite, loss of interest in sex, irregular sleeping habits, fatigue, irritability, sad mood, crying spells, and an inability to concentrate. Many depressed people feel critical of themselves. They despair of ever creating a better life.

Psychologists estimate that in any given year, 15 percent of the population experiences one or more of these symptoms and that between 2 and 3 percent of the general population—some 6 to 9 million people—suffer depressions severe enough to mean a curtailing of lifestyle but not so severe as to require hospitalization.[10] More than 10 percent of the population is thought to seek professional help for depressed feelings at some point in their lives.[11]

Diagnosis of severe depression is not difficult. When a person attempts suicide because of feelings of worthlessness and hopelessness, cries without interruption for days on end, or finds herself literally unable to get out of bed, one can easily diagnose depression. Estimates of severe depression can be derived by counting how many people are currently hospitalized for depression (prevalence) or how many people are newly admitted to the hospital as depressed (incidence).

Milder depressions pose more challenge for the diagnostician; and figures on the prevalence of mild depression can never be precise. Yet, researchers can estimate how common and how serious depression is in any community by asking a randomly selected sample of women and men a standard set of questions, assembled into a "scale" or an "inventory." The questions are established through extensive pretesting with groups of individuals already known to be more or less depressed according to clinical judgments. The scale is then refined by testing whether the questions are equally clear and meaningful to other samples.

For the last decade, the CES-D Scale of Depression has been the method of choice for assessing depression among normal populations.[12] Developed by Leonore Radloff of the National Institute of Mental Health, the CES-D Scale is most often administered by an interviewer who reads out the twenty items and records the person's answers. Sometimes—especially among well-educated people—the scale is self-administered.

A copy of the CES-D Scale appears in Table 3–1. To administer the scale to yourself, simply look at the twenty items on the left, and for each one mark how frequently you have felt a certain way in the last week. Then assess your level of depression by assigning points, using the chart in Table 3–2. If your total score adds up to sixteen or more, you would be classified as depressed and might benefit from professional treatment. If your score is around seven, then you are like the average male in Radloff's original sample. If your score is an eight or nine, then you are like the average female.

Typically researchers find that women are more prone to depression than men. Far more than half of the severely depressed people are women. Women are hospitalized with a diagnosis of severe depression much more often than men are. For those not hospitalized, too, women have been found to suffer more often and more seriously from depression and related psychophysiological symptoms. One well-known researcher reports that in cities across the country, women in the community are between two and five times as likely as men to exhibit the signs of depression.[13]

Why are so many women depressed? The question has propelled a veritable mini-industry of research. Dozens, and possibly hundreds, of scholarly articles and books have examined in-depth the connection between gender and depression.[14] The American Psychological Association has even established a task force on Women and Depression.[15] We are beginning to find answers.

Biology is one of them. Hormones may play a major role in certain

TABLE 3–1
CES-D Scale of Depression

INSTRUCTIONS FOR QUESTIONS: Below is a list of the ways you might have felt or behaved. Please tell me how often you have felt this way during the past week. Please indicate what you felt by putting an X in the appropriate box.

During the past week:

	Rarely or none of the time (Less than 1 day)	Some or a little of the time (1-2 days)	Occasionally or a moderate amount of the time (3-4 days)	Most or all of the time (5-7 days)
1. I was bothered by things that usually don't bother me.				
2. I did not feel like eating; my appetite was poor.				
3. I felt that I could not shake off the blues even with help from my family and friends.				
4. I felt that I was just as good as other people.				
5. I had trouble keeping my mind on what I was doing.				
6. I felt depressed.				
7. I felt that everything I did was an effort.				
8. I felt hopeful about the future.				
9. I thought my life had been a failure.				
10. I felt fearful.				
11. My sleep was restless.				
12. I was happy.				
13. I talked less than usual.				
14. I felt lonely.				
15. People were unfriendly.				
16. I enjoyed life.				
17. I had crying spells.				
18. I felt sad.				
19. I felt that people disliked me.				
20. I could not "get going."				

types of depressions—such as postpartum depressions—and men and women obviously differ dramatically in the composition of their hormones. In the brain as well as the rest of the body, sex differences contribute to differential rates of depression. Scientists have now identified aspects of the neurochemical processes that trigger and sustain some depressions, and some laboratory work suggests that the body's depression-producing chemicals operate differently in male and female brains.[16]

Biology alone does not cause depressions. And so, biology cannot account completely for the excess of depressed women. Social roles are also important. Looking at the prevalence of depression among different types of people, researchers have uncovered some important links between sex-role expectations, life roles, and mental illness.

Here are some pieces of the puzzle:

There is a very strong association between life stress and depression. Major upheavals, such as divorce, job loss, or the death of a family member or friend, produce major depressions. Minor upheavals produce minor depressions. The link is predictable, reliable, and well documented.[17]

Life stresses are most common among the financially insecure. Poverty and problems go hand in hand. A person's economic status is a significant predictor of how likely it is that he or she will suffer from a depression.[18]

Many more women than men in our country are economically disadvantaged. Numerous researchers have documented the discrepancies between male and female wealth. One researcher has also shown that females encounter more life stressors than males.[19]

Some people have assumed that depression is the typically female way to react to life's problems. Either because of biology or because of socialization—goes the theory—a woman is slated to meet difficulties by becoming depressed while a man fights the difficulties or succumbs in ways other than depression. The facts do not jibe with these assumptions. Instead of showing sex-stereotypic differences in people's reactions to stressors, the facts show gender differences in the number and severity of stressors. Women simply face more stressors than men.

Now add to the basic observations, two others:

In the so-called traditional family, wives were much more likely than their husbands to experience depression. Conversely, in dual-earner families, wives do *not* suffer more depressions than their husbands.[20]

TABLE 3–2
Scoring the CES-D Scale of Depression

INSTRUCTIONS FOR SCORING: After completing the CES-D Scale, use this chart to assign points to your answers. Add up all the points. If your score is 16 or more, you might benefit from professional treatment.

During the past week:

	Rarely or none of the time (Less than 1 day)	Some or a little of the time (1-2 days)	Occasionally or a moderate amount of the time (3-4 days)	Most or all of the time (5-7 days)
1. I was bothered by things that usually don't bother me.	0	1	2	3
2. I did not feel like eating; my appetite was poor.	0	1	2	3
3. I felt that I could not shake off the blues even with help from my family and friends.	0	1	2	3
4. I felt that I was just as good as other people.	3	2	1	0
5. I had trouble keeping my mind on what I was doing.	0	1	3	3
6. I felt depressed.	0	1	2	3
7. I felt that everything I did was an effort.	0	1	2	3
8. I felt hopeful about the future.	3	2	1	0
9. I thought my life had been a failure.	0	1	2	3
10. I felt fearful.	0	1	2	3
11. My sleep was restless.	0	1	2	3
12. I was happy.	3	2	1	0
13. I talked less than usual.	0	1	2	3
14. I felt lonely.	0	1	2	3
15. People were unfriendly.	0	1	2	3
16. I enjoyed life.	3	2	1	0
17. I had crying spells.	0	1	2	3
18. I felt sad.	0	1	2	3
19. I felt that people disliked me.	0	1	2	3
20. I could not "get going."	0	1	2	3

Employed women are not exempt from life stress and depression, but employed women recover emotionally from major life traumas more rapidly than do housewives. Thus, when a marriage dissolves or finances take a turn for the worse, everyone feels bad—but among housewives the bad feelings linger longer and are more severe than among jugglers.[21]

All of these findings point in one direction. It seems that traditional restrictions on women's life roles have increased the problems that women face while simultaneously decreasing the available strategies for coping. The statistics corroborate a basic axiom of contemporary American feminist theory. Feminists believe that, despite the apparent ease, to be a housewife (who makes a home and does not work for pay outside it) is often to be burdened, isolated, and psychologically hampered.

Mental Health and the Number of Roles

When making important life decisions, corroborative evidence and feminist analysis do not suffice. We cannot simply be swept along by the tide of currently fashionable ideas, even when the fashion turns feminist. We need hard evidence.

In quest of hard evidence about whether multiple roles enhance a woman's psychological well-being, researchers at Wellesley College's Center for Research on Women interviewed more than 200 women living in a suburb of Boston.[22] In their sample of middle-class women, researchers Grace Baruch and Rosalind Barnett found that the more life roles a woman played, the less depressed she was. Women who were employed, married mothers were less depressed—according to a standard scale like the CES-D—than other women. The jugglers in Baruch and Barnett's sample also exhibited higher self-esteem than other women. Jugglers were more likely than others to endorse positive statements like "I feel I have a number of good qualities" and less likely than others to agree with negative statements such as "I certainly feel useless at times." Jugglers also took a great deal of pleasure in life—more than women with fewer life roles.

Listening with the ears of a social scientist, one hears the refrain articulated by Laura, the young lawyer with the large brown eyes and quick smile, repeated in the detached, impersonal, and numerical data of Barnett and Baruch. The refrain is this: Life's different roles "all contribute to one another." To the busy juggling women in Barnett and Baruch's sample, as to Laura, it would appear that "Life just feels good."

Other researchers have also documented the link between multiple roles and well-being, using standardized measures and statistical techniques. In one study, employed, married mothers averaged a score of 8.8 on the CES-D scale while women who were not in the work force and were not mothers averaged a score of 20.6. The latter group of women were well into the danger zone for depression.[23] In another study, more than 1,000 Californians were asked about their lives and their emotions. For both women and men, employment and marriage shielded people from depression. Unemployed women and men were more depressed than employed women and men; and unmarried people were more depressed than married people.[24] Another study looked at the emotional well-being of Americans between the ages of forty and fifty-nine. Among these middle-aged people, role combination was linked to strong self-esteem and freedom from anxiety.[25] Finally, when men and women across the country reported how happy they felt, researchers found that jugglers were happier than others.[26] By and large, the more roles, the greater the happiness. Parents were happier than nonparents, and workers were happier than nonworkers. Married people were much happier than unmarried people. Married, working parents were generally at the top of the emotional totem pole.

In sum, a sizable number of studies have now shown that women who juggle different life roles are less depressed than other women. The jugglers also rate higher, on average, in self-esteem and happiness. Stress and troubles there are, in no small measure; but in larger measure still are the emotional rewards.

Not only do jugglers feel happier than other women about themselves; jugglers also feel enhanced happiness with many other aspects of life. Involvement in each role seems to increase a woman's satisfaction with her other roles. Having an occupation helps make people content with their domestic situations. Even though they sacrifice leisure time and sleep, employed women often enjoy their domestic pursuits more than do housewives.[27] Traditionally, too, employed women have expressed greater marital satisfaction than have housewives.[28] The evidence indicates that women with responsibilities outside the home appreciate their families and are appreciated by their families.

For the same reasons, employed women with families derive more satisfaction from their jobs than do other women. This pattern was shown very clearly in a survey that I conducted in Newton, Massachusetts.[29] More recent investigations showed the same result in samples representative of the population of the entire United States.[30] Women and men who are married and are parents express higher job satisfaction than other women and men.

Cause and Effect

The fact that contemporary jugglers feel more positive (about themselves, their work, and their families) than other women does not convince everyone about the benefits of multiple roles. The associations between juggling and positive mental health may be strong, but what is the cause and what is the effect? What comes first, some have wondered: a woman's zest for life or her involvement in different spheres of life?[31]

When a survey shows that employed mothers experience less depression than housewives, we wonder which came first—the good mood or the paid labor? Perhaps depression has prevented some of the women from working outside the home.[32] Or perhaps, women with special appetites for life engage in many roles. If so, emotional condition causes life-style. Or perhaps working outside the home has elevated women's moods. If so, life-style causes emotional condition.

The issue is a thorny one, and common sense suggests spiralling effects. For each of us, there are surely times when our emotional (or physical) states produce certain changes in life-styles and also other times when our emotional states are determined by our life-styles. The great majority of the studies have not followed women over a period of time. So we cannot say with certainty whether the juggling or the fulfillment comes first for all women.

But we can take some good guesses. The accumulated evidence contains strong indications that role combination does not simply reflect good functioning but actually produces a sense of enhanced well-being. Juggling, for many women, is the cause; contentment the effect.

Informative is a study conducted by the Survey Research Center at the University of Michigan. In 1976, approximately 2,500 adults were interviewed about several aspects of their lives. A few years later Ronald Kessler and James McRae analyzed a subsample of people to learn about the mental health consequences of female employment for married women and their husbands.[33] Kessler and McRae reasoned that if good health was the cause rather than the consequence of female employment, many women who wished to were prevented from working by ill health—either physical or mental. And, if ill health were preventing women from working, women who were involuntarily out of the work force suffered worse health than other women. One way to test how much of a role good health plays in promoting paid employment, in other words, is to see how much ill health stands in the way of paid employment.

Kessler and McRae concluded that not many women were prevented from working by poor mental health. They reached this conclusion by comparing (1) women who were involuntarily out of work with (2) women who were out of the work force by choice. The first group suffered poorer physical health than the second; but they did not suffer poorer mental health.[34]

Because it sheds light on the question of cause and effect, Kessler and McRae's analysis has important implications for contemporary women. Combining paid employment with marriage and motherhood creates safeguards for emotional well-being. Nothing is certain in life, but generally the chances of happiness are greater if one has multiple areas of interest and involvement. To juggle is to diminish the risk of depression, anxiety, and unhappiness.

The same conclusions are reached in another study that separates cause and effect. In a study mentioned at the beginning of chapter 2, David Chambers examined the career paths of women and men who had graduated from the University of Michigan Law School between 1976 and 1979. His examination included 130 female graduates who responded to a mailed questionnaire in 1986. Of these women, thirty-six had become mothers since responding to a previous questionnaire. "Even with the burdens of a first child," says Chambers, "half of the new mothers reported higher career satisfaction in 1986 than they had reported at the time of the five-year survey (when their satisfaction levels were already high), and only a quarter reported lower satisfaction." Most of the ninety-four women who had remained childless were less satisfied with their careers at the time of the 1986 questionnaire than at previous times.[35]

Thus, when we carefully separate cause and effect, the conclusions of the varied studies remain the same. Stripping away the statistical complexities, the numbers carry some simple advice. First, if you want to like your job, find yourself a family—or at least a significant and long-term involvement outside work. Second, if you want to like your family, find yourself a job—or perhaps a significant, long-term volunteer commitment. And if you want to like yourself, you'd best have both the family and the job—or some suitable equivalents.

Role Quality

We must, of course, resist oversimplifications. Good mental health is not automatically assured simply by virtue of playing multiple life roles. With life roles, as with everything else, quantity can tell only part of the story. The quality of each role also greatly influences well-being.

Quality matters in a couple of ways. When life's roles break a juggler's heart or bend her back, she does not necessarily benefit by juggling more of them. Some jobs are awful; and if possible, she should not take or keep an awful job, no matter what the salary. Similarly, some marriages are terrible. An awful job does not make a terrible marriage better. Nor does a terrible marriage counteract the ill effects of an awful job. If she can, the juggler should leave a terrible marriage or a terrible job.

Note that I say "if." Not all women have the same options. Everyone has some options but life is clearly easier for some than for others. Woe to the woman who must simultaneously face misery in the household and discrimination in the world of paid employment. Such was the predictable conclusion of an intensive study of forty-three Boston women living in poverty.[36] All of the women in the study exhibited fairly elevated levels of depression. On the CES-D Scale, the impoverished sample scored midway between normal samples and samples of people hospitalized for depression. The poorer the woman, furthermore, the more likely she was to be depressed. For the poor women in the Boston sample, every role—even marriage—brought many requirements but few resources. Social interactions were difficult because the women were so often the providers and so seldom the recipients of care. For poor women in Boston and for all women everywhere, adding hardship to hardship brings no psychological advantage. It is only when roles contain enough reward that people gain by combining public and private responsibilities.

When each of a woman's life roles surpasses the minimum level of acceptability—as is true for the vast majority of Americans—quality continues to matter.[37] Several psychologists have documented, in different locations and with different samples, that a woman's mental health depends on the nature of her job, her closeness to her husband, and the tasks facing her as a mother.[38] To accurately guess whether or not a woman will be depressed, inquire about the nature of her marriage as well as about her marital status; about her feelings of job satisfaction or dissatisfaction as well as about her employment category; and about how close she feels to her children, not just whether she has any.

The previously mentioned study of life roles and mental health among middle-class women conducted by Grace Baruch and Rosalind Barnett provides a good example. To measure the quality of roles, Baruch and Barnett asked 238 women about the positive and negative aspects of their experiences as workers, mothers, and wives. Employed women, for example, were asked to rate their jobs on a set of positive items such as "variety of tasks" and "hours fit my needs" and a set of negative items like "job insecurity" and "having too much to do." Married women rated their marriages, and mothers rated the role of motherhood in similar ways. For each role, Baruch and Barnett computed a "balance score" by subtracting the negative feelings from the positive.

Baruch and Barnett included three standard measures of psychological well-being in their study: depression, self-esteem, and pleasure. They calculated the association between role quality indexed by each balance score, on the one hand, and psychological well-being on the other. Satisfaction with the wife role proved extremely important: The associations between the quality of the wife role, feelings of self-esteem, and freedom from depression were strong; and the association between the quality of the wife role and feelings of pleasure were very strong. The quality of the worker role and that of the mother role were also strongly related to all three measures of psychological well-being. Knowing how a woman felt about any one of her life roles—especially the wife role—allowed the researchers to predict the woman's level of depression, anxiety, and life pleasure even better than knowing how many roles the woman played.[39] The strong association between multiple roles and good mental health, in other words, is influenced by how much a woman likes her job and likes her home life.

How much a person likes her job depends on the person as well as the job. Some women are very absorbed in professional work; others are not. In a study of more than 100 new mothers in the Los Angeles area, women varied widely in how they felt in the worker role. Among the sixty-three mothers who stayed home full time with their babies, those who had been very involved in the worker role tended to miss their work, to feel irritable and depressed and to fight with their husbands much more than the women who cared little for working.[40] The effects of high job involvement were also investigated by Rena Repetti. With a sample of forty-four women, Repetti found that those who have high job involvement are more affected by job characteristics such as social climate, supervisor support, and job satisfaction than those with lower job involvement.[41]

Limitations

Observing that the nature of a woman's roles matters at least as much as the number of her roles leads us to remember another qualifier. There is a limit to the number of different roles any woman can enjoy. Nobody can do everything. When flogged repeatedly by the image of the carefree, competent, and ever-gorgeous juggler, some real women begin to wonder at their own limitations. Rather than empowering women, unrealistically positive portraits of role combination can be yet one more way society tells the average woman that she is inadequate to life's tasks.

I was reminded of the importance of limits recently when, after hearing me lecture on the benefits of multiple roles, a member of the audience brought me a cartoon drawn by Nicole Hollander. The first panel of the cartoon showed Hollander's untidy character Sylvia sitting at her typewriter, holding a can of something in her left hand and pecking at the typewriter with her right hand. From the machine come the words, in the bubble of cartoon talk: "Have you always wanted to tap dance like Fred Astaire, play the piano like Fats Waller, perform an appendectomy?" In the next panel the scene remained virtually the same, and the words from the typewriter continued: "The first meeting of the 'It's never too late, but let's be realistic' club will meet at my house on Tuesday. Plenty of refreshments will be served."

Just as we need to encourage women to test life's many options, we need to acknowledge real limits of energy and resources. It would be pointless and cruel to prescribe role combination for every woman at each moment of her life. Life has its seasons. There are moments when a woman ought to invest emotionally in many different roles, and other moments when she may need to conserve her psychological energies.

It is entirely possible that this day, week, month, or year is not the time to juggle different life roles. If a juggler is like Nan, for instance, she may feel that volunteer work is the most occupational involvement she can handle right now. Married to a neurosurgeon and mother of two young children, Nan is currently trying to help her sister through a divorce and to help her brother through the terminal stages of AIDS. Says Nan:

> Here I am. I think I'm doing exactly what I want to do. Yet, I always feel somehow a failure, that I don't do much. You go to a party, and people say "What do you do?" and you say you are a doctor's wife and people say a sort of flat "oh." If you say you just stay home with the kids, most people treat you like a lower, unevolved form of life. So I think, gee, taking care of kids, helping my husband, that maybe I don't do much. Why don't I have a Ph.D.? Why don't I have a job that makes bucks?

Nan both differs from and resembles Naomi, my friend in the Chinese restaurant. On the surface, the two women seem vastly different—one being the image of the self-reliant, feisty, modern woman and the other a vision of the traditional helpmate, trim and demure with a clean apron. Naomi wants to juggle; Nan does not. Yet under the surface, there are striking similarities. Both women are plagued with feelings of inadequacy. Naomi blames herself for any troubles she experiences as she tries to manage her life at work and at home. And Nan blames herself for, as she puts it, "aiming too low." Each woman assumes that there is some absolute standard of true womanhood to which she (and perhaps she alone) fails to conform.

Our insecurities result, without a doubt, from years of sexist socialization. It is hard for a woman to feel fine about herself when she is in a society that devalues and fears women. It is difficult, if not impossible, for her to trust her convictions and credit her ambitions when she is a woman in a culture that restricts women's options.

Ironically, women's self-doubt may help perpetuate the lopsided system in which we find ourselves. When people feel defensive, they often seek to protect threatened egos by criticizing others. It is probably the women (and their partners) who feel most insecure about the new sex-role arrangements who are least tolerant of Nan at cocktail parties. To the extent that we worry about how adequately we are combining all aspects of life, we are unlikely to be sympathetic to women and men who choose options different from ours.

Opening Our Ears and Eyes

Insecurities also have a way of making people frightened of the very information that could release them from their worries. The paradox of self-imposed suffering has interested observers of human nature since ancient times. It does so today.

As I have waded through the voluminous research reports in the social and medical sciences, I have wondered about a curious discrepancy. The beneficial effects of juggling are well documented, and yet, outside the small circles of feminist scholars on college and university campuses, there is little talk of the deep satisfactions felt by today's women as they meet the challenges of simultaneously working outside and inside the home.

That a male establishment should conspire to be silent about the real benefits for women of role combination would be understandable. How safe it is for those who would tether women to show the juggler as either incomparably competent or as bedraggled and defeated. Why have we women ourselves not been clamoring for more accurate information about how real women, women like ourselves, both struggle with and benefit from a life composed of many parts?

The answer came in a memory. Some years ago I organized a conference concerning women and multiple roles. Among the speakers were some luminaries; the preconference plans were many and complicated. My good friend Dana provided weeks of physical and emotional help preparing for the conference. As we worked together, we discussed not only the logistics of the conference but also the issues at hand, the anticipated content of the presentations. Yet, it was not until the very day of the conference that Dana was able to articulate a feeling that had been growing in her over the last few weeks. Minutes before the first speaker was scheduled to talk, Dana tapped my forearm. "Faye," she whispered:

> I'm really confused and ambivalent. On the one hand, I'm hoping to learn all sorts of tips that could help me juggle my different demands. But on the other, something in me does not want to learn how the truly competent women do it all. Something in me wants to learn that there are no truly competent women, or at least no women who are managing any better than I am.

Curiously, it was Dana's fear of inadequacy that momentarily kept her from realizing her own wonderful competence as a working

mother and wife in a contemporary American nuclear family. To lib-
erate her from that fear, Dana needed dispassionate and cumulative
information. It was the sets of systematic studies that reminded Dana
about the benefits of her life and about her talents at living it. I trust
that Dana is not the only woman to find comfort and validation in
what some may think of as dry science.

· 4 ·

Explaining the Link

Back in 1972, when most sociologists were speaking of role strain, role stress, and inter-role conflict, Walter Gove proposed that people—women and men alike—may benefit from having different life roles to play. Gove had come upon the idea in his studies of mental illness. Like many others, he had observed that women were vulnerable to mental illness in far greater numbers than men. Gove also discovered something that had escaped general notice: Namely, that the differences between men and women are sharpest among married people. Among single people, men tended to suffer psychological disturbances as often as women.

Building on these observations, Gove linked the rates of depression and other mental illness to life circumstances. Said Gove at the outset of his article: "I will attempt to show that it is the roles confronting married men and women that account for the high rates [of emotional disorder] among women and not some other factor such as women being biologically more susceptible to mental illness." Gove identified and examined five aspects of men's and women's roles "in modern industrial societies that might produce unusually high rates of mental illness in women." First was what he called women's "fragile structural base." More specifically:

A married man has two major sources of gratification, his family and his work, and a woman only one, her family. If a male finds one of these roles unsatisfactory, he can frequently focus his interest and concern on the other role. In contrast, if a woman finds her family role unsatisfactory, she typically has no major alternative source of gratification.[1]

Walter Gove was a man ahead of his time. True, he was not totally alone in singing the praises of role combination; but even if all scholarly friends of juggling had banded together in the early 1970s, the resulting music would not have been loud. Only recently has the academic community come to see the potentially positive aspects of role combination.[2]

Given the prevailing ideologies, it was to be expected that Gove's thesis about the beneficial aspects of multiple roles did not immediately set off an avalanche of research into the varied ways that people benefit from the simultaneous holding of public and private responsibilities. Twenty and even ten years ago, feminist scholars who, like Gove, looked with favor on working mothers were forced to devote the bulk of their attention and energy to arguing against the negative forces dominant within the social sciences and throughout society. Scholars were so busy trying to demonstrate that juggling was not detrimental that they lacked the time to investigate why role combination brought women benefits.

It is now time to do that. Anyone who loves a mystery might want to know why women, discriminated against in the work force and treated unequally in the home, should nevertheless be better off with dual roles than with a single one. The paradox beckons.

A solution to the mystery is not simply of academic interest. Frayed jugglers who know the reasons why juggling benefits women can minimize the stresses and maximize the benefits. Women whose circumstances do not involve the increasingly common trio of life roles—spouse, parent, worker—who know the reasons behind the juggler's happiness can achieve the same happiness. This was the belief of Bernice, a black single professional woman with whom I spoke. Bernice had recently moved to a new city and was in the process of establishing a support system when she and I spoke about work and family. Given her advancing age and her advanced degrees, Bernice had come to the conclusion "that it is not realistic for me to think of being a wife. I do not think it is in my future." Yet Bernice wanted to know everything she could about the ways in which family life benefits working women. Why? Because she quite rightly thought that she could use the knowledge on her own behalf. "Maybe," she reflected, "there are some things that are good about marriage that I can arrange for myself even without being married."

Hearing Bernice, I was reminded of my father when we were children. "Kids," he used to say, "I don't want to be a millionaire; I just want to live like one." He uttered these good-natured words in the era when millionaires really did live well. It was not until my adolescence that I realized that living like a millionaire on a middle-class budget requires a lot of ingenuity. With ingenuity and with knowledge, all women, even homemakers and career women, can reap some of the emotional benefits that come to jugglers.

Practical Benefits

Juggling produces both practical and psychological benefits. In a material sense, a woman's involvement in one role can enhance her functioning in another. Being a wife can make it easier to function as a mother and easier to work outside the home. Being a mother can facilitate the activities and foster the skills of the efficient wife or of the effective worker. And employment outside the home can contribute in substantial, practical ways to how one works within the home, as a spouse and as a parent.

Benefits to the Family

Working outside the home brings practical benefits to a family member in two ways: First, work directly creates resources that can be put to good use in family living. Second, work provides access to additional resources.

For most women most of the time, the major resource produced by employment is money. Even though the average working woman earns less than the average working man, she earns more than the average homemaker—a lot more. Money is the resource that allows people access to other, more meaningful resources.

Of course, the amount of earnings that a woman can count as profit varies considerably. The working mother typically enjoys a much smaller profit margin when she is starting in her occupation than after she has become established. Her experiences might be like mine; my first year of full professional employment netted me very little hard cash. Babysitting costs alone seemed staggering. I remember calculating my professional expenses, including commuting costs and the costs of supplemental clothing and cleaning, and adding these to the services that I had to purchase to replace myself in the home. When I subtracted the total figure for expenses from my take-home salary, the remainder was less than $2,000. "Swell," said my brain, "I'm working for 80 cents an hour."

As the decades have passed, the time I devote to paid labor has remained fairly constant; but my estimated hourly wage is much more than in the early years—and the need for labor-intensive child care much less. And so today's profit margin is much greater than when I started earning money. Some of the profit goes to the luxury items—a movie here, a dinner out there, a new Nintendo game here and there. Treating the children to these items helps to make me feel that I am a capable mother. Surprising my husband every now and then with his favorite champagne or a new silk tie enhances my sense of worth as a wife. To give my parents and my siblings very nice gifts at birthdays always feels like an act both of love and of self-love. Donating money to worthy social causes makes me feel I am a better citizen.

While some of my salary goes for the treats and surprises, most of it goes for those other little extras like decent clothing, three meals a day, and a place to sleep indoors. Providing these luxuries also makes me feel quite competent as a wife and mother.

Even if money is not a prime motivation for having a particular job, the money that one earns from working surely matters. Jugglers who have employed male life partners may not see their own income as primary. But neither can they ignore that their income exists.

Perhaps, like Miranda Jamieson, you openly acknowledge the importance of money. Miranda works in a greenhouse and her husband Frank is the supervisor at the local lumber yard. They have two children, a teenage boy and a ten-year-old girl. The boy suffers from Crohn's disease, a disease of the small intestine. "When Felix was in sixth grade," said Miranda,

> he started to experience cramping. It was sporadic, but it prevented him from doing the things he likes to do. At basketball practice, he would have to sit down. After the sixth grade year was over, Felix commented that he could see his stomach bulging. Then I knew something was serious. We started to take a more vigilant approach. He had three good months in which he had no problems at all. But when he saw his stomach bulge, we did an barium upper G-I and found that he had Crohn's disease. We went right down to Denver and got a specialist.

As I interviewed Miranda about how she juggles work and family life, given the special stresses in her family, she described her job as flexible and then spoke about the benefits and drawbacks of having responsibilities outside the home when her responsibilities within the home are so grave. Listing the advantages of working, Miranda first noted that the job can take her mind off the serious home problems over which she has no control. Then she turned from the psychological to the practical: "And there's money. There's always that. I work so that I can increase our income. There is always in the back of our heads the idea that Felix might need emergency surgery. We'd have an expense that might come on unexpectedly at any time and we should be prepared for it."

Even women without pressing financial worries find that the money they earn enhances family living and their sense of competence as a mother. Married to an engineer, physician Ellen has few money worries, and thinks that the benefits that her children reap from her working are primarily nonfinancial. She is especially glad to serve as a role model for her girls to let them see "that a woman can have a profession."

Ellen recently changed offices and is experiencing a reduced patient load. The dip in income means that right now her income is, in Ellen's words, "really the icing on the cake to my husband's salary." If you ask her how her salary has enhanced family living, Ellen speaks with appealing understatement of the extras that add up to a "life-style that has a little comfort,"

> It was probably because of my income that we could afford to go to Disney World. We get to do things that we might not otherwise feel that we could do together, like go on trips. We don't feel restricted in doing house projects or buying furniture. And we just bought both girls leather jackets, not something we would do otherwise. If they want to do something, go to the movies, go to camp, they can feel like we can afford it. And a few years ago, my husband was able to purchase his computer because we had some discretionary money.

Asked what the next few years hold, Ellen admits: "[W]hen we're looking ahead toward college, we both contribute." "When it comes to money," her husband chimes in, "if some is good, more is better."

It is not only mothers of young children who benefit their children's lives by earning money. Consider Holly. At age fifty-five, Holly has been a dentist for more than thirty years. She describes herself as someone "who cannot imagine myself not being a professional worker." For Holly, as for Ellen, financial gain is not the primary motivation for working. "I work," says Holly with more than a little vigor, "because I want to work, because work is important to me. I even imagine that I am making a contribution." And Holly also readily concedes: "Historically my working had an enormous benefit for the family. It was my income (and involvement) that took the children and me anywhere we went. We took vacations and went to Europe and all of those things. . . . Now, the children are grown. Yet I am still paying their college debts on my own." Holly's current earnings and the profits on her investments (from earlier earnings) enable her to underwrite the expenses of family life in another way as well. Asked if she and her husband kept joint or separate accounts, Holly replies: "For ongoing, everyday kinds of activities, we each do our own thing. . . . But there is a new development. My husband and I live separately now. I support my own place fully. I also pay half the mortgage on the old place." With the income she earns, Holly can satisfy her own needs and still accommodate the family's need for a homestead. Without an independent income, family friction would be high indeed.

Women who are single and child-free (or childless) can have family responsibilities; and earnings help these women, too, fulfill their obligations. Thirty-year-old Carlotta is a capable administrator whose earnings put her "healthily into the middle class." She lives with another woman, Victoria, and does not expect to marry or have children. Carlotta considers herself partially responsible for the economic well-being of her aging mother.

Carlotta grew up in a working class suburb of New York. Her hard-working parents had been forced to leave a life of affluence in Italy and to start over as immigrants in America. According to Carlotta,

> My mother and my father made a lot of sacrifices in terms of their economic and social life to put my brother and me through school. . . . When we were growing up, in grammar school, we always had pencils and crayons and the little extras. We lived a pretty middle-class life on a lower-middle-class income. . . . Now I feel that it is pay-back time. I would feel very selfish if I could not not share the fruits of my labor. I am lucky. I can do it.

Carlotta shares the fruits of her labor by underwriting some specific expenses and by helping to provide for her mother's economic future. "If there is some time when she needs to be taken care of," says Carlotta,

> I want to be in a position where I can do that for her. . . . Partly I like the notion of being able to give her some luxury, like a really good TV

set. . . . More important than the luxuries is to be able to look toward the future in such a way that if she needs to be dependent, I can handle it. . . . I wouldn't think of the hassle of keeping my pay raises coming if I were just thinking of me. I don't need all that much in order to feel relatively comfortable. But it is not just a matter of me. I am doing all this for someone else as well.

Paid employment produces for women and men several resources besides money that can be used on behalf of the someone elses in their families. On the job, they come into contact with people who then provide services for them and their families outside of work. Jane worked in the same building as a carpenter whom her family later hired to remodel their kitchen. Ethel's workmate was married to a chiropractor who ended up curing Ethel's husband of his persistent backache. Lianna's secretary gave private computer lessons to Lianna's son. And my students have furnished hours of babysitting for Matt and Tim Crosby. With the babysitting has come a fair share of cultural enrichment, as successive waves of students introduced our boys to opera, poetry, art, science, and the joys of scarfing down three Big Macs in a row.

Benefits to the Marriage

What about the other way around? How do family responsibilities help you in your occupation? In what ways do you, as worker, gain from your experiences as a spouse, parent, sibling, or grown child of aging parents?

I asked these questions of a series of friends and acquaintances. The initial answers ranged from awkward silence to barbed jokes. Initially my informants had more to say about incompatible demands, constant interruptions, hectic time crunches, and sullen resistance than about any form of positive influence. Off the top of their heads, most people think of women's families as impediments, not aids, to their occupational efforts.[3]

In an interview with Beryl, a twenty-nine-year-old career woman, the assumptions of incompatibility were evident. Beryl described herself as someone who only very recently realized that "it doesn't work to always follow the career and only the career." When I asked her if she had ever thought about how she might combine professional work and family life, Beryl replied that she had become an avid reader of *Ms.* as a teenager and had, since that time, known that the "superwoman ideal" was not possible.

I had the idea that you couldn't have it all, and I had very strongly decided that marriage and family were just not going to be possible to fit into my life and that it was going to be far more important for me to go with the career. I really didn't start being interested in how to manage work and family until maybe the last year or two. I am now increasingly interested in managing both of those things. But I am not at all clear on how to fit them in. And I am very clear that fitting marriage and family into my life would involve extreme sacrifices in terms of my professional goals for myself.

I asked Beryl in what ways she imagined that family and career interfered with each other. "In almost every way," she replied immediately, "to me they seem totally incompatible." A lively and intense woman, Beryl hesitated not even five seconds when I posed the last question of the interview: "Can you imagine any ways in which family would promote your career?" "No," she exclaimed, "to me it seems that it would only get in the way."

That view is not without foundation. There have been precious few family members who provide the mechanical support for women workers that the women typically provide for them. Most husbands do not act as secretary, bookkeeper, receptionist, chauffeur, and general support staff for their working wives in the same fashion that wives typically do for their working husbands. Even people who seem at one level to have broken through the sex stereotypes seem to crash against domestic limits. A recent study of married union stewards, women and men, for example, documented the persistence of some traditional gender asymmetries among otherwise nontraditional people. Very many of the husbands in the sample acknowledged that their spouses helped them with their speeches and correspondence; not one of the wives was able to make the analogous claim.[4]

Several of the women I interviewed during the summer of 1989 noted the imbalance in their own marriages. Verity runs a crafts boutique and occasionally makes some extra money waitressing. Although quite positive about how much she likes to juggle home and work, Verity voiced a complaint that I heard from other women as well: "There's one thing that I still find very frustrating. . . . Despite everything—you could have a husband that really tries to do his share but there is always more that has to be done by the woman. There is no way that it works out even. There is a frustration there." Yet even in her frustration, Verity noted that her husband had helped as well as hampered her professional development. For Verity, and perhaps for others, there are trade-offs. Husbands receive more from marriage than wives do; but husbands can also give to a woman both practical and emotional support.

The professional support that husbands offer their wives is probably one reason that researchers have found married women, including married mothers, to be as professionally successful as—or more successful than—single women.[5] Often professional women marry men in the same line of work as themselves. Because women tend to marry men who are older than themselves, furthermore, many women are wed to men whose careers are more established than their own. Such women benefit from the good contacts and concrete advice that their spouses provide.[6]

A perfect example is Laura, the young lawyer whom I had interviewed at some length about the sorrows and joys of combining professional and family life. Laura's husband Ned is a tax lawyer. When asked about the sources of support that help her meet the various demands of her job and her home, Laura replied:

> Well, certainly, I feel support from Ned in my role as lawyer. He is very willing to assist me. He is, of course, much further along in his profession, and there are areas where he is much more experienced and knowledgeable. He is very willing to assist me whenever I have a question. It is just a real bonus for me that Ned is willing to help me when I need help. Otherwise, opening my own law firm would be a scary endeavor. What if I didn't know the answer to a question and I couldn't find it in the book? Obviously, I would have to figure something out. But I am wondering if I would be so willing to be on my own knowing that I don't have that source of information so readily available. Also, because of his office, he has on hand some reference books for me.

Researcher Rosanna Hertz found a similar situation among many of the dual-career couples whom she interviewed. Hertz claimed that at least a portion of her sample could "provide support for each other because they share similar work and organizational experiences. . . . They offer each other advice and counsel about career decisions, occupational stumbling blocks, and personnel matters, such as how to handle a boss or how much of a pay raise to ask for."[7]

Nor need the jobs be identical to each other. Sometimes occupations call for complementary skills. Take Eileen, a professional writer married to Jake, a college teacher. Eileen edits Jake's papers; and Jake coaches Eileen whenever she has to give a talk. His teaching skills are invaluable whenever she needs to make an oral presentation. Eileen and Jake are not rare. In Lisa Silberstein's study of twenty dual career couples, one-third of the women mentioned that their spouses had given them substantive or concrete input over and above emotional support.[8]

Truth to tell, marriage benefits men more than it benefits women. Most married women no doubt receive less support and material help than they would like. And certainly women receive less support than they are entitled to given the generally substantial support they provide to their husbands.[9] To say that women receive less than they should is not to say they receive nothing. As more and more women acknowledge, a husband can be a great professional resource.[10]

Children, Too

And what about children? Middle-class mothers are supposed to and generally do help their dependent children with their school work and extracurricular lessons. It would be absurd to expect repayment in kind—at least until such time as the child, mastering the technology of VCRs, home computers, seeing-eye garage doors, microwave ovens, and cellular phones, begins to act as technological consultant to her or his bewildered parents. What practical benefits do children bring to the working mother?

Children are a source of information and inspiration for women in many occupations. Congresswoman Pat Schroeder has described family life as a training ground for communicating with the public. In *Champion of the Great American Family*, Schroeder recounts:

> How to phrase things with the vividness necessary to get through to a child who is not studying for his final exams is always a challenge, as is surviving the daily crunch at the breakfast table. One morning a few years ago, I stood scrambling eggs in my kitchen, thinking with irritation about how President Reagan seemed to escape unscathed from all the failures and scandals of [his] administration. A moment later, when I looked down at the Teflon frying pan I was wiping clean, my face broke into a grin. That's what the Reagan presidency was like! Nothing stuck to it . . . *Ronald Reagan was a Teflon-coated president.* I couldn't resist the phrase, and later that day I trotted it out in a speech on the House floor. At least the term stuck—so to speak.[11]

Out of the limelight, working mothers who are less nationally prominent than Representative Schroeder find the same as she. Meredith teaches fourth grade. Her own child, Steven, has not always had an easy relationship with school. Steven's experiences allowed Meredith to develop a special perspective on some aspects of her occupation.

> My ups and downs with Steve have in particular given me a sense of what life is like for kids who are not necessarily just taking school by storm, with everything moving along and everybody feeling enthusiastic about it. I think I see the power of the teacher's word more than a lot of teachers do. Sometimes at school, when I hear other teachers' discussions, I am struck with the authority that a teacher has, the power in the life of the child and the child's family. I know how much of what is said is taken to heart. I know from being a parent how it is hard to argue with the teacher or take a different point of view. So, if you say to the parents, "This child is such-and-such and just can't seem to do this or that," it is like a self-fulfilling prophecy. . . . Until I was a parent, I never realized what it meant to have a teacher telling you things about your child that you didn't want to hear. So perhaps more than some [other teachers] I try to remain sensitive to the complications of life for all different children—no matter what their learning styles.

In short, Meredith's experience as a mother helped her fulfill her professional obligations. Even women who do not have professional contact with children find that being a parent helps them to do their job well. In the early 1980s, psychologist Paula Derry surveyed women therapists living in North Carolina. Nearly every mother in Derry's sample believed that she had become more empathic and understanding about parent-child issues after having given birth herself.[12] One respondent noted: "Having a child in terms of helpfulness as a psychotherapist is very much like having been through therapy. Theory is one thing, intimately experiencing it is another."

"Once I had children," offered another therapist, "I was much more sympathetic to the difficulty of rearing children." The same sympathy with well-meaning parents was voiced by another woman: "I can see that parents can be caring and still make mistakes, as I can already see the kinds of mistakes I'm making that I don't really want to be making. So I'm not as hard on parents."

The insights gained from motherhood extended beyond sympathy with the difficulties of parenting. Having children at home also helped the therapists understand some of the childlike behaviors of their clients. Said one: "It's very easy for me to see grown-up versions of certain kid developmental stages by virtue of having a kid." And another: "When people are dealing with those phases, I can spot it and work with it much better since I've seen my children go through them."

What about women who are less directly and powerfully under the influence of the clock? What help might children be to women whose work involves creativity in its most concentrated form: writing, painting, composing music?

Interviews published in *The Woman's Review of Books* speak to the question. Reporter Ruth Perry asked women poets how they managed to balance motherhood and writing.[13] "How," asked Perry, "has being a mother, that is, in some sense relinquishing your position at the center of your world, changed your writing?" One poet described how she had become "less interested in the kind of poetry which is beautiful for its own sake or concentrates on style for its own sake; I care more about the kind of poetry that has a vision, that speaks for and to a community."

The other poet interviewed, Marea Gordett, added:

> I'm much more interested in writing fiction now, because of this urge to reach a larger audience. In fiction, I think, I can respond to some of the issues of motherhood or of being a woman. . . . [For example] when I was pregnant, I was somewhat obsessed with the fear of having a child who had some handicap, and I wrote a story about it and it helped me tremendously. I no longer have this terrible fear that maybe it will happen. I don't know if that fueled the emotion in the story or not.

A somewhat different approach has been taken by the famous novelist and essayist, Alice Walker. In a review of *Second Class Citizen* by Buchi Emecheta, Walker poses the question of how a woman can create good prose when she has a baby screaming at her.[14] The question arises from Walker's musings on the dedication of the book that she is reviewing. The dedication reads:

> To my dear children,
> Florence, Sylvester, Jake, Christy and Alice,
> without whose sweet background noises
> this book would not have been written.

Walker praises the book for raising "fundamental questions about how creative and prosaic life is to be lived" but confesses that she herself has "always required an absolutely quiet and private place to work." She balks in particular at the word "sweet" and strongly implies that the early years of motherhood made it hard for her to practice her craft. Happily, no child remains young forever. Whatever problems Alice Walker's young daughter had posed for her as artist in the early years, the problems appear to have been resolved by the time Walker's review is published in a collection of her writings. How lovely is the way Walker dedicates her collection:

> TO MY DAUGHTER REBECCA
> Who saw in me what I considered
> a scar
> And redefined it as
> a world.[15]

Psychological Benefits

To differentiate between the material and the psychological aspects of living is, in some senses, overly simplistic.[16] But if you do separate the material from the psychological, you find that the practical benefits of multiple roles pale in significance next to the emotional ones. Women and men derive psychological fulfillment from having, simultaneously, paid employment and family roles. Circumstances allow men to reap the benefits at less cost; but women derive satisfaction and fulfillment as much as men do.

There are three major reasons why the juggling life makes people happy. The reasons have become apparent to me in the course of interviewing adult women of all ages in a number of different occupations and with a number of different family configurations. They can be summarized as:

- ✦ variety
- ✦ amplification
- ✦ buffering

Variety, amplification, and buffering explain why so many women benefit from juggling home and work despite the obvious difficulties and impediments that face them within each role. Let us consider each factor in turn.

Variety

Imagine a buffet table with meats, vegetables, fruits, and breads. Now imagine that the host decrees that all the guests in one corner of the room must eat meat and nothing else while all the guests in the second corner must eat vegetables and those in the third corner fruits and the last corner bread. Imagine that the banquet goes on continuously, so that all their lives each group could only eat the meat, the vegetables, the fruits, or the breads. Such a scheme is boring and fundamentally unhealthy. One does not have to be a nutritionist to know that the body needs variety in food.

It is the same with psyches. If we confine ourselves to one life role, no matter how pleasant it seems at first, we starve emotionally and psychologically. We need change and balance in our daily lives. We need to see many different faces and hear many different voices. We need sometimes to dress up and sometimes to lie around in torn jeans. We need a change of rooms and places. Even a grimy factory can afford some relief from a grimy kitchen and vice versa. The office tedium can provide a healthy change from domestic tedium.

Sophia's situation is a case in point. Raised in a New England mill town, Sophia married a local boy, Ernest, and in the 1940s they had two children. In due course Ernest took over the operation and ownership of his family's office supply shop. The store did well enough at times, but both Ernest and Sophia thought that Sophia ought to return to work to supplement the family income. Sophia became a secretary in a local insurance company. The work was not exciting but it was not unpleasant. Sophia liked the people with whom she worked and was glad to be associated with the company. Some weekends Sophia helped Ernest at the shop.

In the late 1970s Ernest's fortunes changed. Home computers had made their appearance, and Ernest had the foresight to expand. He included in his inventory home computers and all the paraphernalia that go with them; and he became rich. By this time, Sophia had the option of retiring from the insurance company. Ernest thought that he might like Sophia to retire. Her grown children, with children of their own, thought that they too might like it. And Sophia herself felt drawn to the idea. "But," she recounts, "I decided to keep working. I'm going to stay at the insurance company until they kick me out. I like the variety. I need it. A lot of the stuff that I do here—the filing and arranging and tidying up—I would be doing there if I weren't here. So I might as well stay here and get a little change of scenery."

The importance of change of scene was noted by several of the women I interviewed. Verity, the owner of the crafts shop, summed up her feelings saying that her family and her career "are outlets for each other. When one gets to be too much, you have something else. If I were to be at home all the time and not have anything else to do other than my arts and crafts, I'd go antsy. I do like what I'm doing."

Other researchers, too, have found that working mothers mention variety as a major reason that they benefit from the juggling life. David Chambers, for example, asked women lawyers about how they balance their careers and their private lives. As mentioned in previous chapters, the women in Chambers' survey were not mute on the subject of difficulties, but most felt the benefits outweighed the problems. They cited variety as a crucial factor: "I've tried the 'total immersion' approach," one respondent wrote, "and find I cannot stay sane for very long. I have another activity separate from 'the law' where I can clear my mind of all the debris and frustrations of my job."[17]

Similarly, several of the women in Lisa Silberstein's study said that they tried staying home after the birth of their children but that the lack of variety posed difficulties. "I went so bonkers," said one woman.[18]

Variety in the type of activities you do is as important as a change in scene. A choice of different types of activities is available to the woman who has both a family and a job away from the family. She has choice and variety in the very contours of her actions.

Psychologist David Bakan has distinguished between two basic ways of being: agency and communion. When a person behaves "agentically," she or he is involved in accomplishing tasks, striving toward goals. When a person is in the communion mode, she or he forgets about striving and concentrates more on experiencing the moment. In Bakan's words: "Agency manifests itself in self-protection, self-assertion, and self-expansion; communion manifests itself in the sense of being at one with other organisms. Agency manifests itself in the formation of separations. . . . Agency manifests itself in the urge to master; communion in noncontractual cooperation."[19]

The demands of postindustrial American life too often dictate that we split the agentic and communal modes of being and exercise different modes in different roles. Agency is more or less reserved for the world of work, communion for family life. The split is not perfect, of course. Researchers Abigail Stewart and Janet Malley point out in a study of agency and communion that:

> [s]ome aspects of jobs are clearly communal. Drawing on our own experiences, it seems clear that even collaborating on papers are activities which at least sometimes demand communication, closeness, and caring. . . . Similarly, in our family lives we could see elements of agency (scheduling doctor's appointments, choosing schools and camps, handling emergencies) and of communion (taking walks, reading stories, and bedtime chats).[20]

Yet, often there is a large difference between activities that require agency and those that require communion. To be competent, workers need to strive actively and effectively toward goals, whereas wives and mothers need to be open and receptive to the needs of others to be competent.

It is the variety in the essential mode of being that protects women. A sample of women graduates from an elite college in Massachusetts was contacted by Abigail Stewart and her colleague, Patricia Salt.[21] Surveying the graduates a dozen years after college, Stewart and Salt divided the women into different categories on the basis of their work and family patterns. Some of the women were single and had careers. These women were classified as agentic. Others had husbands and children, but no careers. Stewart and Salt called these women communal. The women who combined a career with a family were considered to have both agentic and communal aspects to their lives.

Stewart and Salt discovered that most of the women had encountered some difficulties since graduation. In times of life stress, the agentic women developed physical illnesses. The communal women met life stresses with depression. The women who combined agency and communion became neither ill nor depressed when misfortune (such as divorce) occurred.[22]

In a related study of women who had gone through divorce, Stewart and her associates returned to the idea that every role can entail both agency and communion. They identified some women who took an agentic approach to home as well as to work.[23] These were the managerial moms. They saw to it that all the household tasks were mapped out, that each member of the family knew his or her obligations, and that goals were met. Also present in the divorced sample were the women who took a communal approach to the workplace as well as to the home—the kind of woman who mothered her coworkers, her subordinates, and even her superiors at the office.

Abigail Stewart's work shows that variation is beneficial and necessary. Both the managerial moms and the office mother hens recovered from the stress of divorce less well than the other women in the sample—women who had some variety in their modes of experience. Neither unmitigated agency or unmitigated communion was good for a woman's mental well-being.

There are some fundamental lessons here. If you juggle work and home but yet have little or no sense of variety in your daily life, you may be at risk for discouragement. And if you, like Bernice, do not have it within your power right now to combine the roles of spouse, parent, and worker, you can at least plan for variety in your week. If your life at the office is full of competency and agency, you can join a choir or a ski club or a cooking class where the emphasis is on relaxation and enjoyment. Or you can volunteer your time to a social cause in a way that allows communion among like-minded people. If you do not, you may be heading for trouble.

Not Interruptions

Variety is not the same as interruptions. The distinction is obvious and simple but some people confuse the two. When they break your concentration, these people mistakenly think that they are giving you a break.

The critical distinction lies in control. When one is in control of the schedule, variety feels like an escape from monotony. How soothing to be able to stand up from the typewriter, stretch, stroll into the den and water the plants while mentally formulating the next paragraph for an article. How refreshing to turn from the necessary tedium of the footnotes to a lighthearted philosophical discussion with the seven year old. And how relaxing after the intensity of helping your eight year old with the multiplication tables to pick up the phone and contact a colleague about some bland office matter. So long as the juggler is the one to control the shift in activity, variety feels fun and wholesome.

But when someone else controls the pace, variety can doom you to frustration. Imagine it. No sooner have you gotten into the rhythm of the article that you are writing than your mother phones needing some advice. Just as you are about to land on Park Place (where your daughter has not one but two hotels), your spouse shouts for you to help move the lawn furniture.

Interruptions are irritating. A life of constant interruptions is obnoxious.[24] The worst possible situation is to be near completion of a task when an interruption occurs. Indeed, according to social historians, the creation of unpredictable interruptions is a basic technique of "thought control" and "thought reform." If you allow a prisoner to start a task and then intervene and set him on another task just as he is on the verge of finishing what he started, sooner or later you can totally disorient the prisoner. Interruptions can break someone's will.[25]

Motherhood in contemporary America gives a woman a life of constant interruptions, especially when her children are young. When she is the only adult in charge of one or more small children, she is likely to spend her days starting many more tasks than she completes. Even very placid children do not typically conform to the rhythm of household tasks. A single pair of hands to pat, hug, guide, soothe, or restrain a child may suffice as long as the hands are not also responsible for performing other tasks—such as keeping the house straightened or the other children out of harm's way. With multiple demands, the interruptions proliferate; and motherhood becomes a great burden.

Paid employment does not generally involve as many interruptions as motherhood. Thus, a young mother often finds happiness working outside the home because she needs the break from living the totally interruptible life. Meanwhile, the worker experiences delight in the company of a baby or young child because it is a relief and pleasure to yield oneself up to the rhythm of another for a short time and as long as no other concerns intrude.

Amplification

Amplification is the second reason why multiple roles bring emotional health. When a woman has different life roles, she comes into contact with different casts of characters, usually on a daily basis. These different characters can act as audiences.

Audiences provide an opportunity to recount stories. Some stories are told to help a person sort out problems or get beyond disappointments. When a juggler's husband forgets her birthday or seems to be spending too much time with his attractive colleague, she might talk the situation over with a friend simply to evaluate if she really should worry. If she suffers a reversal at work, she may tell people at home. "Let me tell you about the terrible day I had today," is a phrase heard at dinner tables around the globe.

But many stories are happy. Many involve good luck. Many involve accomplishments. We tell our triumphs and our joys. The triumphs need not be earth shattering. They can be on a small, even domestic scale. When Matt Crosby was eight, he learned to ride a bicycle. All of his friends had learned to ride their bikes earlier. At six, Matt was still too uncoordinated and timid to survive without training wheels. The next year Matt lived in London, halfway up a steeply inclining hill. Ferocious juggernauts from every country of the Common Market rumbled down the highway at the bottom of the hill: To ride a bicycle there would have been suicide. We moved back to New Haven for

Matt's third grade, and lived opposite a city park. Mornings, waiting for the school bus, Matt practiced riding his bicycle, and I huffed and puffed alongside. At first, I could let go of the bicycle only for a few seconds.

And then, abruptly, on the eighth morning of practice: Click, the moment of mastery came. Sudden and complete triumph! "I've got it!" he yipped, and he picked up speed and rode from one corner of the small park to the other. His jacket flapped in the wind as he circled back toward me, and I could see the expression of sheer bliss and victory on his face. I watched him, my heart pounding, my hands clapping, and my voice shouting "Ya-hoo Matty! Ya-hoo! Attaboy! Go, Matt, go!"

The bus came soon after. Matt went to school. I wheeled his bike home, locked it up, picked up my briefcase, and strode off to work. Everyone along the way received a broad smile and a cheery "hello." I must have looked like a character out of a Walt Disney film.

The mood was still on me when I entered the building that contained my office. I ran into a secretary in the photocopy room and immediately shared with her the vision of Matt sailing across Wooster Square. In the space of 10 minutes, I saw and told five other people. With each retelling, I felt renewed joy. Later in the week, I even managed to work the story into the lecture for my Introduction to Psychology class, a class that some students affectionately renamed "Introduction to Matthew."

By recounting joyous stories, we can experience anew the happiness felt when the action and events occurred.[26] (Right now, as you might guess, I am smiling broadly at the screen of my word processor.) If you dwell on happy news, you actually can induce a good mood in yourself.

And what about the mood of the person who hears of our triumphs? It is simply part of human nature to sometimes feel envy and jealousy.[27] One happy consequence of playing different life roles is that the woman with many audiences is more likely than others to be able to share her joys and triumphs without engendering jealousy.

Some situations make it easy to enjoy another's good fortune with no hint of jealousy. Some situations make it harder. When you are present at the moment of another's triumph and can imagine that you yourself might have been the recipient of the good fortune, there is bound to be at least a whiff of envy in the air.

How happiness for a friend can mix quite painfully with an unhappy comparison to the self was recalled to me two years ago when a seven-year-old Tim and his great friend Jack (then eight-going-on-nine) went to the amusement park. Tim, Jack, and their brothers had gone with a friendly adult for a day's outing. They were gone all day. Around dinner time, they arrived home with an enormous white furry lion, five feet long and three feet tall. Jack had won the creature when he tossed a dime into a milk bottle. Tim was happy that his friend had experienced such a triumph. It was he who told me in fine detail about how the dime had teetered on the rim and then fallen into the bottle. But a little later his chin trembled as he piped out, "Gee, Mommy, why don't I ever win anything like that?"

Listening to stories of good fortune is an easier enterprise for those who were not part of the central action. Better yet is a situation where the listener could not have been involved in the action, where she could not have either succeeded or failed.[28] A young female academic had to choose her words carefully when she told her fiancée that a certain journal had accepted her article for publication. The fiancée had recently had a piece rejected by the very same journal. George met the news of Mary's success with more than a little sourness.

Evidently, having multiple life roles does not automatically ensure that a juggler will have many opportunities to speak of good happenings. Her good fortune can still provoke mixed feelings in others. Jealousy is a basic fact of life; it is hard to contain.

Nevertheless, interacting with different clusters of people at least increases the probability that one may freely give her own glad tidings. To speak of good happenings is at least partially to reexperience them. When things are going well in your life, being able to share the good news helps multiply its positive effects.

Buffering

Not only does involvement in multiple roles help augment the good; the juggling life also offers ways to dampen the bad. Paid employment, or other responsibilities outside the home, usually buffer the impact of negative events within the domestic sphere. Family responsibilities usually buffer the impact of negative events at work.

Julie is a thirty-five-year-old administrator who will tell you how she feels stretched and pulled by her family and her occupation. ("There is not enough of me. Everybody needs so much of me.") She will also tell you how each role buffers her from the stresses of the others.

Sometimes I have a really rough day at work and then I come home and these two little kids run to the door. My older daughter says, "I'm really glad *you* got picked to be my mother." [Julie laughs.] Then, I forget the day at work and put all that bad stuff in its pocket. If I didn't have these kids, if I weren't juggling, I'd probably sit there and think about the rotten day for five hours.

Many studies have now been done that document buffering.[29] One was conducted by Rena Repetti and myself.[30] We concentrated on information related to depression from a larger study that I had conducted in Newton, Massachusetts. Each woman in the sample was given a depression score based on her answers to the CES-D scale, a copy of which is in chapter 3. Each woman was also rated on role satisfaction. Through a series of standardized questions, we determined how satisfied or dissatisfied each married person in the sample felt with her home life. Standardized questions also allowed us to record a numerical measure of job satisfaction for each employed woman.

Repetti and I thought that feelings of satisfaction or dissatisfaction with home life would correlate with feelings of depression. We were right: The more dissatisfied a woman was with her home life, the more depressed she felt.[31] But paid employment modified the association. Among housewives, the association between domestic dissatisfaction and depression was very strong. The housewife who felt really good about her home life felt quite elevated, but the housewife who felt dissatisfied about it felt depressed. Among jugglers, negative feelings about the home resulted in less depression than was the case for the nonjugglers.

Job dissatisfaction also bore a predictable relationship to depression. Here, the strength of the relationship depended on marital status. Job satisfaction correlated with depression among the single women more than among the married women. The woman who felt very satisfied at work was more likely to feel more elated if she were single than if she were married. But the woman who felt dissatisfied at work was more likely to feel depressed if she had no family. For all the women in the study, then, involvement in one arena offered psychological protection when there were disappointments in another arena.

No role of any real significance can be absolutely free of negative events and circumstances. Unless one's life is totally sanitized or totally stagnant, she is bound to encounter disappointments and upsets, sometimes of great proportions. A diversified emotional portfolio buffers losses in any given life role.

Time-Out

Buffering operates in three ways: First, neutral activities can offer time-out from negative or difficult situations. Introspection and reflection constitute excellent activities; but sometimes one ought to refrain from engaging in them. A juggler who has a problem that she cannot solve no matter how hard she thinks about it, does not benefit by ruminating on it.

Miranda Jamieson, mother of the boy with Crohn's disease, differentiates between the parts of her son's illness that call for vigilance and the parts that simply involve waiting.

> If he needs to have an X-ray right away, or to get to the doctor's, that is primary. If you have a job, there is a certain amount that you have to think about. Scheduling can be a worry and a concern. But then there's the flip side. If you didn't have a job, you'd spend a lot more time brooding about the situation. When you go to work, you're so piled up with work that you tend to forget about the illness. In that way, I think a job is great. I am not always dwelling on Felix's health. If I were home all day with nothing to do but clean and organize things, I would think about it a lot more.

Time-out has also been identified as an important aspect of dual-career marriage by the professional people in Lisa Silberstein's study. As a respondent said, "One of the wonderful things about the family and coming home is that you have to shift gears and leave work behind or at least leave most of it most of the time. And if things are nuts at home, I'm more than happy to go into the office. You have no choice but to shift gears."[32]

A change in physical location is often part of the time-out process. Literally leaving the house in the mornings to go to work proved emotionally helpful to managers who were going through divorce.[33] "I can remember days, weekends," recalled one woman who participated in a study at the Southern New England Telephone (SNET) Company "when I couldn't wait for Monday to come so that I could get my mind off the problems I had no control to solve." For this woman and for seventeen other women managers interviewed in depth, at one time or another, employment provided the reason to get out of bed, get dressed, put on some makeup, and leave the house in the morning. "I was just showing up [at work] to avoid being by myself," confessed a manager in her forties. "It gave me some place to hide."

According to almost everyone in the SNET study, to be in the office was a great means of diverting attention away from unpleasant matters. The press of daily business helped people through one day after another. "When it hurts to think of certain things and the phone rings, you answer it and say hello. Unless you're really out of it, you'll listen to what they have to say." When problems do not admit of ready solutions, time-out from the pain can help buffer the damage.

Perspective

The second aspect of buffering concerns perspective. Events in one life role typically help people put into perspective worrisome events in other life roles. Competing urgencies—that is what my pal Dana calls the juggling life. For her, every crisis at home seems to put into the proper scale crises at work and vice versa. One day the dog was stolen, and the house filled with worry. The recent personnel squabbles at work diminished in importance. After the dog was retrieved, the squabbles still seemed minor.

Sometimes, too, a disagreeable turn of events at work can make us see that some domestic problem is not as large as we had thought. Patty was part-owner of a trendy boutique outside of Seattle. In the spring of 1989 she was feeling a little disgruntled with her husband, who was constantly renovating their house. Additionally, she was more than a little worried about her teenage daughter. Her domestic preoccupations shrank into their proper proportion one day in March when her business partner announced that he had been growing discontented with the business and had become increasingly resentful. Patty was forced to buy out her partner. As she worked through the legal and emotional issues at work, the mother-daughter squabbles over hair-gel and telephone calls seemed less and less involving.

The events that put others into perspective are sometimes very major ones that cast a long shadow. People who suffer trauma usually look for positive meaning in the negative events.[34] After suffering trauma, people tend to compare all future life stresses against the traumatic events. They can eventually manage, in this way, to incorporate the trauma into an integrated life. At the same time, they manage to dampen the negative aspects of other events.

The significance of domestic trauma has been evident in the life history of the feminist Sylvia Hewlett. In 1986, Hewlett published an

account of the women's liberation movement in America and concluded that women's liberation was a myth. Hewlett showed how
societal conditions in the United States condemned women to "a
lesser life."

The condemned included Hewlett herself. Admitting that the personal was the political, Hewlett described without restraint how Columbia University had mistreated her. In apparent disregard of her
record as a scholar, they denied her tenure—the coveted stamp of
approval by which professors become permanent members of their
universities. Hewlett was shocked and outraged.

> Everyone [writes Hewlett] was surprised, especially since I had been
> unanimously recommended by my department and by the Appoint-
> ments and Tenure Committee of Barnard College [a division of Co-
> lumbia University]. It was the final committee, the Ad Hoc Committee
> of Columbia University, that turned me down. . . . There were student
> demonstrations and faculty appeals; but the decision stuck, and I was
> given notice.

Hewlett suffered "massive psychological rejection" but several factors helped her cope. The memory of an earlier trauma, the stillbirth
of twin babies, allowed the professor to see the unhappy moment in
her career in the proper perspective. The denial of tenure "was, after
all, so very, very much less painful than losing the twins."[35]

It may seem odd that one negative event should cancel out another.
Yet the struggles—large and small—inevitable in one moment or place
can put into perspective other struggles. Because each role contains its
own separate set of problems, she who juggles different responsibilities is somewhat shielded against pain.

Protection to Self-Esteem

The final mechanism involved in buffering is the protection to
self-esteem that comes from having several selves.[36] Having an identity at work separate from an identity at home means that the work
role can help absorb some of the emotional shock of domestic distress. Even a mediocre performance at the office can help a person
repair self-esteem damaged in domestic battles. Said one woman in
the SNET study:

In divorce . . . you're so beaten down that you begin to feel awful. You have somebody telling you, "you can't do this, you can't do that." You get to the point where you say, "How could anybody survive and be as stupid as I am?" My feeling is that you have to start building yourself back up again so that you have some respectable self-image. And I think that's where the job comes in. I don't think you can feel good about yourself just because you can clean the house well.

Other women concurred. "The fact that you can do a good job," declared a manager in her thirties, "means that you can't be all bad." Yet another woman added: "Even though my job right now is not very rewarding, I get a great deal of satisfaction out of knowing that I can support myself and my daughter."

The findings of other researchers point in the same direction. A study of women in unusual transitions looked at (among other groups) older women returning to school. As many women could attest, scraping the rust off a middle-aged mind can produce some stress. Of special interest were the friendship patterns of the women. Women with nonoverlapping circles of friends coped better with the stresses of school than women who had one closely knit group. Presumably, a woman benefits if she has friends at school with whom to study and friends away from school to buffer the pressure.[37]

Limits to Buffering

As with variety, so with buffering: There are limits to the phenomenon. When a juggler loses control over her time, and what is called variety is really a series of interruptions, multiple roles do little or no good. Analogously, when the separation between work and home weakens, each sphere of life loses some of its ability to buffer the impact of negative events in the other sphere.

The study of divorce in the telephone company and follow-up studies among a variety of professionals have revealed some of the factors that limit buffering. If performance at work deteriorated too drastically, especially for very high achievers, occupational failures could be taken as just one more indication of personal inadequacy. Amorphous, unstructured, high-status professions—such as writer or management consultant—seemed to offer special problems because the indicators of good performance could be unclear at the very time when a job offered no protection from depression by structuring the day. If the demands of the job grossly interfered, furthermore, with the demands of parenting, the worker role did not help buffer disappointments in the marital role.

One factor actually neutralized the positive effects of employment for the divorcing professional worker: contact on the job with the former spouse. Coming into contact with the former spouse and with friends, lovers, and associates of the former spouse tended to retard the adjustment to divorce and to make work life an unpleasant and distressing irritant rather than a balm.

I have also seen in contexts other than my SNET project the negative effects of involuntary professional association with a husband or former husband at whom a woman is angry. An acquaintance named Jane is a case in point. At one point in her marriage—her now reconciled and reconstituted marriage—her husband Wallace experienced the proverbial mid-life crisis. What really made matters intolerable was that the flower shop Jane owned was located in Wallace's building. She saw him enter and leave his office every day. When Wallace moved out of their home and into the apartment of "that Eleanor woman" as Jane called her, Jane went through an intensely anxious time. She found herself monitoring Wallace's movements.

Jane went to the shop every day. She had no choice. Especially as her economic future began to look uncertain, she felt she could not let her business founder. But the proximity to Wallace turned her into a sleuth. Jane became obsessed with Wallace and Eleanor and began to involve even casual acquaintances in her constant ruminations. She would show us scraps of old phone bills or report Wallace's movements in minute detail. When she found herself one day interrupting a sale and rushing out of the shop to observe where Eleanor's car was heading, Jane realized how extreme her obsession had become. She hired someone to take over the shop and went on vacation. What Jane could afford emotionally and what she felt she could afford financially were diametrically opposed. Fortunately, the emotional side won out and then the financial side eventually fell in line, too.

Jane's story and the plight of divorced or separated people who need to interact in their professional life with the source of domestic problems illustrate some of the limits of the buffering function of multiple roles. The story also contains a moral: The effects of multiple roles may depend on having different sets of actors. Work and love represent the two great aspects of life. Often—although not always—it helps our emotional well-being if we can keep some separation between the two. If all the work that you do is for people whom you love, the balance of life becomes precarious.

In Sum

More than fifteen years have passed since Walter Gove first proposed that multiple roles are psychologically beneficial to women and men. In the intervening years, precious few investigators have pursued the notion. Rather than probe why it is that multiple roles foster health, most researchers and commentators have dwelt on what it is about multiple roles that interferes with health.

The orientation toward stress is entirely reasonable in some senses. To be sure, women are still discriminated against at work and burdened at home. Recognizing the special stresses of women is a basic task of contemporary feminism.

In another sense, however, the orientation is curious. Although more burdened than men, most women in America express satisfaction with their major life roles.[38] When asked to list the problems and the rewards inherent in the roles of mother, spouse, and worker, women typically list more rewards for each role than problems.[39] Problems there are; but benefits (in each role) occur in greater abundance than the problems.

Nor is it difficult to generate reasons why involvements in different spheres of life should promote well-being. In a material or practical sense, different roles benefit each other. The psychological benefits of multiple roles include variety, amplification, and buffering. Buffering, in turn, operates in a number of ways including time-out, perspective, and protection of self-esteem.

So why have the commentators and researchers been relatively lax in their efforts to explore the mechanisms by which multiple roles enhance well-being? The focus on roles stress can in part be understood as what sociologist Cynthia Epstein calls "an objection to women experiencing multiple successes." In 1987 Epstein wrote, "The current focus on role strain no doubt results in part from an honest recognition of the difficulties of meeting conflicting demands. But, in my view, it also results from the fact that some people feel threatened by the vitality and productivity of women with accomplishments in different life roles."[40]

Added to the threat that Epstein identifies is another. In acknowl-
edging frankly that most women benefit psychologically when they
add the worker role to the family role, we advance toward a huge and
terrifying question: Who will raise the children? We are devoted, as a
nation, to the concept of the small, self-sufficient family unit. Given
such a family unit, is it possible for a mother to function outside as
well as inside the home? If not, who should make what sacrifice for
whom?

· 5 ·

What About the Children?

"Those are very pretty sentiments. But . . ." the middle-aged woman smiled frostily, "what about the children?"

What, indeed? The question was the first one to come from an audience of mental health professionals whom I had just addressed. At one point in the talk, entitled "Gender and Connectedness," I had proposed that the divorced woman can benefit psychologically from the rigors of career life.

"I have no doubt," continued the woman, "that all of us here care about the development of women. But I, for one, have seen too many casualties of maternal neglect in my practice to condone mothers' professional ambitions. So, I do not think it is fine for a woman to 'juggle' when she has school-age children. And if her children are younger, I am even more against it."

The question was asked in September 1986. But it had been asked many times before that, and it continues to be asked daily. Women from all walks of life display a marked concern about their children and an insecurity about whether or not they are doing the right thing for their children.[1] Any woman who has the financial option to reduce the hours she spends working outside the home is likely to ask herself if her own involvement in paid employment puts her children at psychological risk.[2]

Men do not seem to question their involvement in the paid labor

111

force. Socialized into the bread-winner role, men do not typically worry whether their commitment to work comes at a high emotional cost to their children. "I shot out of here to the New York office. My wife's company whisked her off to Denver, and Lord only knows what happened to the children," read the caption on a *New Yorker* cartoon.[3] Even in a cartoon, such a callous attitude from a mother would be almost unthinkable.

Social Scientists and Their Values

Certainly, a long line of social and behavioral scientists have opposed maternal employment. Since World War II, psychologists and psychoanalysts in particular have been studying its effects on children; and in the early days, the conclusions psychologists reached gave cold comfort. Anna Freud, daughter of Sigmund, set up a nursery in war-time England to care for refugees and for working-class children with fathers dead or on the battlefields and mothers dead or in the war factories. Given the emotional devastation that she saw among the small children in the clinic, Anna Freud decided that children are almost inevitably wounded by what she termed *maternal deprivation*. Her view was that children suffer more from the separation from their mothers than they do even from the terror of bombing.[4]

Anna Freud's ideas about maternal deprivation stemmed, of course, not only from her observations but also from psychoanalytic theory, which she herself was refining and extending. Psychoanalysts see the family constellation as critical to emotional development and tend to downplay, even ignore, the importance of wide social events. Perhaps the children in Freud's care were fearful and clinging because their mothers left them each day for work, but perhaps they were also fearful and clinging because of the sirens and bombs and the great, general anxiety of war.

Whatever their validity, Anna Freud's views proved extremely influential in both England and the United States after the war. In the United States, Dr. Benjamin Spock disseminated the Freudian point of view. His *Common Sense Book of Baby and Child Care*, originally published in 1946 by Duell, Sloan, and Pearce, advised in no uncertain terms that children need mothers who stay at home full time. The 1950s and 1960s editions of Spock's *Baby and Child Care*, a major reference book in many homes, softened the message only slightly.[5]

The book sold more than 30 million copies, and generations of young mothers came to worry about the psychological consequences for their children of their own actions. Of course, the notion that children need an at-home mother also accorded with the requirements of the post-war economy, an economy in which married women were supposed to stay at home.

The cult of domesticity could not last forever.[6] In 1963, just as Betty Friedan was holding up the feminine mystique to close scrutiny, two psychologists at the University of Michigan, F. Ivan Nye and Lois Hoffman, edited a seminal collection entitled *The Employed Mother in America.* An updated edition entitled *Working Mothers* was published in 1974. *Working Mothers* has served as the standard reference for researchers and policy planners for over a decade. Said Hoffman and Nye in the preface to their 1974 volume: "One goal [of this book] will be achieved if the reader at least learns to avoid the question 'Is maternal employment good or bad?' and to ask instead, 'What is the effect on specific attitudes, behavior, or health under specific conditions?' "[7] Hoffman and Nye, in other words, had moved—already in 1974— away from the bold question, "Does she harm her children by working?" They had not, however, moved far away, for the new set of questions might be phrased: "Given certain conditions (say, for instance, that she is working class), does she harm her children by working?" At the time they published *Working Mothers,* to have asked any more radical questions would have left Hoffman and Nye talking to themselves.

In the ten individual chapters of *Working Mothers,* it is clear that Hoffman, Nye, and the other scholars were trying to lay to rest the ghost of the still warm attitude that "the working mother's child is a victim."[8] Nowhere is the defensive posture more evident than in Hoffman's own chapter bearing the crisp title "Effects on Child." Hoffman examined with minute and skillful care five hypotheses "implicitly involved in the expectation that maternal employment affects the child." More specifically, she assembled and evaluated the evidence that social scientists had collected at that time concerning five central questions. Of the evidence, Hoffman asked whether or not: (1) working mothers provided role models for their daughters; (2) the maternal employment affected a woman's emotional state which, in turn, affected her children; (3) child-rearing practices differed in families where the mother worked and in families where she didn't; (4) working mothers supervised their children inadequately; and (5) children mourned for their mothers, as the Freudians claimed, if work took the women at least part time from the home.

Hoffman concluded her chapter with this sentence: "Over-eagerness to demonstrate that maternal employment is good, bad, or has no effect may result in misleading conclusions."[9] Pretty indecisive, one might say. Such a conclusion seems quintessentially academic. Given the prevailing norms, the claim that the evidence did not prove a negative effect of maternal employment was quite bold indeed.

Two factors prevented firm conclusions: First, some of the studies contradicted each other or showed that what was true among middle-class women was not true among working-class women. Take supervision, for example. The research showed, at the time of Hoffman's review, that middle-class mothers who worked outside the home granted their children greater independence than full-time homemakers, whereas the opposite appeared to be true among working-class mothers. Second, the evidence was fragmentary and incomplete. Not many studies existed, for instance, that traced the complete sequence from employment to a woman's emotional state to the emotional state of her child.

Lois Hoffman's aversion to overstatement has made any number of researchers all the more convinced of the soundness of her conclusion, conveyed more implicitly by the data than explicitly by the author. To the hoary question, "Isn't maternal employment really bad for children," came the firm answer: "No, not consistently." Working mothers, like at-home mothers, can be and often are bad mothers. But they are not bad mothers by virtue of their employment status.

One very authoritative researcher to be convinced by Hoffman was Sandra Scarr, who like Hoffman is a leading developmental psychologist. In 1984 Scarr published *Mother Care/Other Care*, which in 1988 was awarded a prize by the American Psychological Association for its distinguished contribution to psychology in the public interest.[10] Scarr's analysis drew both on research—hers and that of others—and on her own experiences as a professional woman and mother of four.

One of Scarr's central aims was to free mothers, and especially working mothers, of some of the burden of guilt. We worry about whether we are good mothers and, indeed, whether we are good women, suggests Scarr, because "society sends mixed messages about women's rights and about women's proper place."[11] We look for standards, but the very fact that experts cannot agree among themselves ought to tell us that there is no one mode of perfection. "Closely linked to the politics of what women ought to be" furthermore "is the psychology of what children are supposed to need."[12] It is here, in children's supposed needs, that Scarr most effectively describes the vicissitudes of expert thinking. Watson advised this; but Gesell advised that; and Freud, his followers, and Dr. Spock, articulated ideas that were altogether different.

Scarr offered women a way out of the guilt that many experience when they relinquish exclusive care of their children. It was to say, in effect: Don't adhere slavishly to what the experts tell you because we experts cannot even agree among ourselves. Note that this advice parallels very closely Hoffman's earlier observations about inconsistent evidence. While the content of the authoritative advice has not changed, Scarr's entire thrust differed from that of Hoffman. Hoffman had had to defend the working mother and did so essentially by demonstrating that the working mother's child did not lose much. Scarr, in contrast, spent less time and ink on what the child loses from alternative care, as contrasted with home care, and more on what the child gains.

What were the gains Scarr had in mind? First and foremost, children gain by learning to trust many adults, and not just one. "As experienced parents know," Scarr reminds us, "young children can love more than one person. In fact, it is probably better for them not to be at the emotional mercy of just one mother."[13] Another advantage of other care over mother care is especially relevant to the first-time parent. In our society people have little firsthand exposure to the day-to-day realities of parenting until they become parents themselves. Child-care specialists often know a lot about the developmental needs of children, and their expertise can help a child to grow. "If you knew nothing about vegetable gardening," Scarr muses, "would you buy a bunch of seeds and throw them on the ground, hoping for a bumper crop?"[14]

Not only can child-care providers help instruct new parents in the art of parenting they can also often prove more effective instructors of the children, especially older children, than the parents themselves. Parents can (and Scarr hints, should) provide the child with "unconditional positive regard." Parents, in other words, can love the child unconditionally. Parents can (and perhaps should) communicate to the child that she is valued and cherished no matter how well she performs. But effective instruction depends on rewarding only correct performance. Wrong answers are not to be rewarded if the child is to distinguish rapidly between the right answer and wrong answers. To instruct, in other words, one has to be conditional.[15] Because they are not in the business of communicating unconditional positive regard, noted Scarr, strangers may have an advantage over parents as teachers.

While attentive to what children gain from other care, Scarr was careful not to denigrate mother care. Just as we should encourage the woman who wishes to work, so too must be encourage the woman who wishes to stay home full time with her infant or young child. It was wrong in the past to condemn mothers who wished to hire other people to help them raise little children, and it is wrong, says Scarr, to condemn mothers today who wish to reserve the job for themselves.

What accounted for Scarr's permissive attitude? The evidence does. There is now a storehouse of systematically collected evidence on children's social and academic lives. It shows that no one form of child care is always superior to any other. As long as they receive good care—at home or elsewhere—children thrive.

A number of researchers have studied the social development of children raised exclusively at home and children attending preschool child care. By and large, no one could tell the former from the latter. The other care children may be more socially competent when they reach elementary school than are the children who have been cared for exclusively by their mothers, but the advantage is not overwhelming.[16]

Some critics of child care have suggested that these children are more aggressive than others, but the evidence is more mixed than the outspoken critics would pretend. According to Scarr and other experts such as Kathleen McCartney, the early reports of aggressiveness were due to the fact that children from one particular child-care program had, in fact, acquired aggressive habits. Children from other programs had not. In any event, by third grade, even the children from the one problem child-care facility were no more aggressive than any of the other children.[17]

One explanation for the small contrasts, on average, between other care and home care is the great degree of variation among both types of care. Thousands of American children are in child care; some of the centers offer high-quality care while others are less well staffed and equipped. Studying intellectual development, psychologists have found that children acquire better language skills in high-quality programs than in poorer programs. In this regard, other care replicates home. Children from advantaged homes acquire better language skills than children from disadvantaged homes; attendance in a reasonable program gives the child an academic boost.[18]

Emotional development, like social and intellectual development, shows no dramatic effects when other care and mother care are compared. When tested with one particular (and somewhat artificial) method, infants and toddlers who attend child care do behave differently than children who are raised exclusively at home; and some researchers have interpreted the results as an indication that children in child care are less secure than other children in their attachment to parents. More specifically, children in group care can cling to their mothers after brief absences in strange rooms or in the presence of strangers during controlled experiments. But no one has documented differences in any other indicator of attachment.[19] Observed during free play periods (rather than in the artificial situation), for example, child-care children cling to their mothers no more and no less than other children do. The accumulated evidence has not led researchers to call for an end to other care during infancy and toddlerhood on the grounds that it disrupts the mother-infant bond. On the contrary, controlled studies have reassured most educators and researchers that children suffer no psychological harm, and may reap some emotional benefits, from child care and other nonfamily care.[20]

Basically, then, the evidence indicates that small children develop nicely under a variety of circumstances. Children need good and fairly stable care. The number of caretakers does not much matter. What does matter is that the people in charge of the child wish to be in charge, that there is continuity of staff, and that the facilities are ample enough to make the interactions enjoyable and relaxing as well as instructive.

Another line of evidence is also relevant. Even very young children are less dependent on their own biological parents than we usually imagine. "As the twig is bent," we tell ourselves, "so inclines the tree." Like Doreen, the speech pathologist in chapter 1, we worry that any little mistake now can have large ramifications later. Our worry is not totally rational. For one thing, parents are not the only influence on children. Also, children come somewhat preprogrammed. On the latter point the observations of the eminent developmental psychologist, Edward Zigler, bear repeating here:

> Parents must . . . recognize that their child's development is not entirely in their own hands. . . . The child is endowed by nature with individuality and unique potential. One can provide a child with . . . [enriching] experiences. But parents must be clearly aware that there are individual differences between children . . . and that the impact of a child's experiences is determined in a large part by the child's own nature.[21]

Persistence of Old Values

Not all psychologists have traveled as far as Scarr and Zigler. A great number—even of those who favor child care outside the home—

still assume that there is only one kind of parenting: the kind called mothering. The December 1986 issue of *The APA Monitor,* the newsletter of the American Psychological Association, carried a long article on latchkey kids. Here is how the article starts: "When junior high and intermediate schools across the country release their energized charges each afternoon, a growing number of them are on their own until almost suppertime."[22] The second paragraph begins, "Some prowl the local shopping malls while others head for an empty home"; and the topic sentence of the third paragraph reads, "Even the number of latchkey kids is a matter of debate." Then comes the fourth paragraph: "In 1985, more than three-fifths of the 24.2 million married women with children under 18—and more than two-thirds of the approximately six million single-parent mothers—were in the labor force. In all, nearly 33.5 million children in 1985 had mothers who worked."

Did you catch that? It is so much a part of our thinking, so integrated into the conceptual wallpaper of our theories, almost anyone might have missed it. Many people might think nothing about the fact that the *APA Monitor* spoke only of maternal employment and not of parental employment. In case the excerpt from the *Monitor* seemed perfectly normal and unremarkable to you, try reading it again and again with one minor modification. Switch from a recitation of statistics about maternal employment in the fourth paragraph to one about parental employment. Children, after all, have fathers as well as mothers. Why must only mothers be the parents to provide child care?

One reason, possibly the most important reason, that mothers are so often designated for the caretaker role after infancy is that we keep a deep-seated cultural belief in feminine powers of human connection and intuition. In a world that devalues women, many like to dwell on the special talents and interpersonal skills of females. To declare that women have better interpersonal skills than men seems to give women a pat on the back.

The importance of celebrating women's talents is known to those who make their way through the corridors of power and finance. I recently interviewed a woman who had carved out a successful career as a financial consultant. "Would you say," I asked, "that women bring any special strengths to a business career?"

"Yes, I would," replied Charlotte. Speaking of women bosses as they function as managers of other people, she continued:

> I think that a women has a greater capacity to understand all the factors that can affect a man or a woman's life and can influence their work environment. That ability can pose a problem for a woman, but not

necessarily. A woman manager can open up other people, take in other factors, bring in those home factors. A man would not necessarily be able to do that. A woman can intuitively know what outside factors are influencing their employees, both for men and for women.

It is not just the people on Wall Street who believe in women's superiority in matters relational. So do the members of the Women's Auxiliary of the Lake Wobegon Chapter of Our Lady of Perpetual Responsibility. So do some reporters for the *New York Times*.[23] And so do some of the ivory tower academics about whom the reporters write.

Of all the academics who subscribe to the view that women and men are essentially different, rather than similar, the one most famous among nonacademics is surely Carol Gilligan, a psychologist at Harvard's School of Education. In 1982 Gilligan published a book that brought together years of theorizing and research. *In a Different Voice* became an instant success in academic circles and among feminists in the world at large.

Gilligan sees herself, and is often seen, as writing against the masculine bias of psychology, and especially against the bias of her erstwhile mentor, Lawrence Kohlberg, whose theory of moral development has been very influential.[24] The effort does not entail a denial of sex differences but rather a rediscovery and reevaluation of them. Although Gilligan denies at certain points throughout the book her interest in gender differences, she sets out her comparative frame quite clearly in her introductory chapter, curiously called "Woman's place in man's life cycle." At the crux of her argument is her view of women as more relational than men. To quote Gilligan:

> For girls and women, issues of femininity or feminine identity do not depend on the achievement of separation from the mother or on the progress of individuation. Since masculinity is defined through separation while femininity is defined through attachment, male gender identity is threatened by intimacy while female gender identity is threatened by separation. *Thus males tend to have difficulty with relationships, while females tend to have problems with individuation.*

Elsewhere in the introductory chapter Gilligan refers to "women's moral strength, an overriding concern with relationships and responsibilities," and asserts that "women not only define themselves in the context of human relationships but also judge themselves in terms of their ability to care."[26] In a later chapter Gilligan proposes that girls and women progress through the stages of moral development differently than boys and men. More specifically, in Gilligan's model they move from a stance in which they place their own needs above all else to a state in which everyone else's needs take precedence to the final and best stage, in which they recognize the rights and needs of all persons, including themselves, for care.[27] Each stage marks a new view of the self in relationship to others in the world.

Gilligan is certainly not alone in her views. Several prominent feminists endorse the relational view of women. One of the first theorists to emphasize gender differences in connectedness was my friend and colleague, the late Helen Block Lewis. In *Psychic War in Men and Women*, Lewis wrote about how women have come to devalue their natural "affectionateness," and implied that men lack affectionateness.[28] As we saw in chapter 3, her conviction in the female capacity for attachment led Lewis to her view of depression as the female malady.

Equally convinced of the link between gender and affectionateness are other quite prominent feminist psychoanalysts and psychotherapists. Wrote Nancy Chodorow in *The Reproduction of Mothering*: "The basic feminine sense of self is connected to others in the world. The basic masculine sense of self is separate."[29] Says another well-known feminist, Lillian Rubin: "For a man the heart of identity lies in his ability to master, to achieve, to conquer—qualities that are most likely to be given expression in the world of work."[30] While: "For a woman, it's the other way around. Her sense of herself is importantly connected to the world of interpersonal relationships, therefore, that's where she will compete most intensely."[31]

The New Sexism

The notion that women are more capable of affiliation than men makes me extremely uncomfortable. I am not alone in the feeling. Rachel Hare-Mustin and Jeanne Maracek, two prominent feminist academic psychologists, hint at the same discomfort in an elegant article entitled "The Meaning of Difference." They conclude the piece with the apt warning: "[A]s observers of gender, we are also its creators."[32] Elsewhere, Hare-Mustin and Maracek elaborate on the need for caution about supposed gender differences. Whether we focus on sex differences directly or approach them indirectly through our concern with the "special" gifts of one gender or the other, the preoccupation with gender differences causes us to overemphasize one abstraction—namely, gender—and give insufficient attention to the context in which behaviors occur.[33]

Another feminist, contemporary philosopher Elizabeth Spelman, bluntly questions the value of some of the current portrayals of women's ways of being. While attacking the male bias of traditional scholarship, says Spelman, some of the contemporary

> critiques of . . . sexism are equally exclusionary in their focus and concerns. Most philosophical accounts of "man's nature" are not about women at all. But neither are most feminist accounts of "women's nature" or "women's experiences" about all women. There are startling parallels between what feminists find disappointing and insulting in Western philosophical thought and what many women have found troubling in much of Western feminism.[34]

The new sexism seems as potentially crippling as the old sexism. If we accept the view that men and women differ in their need to attach themselves to others and in their skill at relationships, we have only a tiny distance to go before we decide that mothers make the best parents. We would see mothers as more involved with their children than are fathers. And, after all, who do we want raising our children—someone who is detached and uncaring or someone who is tuned-in, emotionally available, and sensitive?

Notice, too, how very difficult life becomes for American women if we accept the view that they, but not men, are relational. As a culture, we admire individualism and shy away from communal solutions to life problems. Remember the Efe? How unthinkable is their collective orientation toward social welfare in our own individualistic minds.

To make matters worse, American women today appear to be isolated in ways that our mothers and grandmothers may not have been. There has been a drastic and dramatic decline in the number of women who do volunteer work.[35] While it is proper that women be paid for their labor, it is too bad to wave farewell to the comradeship that volunteer associations brought to women. Anyone who tries to organize a bake sale these days can immediately feel the isolation of woman from woman. In a world where woman rarely congregate, any rule—spoken or implied—that leaves all the parenting to women puts each woman in a terrible spot, on her own with enormous responsibilities.

Being the only adult in charge of small children for long periods of time can be difficult. The tedium of prolonged one-on-one contact may explain why even full-time housewives spend many hours a day in the same house with their preschool children without any adult-to-child interactions. A detailed and in-depth study of mothers and children documented the hours per week spent by the mothers in contact with the children. On average, mothers and children in the study spent three hours per week watching television together. Mothers and children spent less than two hours per week in teaching and learning activities (including activities aimed at preparing the child for kindergarten) and mothers read aloud to their children for an average of one hour per week. The at-home mothers in the sample spent the same number of hours on the three activities with children as did the employed mothers.[36]

Implications

Not only is the new reverse sexism troubling for its policy implications. It is also troubling because it does not accord with the evidence. Just as the evidence did not really support the views of Anna Freud, so too is there a lack of good evidence to support the orthodoxy that views the female sex as the social one.

Think about the views of Lillian Rubin, just quoted. They seem valid enough on the face of things. Who doubts that men care more about their careers than women do? Who doubts that men care more about their careers than about their families? While Rubin's claims accord with our cultural mythology, they are not supported by empirical evidence.

In *Working Wives/Working Husbands,* for example, Joseph Pleck reviews surveys of the place of work and family in the lives and hopes of women and men. Twelve separate studies of diverse populations, published from 1956 to 1981, revealed virtually no data consistent with the belief that men's identity is more bound up in their work lives than in their family lives. Only one item in one study could be taken to suggest that men are more psychologically invested in work than in home life. A study published in 1966 asked young men in college how "a person can make his most significant contribution to society"; 56 percent of the sample identified work and 41 percent chose the family. Yet, as Pleck notes, the item referred to a generalized other person and not to the self and might, thus, be more an indication of stereotypic notions (myths) than an affirmation of what is true for the individual. Traditional college-aged students, furthermore, have had no opportunity to test their beliefs about the importance of work and of family.[37]

To assume that work is central in the life of a man while home is central in the life of a woman is contrary to the data. The issue is not just academic. Persisting in the assumption does violence to the experiences of many women, men, and children. To perpetuate such assumptions, especially in face of the evidence to the contrary, seems a surprising action from people who value gender equity.

This public airing of in-house disagreements about gender differences makes the academic in me feel both vulnerable and lacking in graciousness. The image of one sister debunking another's ideas is not an attractive one. The fact that some of the women who propose sex differences in affiliation have been personal friends or professional colleagues increases my sense of discomfort. But to avoid intellectual confrontation because I do not desire to break ranks with my sisters would only be to reproduce the worst aspects of the old-boy system.

Muzzling my disagreements with some of my intellectual sisters would also make me a passive participant in what Cynthia Epstein has called a conspiracy. Noting how the culture has accepted the myth of male superiority, Epstein says: "Women participate in the conspiracy; they protect men and help maintain the myths. For example, they argue that men do not exhibit feelings and will not cry. But men do cry and express emotion, usually in the presence of women."[38]

Even as I sound my strong protests, I think it is important to remember that Carol Gilligan and other like-minded theorists have done women an enormous service by giving voice to the ways in which female development differs from the stereotypic view of human development. Women are different from what psychologists have claimed. It is helpful for all of us that such scholars as Carol Gilligan, Helen Lewis, Nancy Chodorow, Lillian Rubin, and Jean Baker Miller have eloquently proclaimed that women are to be appreciated. Until recently, psychologists have misunderstood and underappreciated women.[39]

It is also possible, oddly enough, that psychologists have not appreciated men. Clearly women speak in a voice different from the one psychologists have heard (or imagined). Yet so do many men.[40] And thus the question remains: Do women speak in a different voice than men? The facts suggest not.

The Relational Self

Let us look first at the data from which Gilligan claims to argue. Gilligan outlined at the start of her book three studies that "reflect the central assumption of my research" and that supposedly show women and girls to be more relational than men and boys.[41] Her first study of college students included twenty-five college seniors who had taken a course on moral and political choice at Harvard. The second study, labeled the abortion decision study, included twenty-four women who had been referred to Gilligan's research project and interviewed during the first trimester of an unwanted pregnancy. The respondents' sexual partners were not interviewed. Finally, data were collected from 144 people studied at nine points in the life cycle from middle childhood (six to nine years) to late middle age (sixty years old).

Gilligan referred throughout her book to the information obtained in her studies but did not present any tabulations. Indeed, she never quantified anything. The reader never learns anything about 136 of the 144 people from the third study, as only 8 are quoted in the book. One probably does not have to be a trained researcher to worry about this tactic. Questions that might occur to readers include: Were there no quantified data from the study that speak to her hypotheses? Did they not support her conclusions? And how did she select the particular eight people to quote? Were they the only ones to say the words she wanted to hear?

Nor should we leave unquestioned the lack of a comparison group in the abortion study. Granted, the women were upset. Granted, they were thinking about their relation to and responsibility for the fetus. But how do we know that the women in the sample were more upset and bothered than men would be? Gilligan did not interview the men who had fathered the fetuses. In the absence of comparative data, no comparative claims are justified.

Finally, when Gilligan did quote her respondents, it became clear that she sometimes characterized what the people are saying in unusual ways, ways with which we might not always agree. For example, Gilligan reproduced portions of the transcripts of, among other children, two eleven year olds named Jake and Amy. Each child had been told a moral dilemma story, developed by Lawrence Kohlberg, about a man named Heinz whose wife is fatally ill. The local pharmacist, goes the story, has invented a drug that could save Heinz's wife but is charging an outrageous price for the drug—far in excess of what Heinz can afford. The question is, should Heinz steal the drug? The point of the dilemma is not to look for a simple yes or no answer but rather to examine the process by which the child reaches a determination. Gilligan quoted Jake's answers to the original question (should Heinz steal the drug?) and to a series of probes; she then characterized Jake as treating the dilemma like a math problem and, later, as envisioning the conflict to be one between life and property. In contrast, Amy's response was portrayed as "a narrative of relationships that extend over time."[42] Amy's "world," said Gilligan, "is a world of relationships" and she conceived of "the actors in the dilemma arrayed not as opponents in a contest of rights but as members of a network of relationships on whose continuation they all depend."[43]

To determine whether Gilligan's characterizations strike you as apt, read the following passage and deduce from the preceding descriptions whether the child quoted here is Amy or Jake:

[Q: Should Heinz steal the drug?]
Well, I don't think so. I think there might be other ways beside stealing it, like if he could borrow the money or make a loan or something, but he really shouldn't steal the drug—but his wife shouldn't die either.
[Q: Why should he not steal the drug?]
If he stole the drug, he might save his wife then, but if he did, he might have to go to jail, and then his wife might get sicker again, and he couldn't get more of the drug, and it might not be good. So, they should really just talk it out and find some other way to make the money.[44]

Jake or Amy? Such was the question I asked the ninety female students in my Psychology of Women class, before they read *In a Different Voice*. Less than 10 percent of the class perceived the child to be treating the dilemma like a math problem. And, as the child quoted actually is Amy, you might wish to chalk one up for Gilligan—until you learn that less than 20 percent of the students inferred from Jake's response that he treated the dilemma as a math problem. Only two-thirds of the students, furthermore, saw in Amy's response a narrative of interdependence. And one-third of the class felt that the response they read was a conflict of life and property, even though Gilligan offered the passage as an example of how girls do not pit life against property. My sample was limited, but such figures hardly constitute a thumping endorsement of Gilligan's characterizations.[45]

My attention to the details of Gilligan's argument is not an exercise in esoteric academic nit-picking. Splitting conceptual and methodological hairs, we can lose sight of the reason that such details matter. The reason has to do with knowledge and with empowerment.

To see why, review the situation. Carol Gilligan believes that the female self revolves around connections with other people. She proposes the idea in a book published by the prestigious Harvard University Press. In the same book she presents what appear to be data.

The book is well written, and it strokes our cultural preconceptions the right way.

Now imagine: Along comes the average unsuspecting college graduate. She reads the book and thinks: "Oh, my gosh, women are more relational. I knew it. The scientific data say so." Gilligan's ideas are spread further abroad by columnists and commentators. The media line becomes: "Scientists prove that women are the social sex." This is read and remembered by the woman who is struggling to keep her own career afloat without detriment to her husband's and at no cost to the children. When push comes to shove, she decides that she, not he, should stay home with the sick children because she, after all, is the one who responds best to their needs. Could he be trained to respond to their needs? Probably it would be a uphill battle because, she reflects, "you know how men are."

Is it worse to propose interesting ideas when there is the illusion of data than when one makes no pretense at scientific validation? I believe so. In any book about human nature, even the most scholarly, values are unavoidable. Ideas and theories often derive from insights gained in daily living. And that is fine. But truth in advertising requires that we label things as accurately as we can. As an author, do not claim that the data support a conclusion when, in fact, the data are only tangential to the point. As a reader, do not assume that every conclusion is reached through a pure process of impartial scientific inquiry.

The long and short of it is this: If a juggler thinks that her children need her more than they need their father, she may be right. Or she may be mistaken. If she is right, it is not because scholars have proven that female nurturance is superior to male nurturance. Researchers such as Carol Gilligan may share her beliefs about gender and connectedness. It is always a comfort to know that our beliefs are also held by very bright people. But for Professor Carol Gilligan, as for the juggler, the belief may or may not have anything to do with hard data.

Evidence on Gender and the Positive Aspects of Relationships

If empirical support for Gilligan's conceptualizations does not come from her own research, how well does her view of females square with the data of other researchers? The first problem that we face now is in deciding which data to consult.

It sounds erudite to speak of natures that define themselves in relation to the world. Adjectives such as *connected, attached,* and *affiliative* have such a beautiful ring to them that it gives us pleasure to read the text in which they figure. Or it does until one asks: What, exactly to these words mean? What does an author have in mind when she says that someone is affiliative? What does it mean to be connected to other people? What does she mean when she claims that women are the social sex?

Perhaps it is a simple matter of the amount of time devoted to socializing. Let us assume that when Gilligan, Chodorow, Lewis, Rubin, and all the other new-wave theorists speak of females as being more relational, they mean that women socialize more than men do. Is there any evidence that shows who spends more time in the presence of others—men or women? Yes, there is. It shows that, throughout the life course, boys and men spend as much time interacting with other people as girls and women do.[46] Also, young males—especially on the school playground—tend to congregate in large groups while young girls do not.[47]

Such information certainly flies in the face of the prevalent preconceptions. So, let us push a bit further. Perhaps the female relational self is manifested in the importance that women accord to the interpersonal world and the unimportance that men accord it. Perhaps social interactions matter more to women than to men.

To test the notion that the interpersonal world matters more to females than to males, we can seek answers to a series of specific questions. We can ask, for example:

1. Is the female's self-concept wrapped up in social interactions?
2. Do females need and enjoy the company of other people?
3. Do females learn in social situations better than impersonal or mechanical situations?
4. Are females swayed in their attitudes and opinions by others?

Answers to specific questions such as these have been found by psychologists. An authoritative source, *The Psychology of Sex Differences,* appeared about fifteen years ago and inspired a generation of researchers. In the 600-page volume, two leading experts, Eleanor Maccoby and Carol Jacklin, reviewed a prodigious amount of empirical evidence to see where gender differences exist and where they do not. It is a huge compilation of all the relevant research published in scores of journals prior to 1972 or so organized by such topics as aggression, intellectual functioning, and prosocial behavior. Maccoby and Jacklin scoured the field and then lined up all the studies in charts such as the one for studies of "Self-Report of Liking for Others and Rating of Others" or "Positive Social Interaction with Peers."

Each chart lists the names of the investigators and the dates of their studies, the age and number of subjects in the studies, and a brief comment (such as "evaluation of partner, pairs of friends, or acquaintances") that illustrates precisely what the investigators measured. For each entry in each chart, Maccoby and Jacklin also report whether or not there was a sex difference and, if so, the direction of the difference.

Anyone opening Maccoby and Jacklin's book to the chart on self-reported liking, for example, would see from the charts that there had been twenty-four publications, yielding twenty-eight studies, in which people reported their ratings or likings of others. The studies had all been published between 1966 and 1973. The ages of the people studied varied from three years old to twenty-two years old. More than half of the studies—fifteen to be exact—showed no difference between males and females. In most of the remaining thirteen studies, females exceeded males in self-reported liking, but sometimes males exceeded females. Turning to the chart on positive social interactions, we could count one comparison in which girls outperformed boys, thirteen in which there was no sex difference, and ten in which the boys outperformed the girls.[48]

From this and much other material contained in Maccoby and Jacklin's book, here are the answers to the four specific questions:

1. Female self-concept does, in fact, depend partially on social approval but no more than does male self-concept.
2. And females need and enjoy company in equal measure to males.
3. And yes, again, social factors—such as teachers' approval—matter for females; they matter equally for males.
4. And, unless one is dealing with traditionally masculine issues like those to do with car engines, females are not easier to persuade than are males. Under some circumstances, everyone acts like a spineless jellyfish; and under other circumstances, everyone shows strength and independence.

The conclusion? Assuming that the "relational self" likes to spend time with other people and derives a sense of well-being from pleasant social interactions, males and females are equally relational. More recent investigations and analyses have confirmed the conclusion that males need and want to be with other people as much as females do.[49]

What is the implication? The implication of most immediate concern to jugglers is this: When they require that their husbands spend time with the children, they should not imagine that they are automatically depriving the children of the one who can understand and relate to them. According to the data, males and females are equally socially oriented—if we agree that social orientation can be captured by seeing how much people want to be with other people.

Perhaps the sexes do not differ in how much they socialize or wish to socialize but do differ in how *well* they socialize. After all, mothers and caretakers would think about the quality of interactions, not the sheer quantity. Perhaps females are more empathic, more altruistic, more cooperative, more nurturant, and better at intimacy than males.

The idea that females relate to other people better than males do is one that contributes to the kind of disapproval of working mothers shown by the therapist at the beginning of the chapter. She spoke of maternal neglect, not parental neglect. She declared herself unable to condone working outside the home while the child was young—but only if the working parent were female, not if the working parent were male. In her book, mother love differed from father love. The belief that mother love differs from father love is, in turn, part and parcel of the ideology that sees females as better at social interactions than males.

Using the same process I used to assess gender differences in the amount of affiliation, I looked for gender differences in the quality of interpersonal interactions. I methodically examined all the systematically collected information comparing how empathic, altruistic, cooperative, nurturant, and intimate males and females are. My search revealed many controversies, but there was virtually no conclusive evidence to show that adult women and men differ from each other in the extent to which they attend to and are good at interpersonal relations.[50]

Consider empathy. It does seem to be true across a number of studies that women are better nonverbal decoders than men. Women are better, that is, at reading nonverbal signals of, say, someone's mood than are men. An interesting point is that the female superiority in nonverbal sensitivity is most pronounced when the subjects know that they are being evaluated for nonverbal sensitivity.[51] So perhaps women are more skilled than men at "reading another person like a book" in certain circumstances but not in others. There is not any conclusive evidence that they can put themselves in another's emotional shoes more easily than can men.[52]

The social scientific data also show women and men to be matched in helpfulness and altruism. In fact, in experiments where the subject is given an opportunity to help a stranger or not help a stranger, men are reliably more helpful than women. Alice Eagly, a social psychologist and a foremost researcher in the area of gender difference, interprets the findings as an expression of scripted behavior. We all simply play out social roles, says Eagly, and helpfulness toward strangers, as opposed to shyness around strangers, is certainly more masculine than feminine.[53]

As for nurturance, systematically collected information is in short supply. The little that there is suggests that gender differences need to be seen in the context of cultural and subcultural differences. Especially interesting in this regard are the studies of Beatrice Whiting and John Whiting, two anthropologists at Harvard. Their work in Africa shows cultural variation in the kind of behavior we expect from boys and girls and also the behaviors deemed appropriate for men and women.[54] For example, some cultures expect older brothers to manage young siblings and handle them tenderly, while others encourage boys to fight with each other.

What are we left with? Intimacy. The stereotype, promoted by conservatives who would keep women out of the labor market and constantly by the child's side, and further bolstered by sociobiologists and by researchers and theorists such as Gilligan, is that women care more about and are better at intimate relations than are men. According to the stereotype, one who needs intimacy, had better find a woman. If a child needs intimacy—and what child doesn't?—she had better find herself a mommy. A daddy will not do.

But what hard data support the stereotype? The evidence is inconclusive. Many—maybe even too many—studies have shown that women stand closer together and touch each other more than do men. But before you conclude from this that males fear intimacy and women do not, you should also know that the variations between cultures exceed the variation between the sexes in any one culture. I might stand snugly close to my friend Dana. Dana and I might stand closer together than two close male friends would. So what? The gender difference is not nearly as great as the difference between me as an American and my Italian friends, male or female. Take a look at two Scandinavians and at two Spaniards.[55]

A better indicator of intimacy is someone's willingness to disclose personal information. Our preconceptions may suggest that women disclose more personal information than do men. But there is only a little evidence that tests our preconceptions, and most of it comes from one source: Harry Reis and his colleagues at the University of Rochester. Reis enlisted the cooperation of college students who kept records of their interactions over a two-week period, noting the times and places and also rating how intimate the interactions felt. Male-male interactions involved less disclosure of an intimate nature than did interactions between female friends or between a male and a female. Reis's research is of excellent quality; yet, it has been conducted entirely with college student volunteers and mostly or wholly concerned with verbal exchanges. In a recent follow-up study of women and men after college, the effects of gender were minimal.[56] In this regard it is important to remember, too, that people disclose personal information to those whom they trust and that there is some evidence that each gender expresses greater trust in itself than in the members of the other gender.[57] So it is possible, likely in fact, that women experience emotional intimacy with other women and men experience emotional intimacy with other men. Small wonder that many female authors, like Carol Gilligan and Lillian Rubin, praise female closeness, while most male authors, such as Lionel Tiger, wax lyrical about the beauties of male bonding.[58]

Male bonding is not a concept that speaks to me personally. But it does bring me to the last point in my long review of the facts about women and affiliation. The final reason that I disagree with the point of view made so popular by Gilligan and others is that I think it unfair to men. We have been busy asking: Who is better at relationships, men or women? What if we were to change our approach and start by taking as self-evident the truth that all people need other people? Let us assume for a minute that we cannot determine who is better at relationships. Now we are free to ask: Are some patterns of relationships more frequently seen among men and others among women?

This alternative kind of approach has been developed by Francesca Cancian. In an insightful essay, she writes:

A feminized and incomplete perspective on love predominates in the United States. We identify love with emotional expressions and talking about feelings. . . . At the same time we often ignore the instrumental and physical aspects of love . . . such as providing help, sharing activities, and sex. This feminized perspective leads us to believe that women are much more capable of love than men and that the way to make relationships more loving is for men to become more like women. [We can] propose an alternative . . . perspective. From this perspective, the way to make relationships more loving is for women and men to reject polarized gender roles and integrate "masculine" and "feminine" styles of love.[59]

Nonverbal means of establishing intimacy and trust can, indeed, be very powerful. Quite apart from sexual intimacy, there is the warmth that can develop when one moves or works in synchrony with another person. By marching together—literally—we can come to experience a feeling of oneness. Jugglers who have swayed in unison with a whole group of people—say around the camp fire at the close of Girl Scout Camp—have felt a special sense of oneness with the universe. They would disagree with the people who scoff at the so-called intimacy of two men sitting all day together in a rowboat, holding their fishing rods and exchanging no words. Words, we must agree with Cancian, are but one way, and not always the best way to communicate.

Evidence and Convictions

Why are Carol Gilligan, Nancy Chodorow, Helen Lewis, and Lillian Rubin so widely read by women if what they have to say is as conservative and as unsupported by the facts as I claim? The answer is that Gilligan and the others are right as well as wrong. They are ultimately wrong about the differences between men and women. But they are right in their contention that current models of human development do not describe the ways in which the female psyche develops. And it is extremely validating, I think, for us women to hear Gilligan, an esteemed Harvard professor, tell other Harvard professors that when it comes to women, the old androcentric models simply will not do.

Do the current models of human development describe men any better than they describe women? This question was posed by a clinical psychologist to Jean Baker Miller, a pioneer in the psychology of women, at a talk Miller delivered in June 1985. "An excellent question," replied Miller (and it was!) "but I'm only one individual with limited time and resources. My time and resources I'm devoting to the understanding of women." Miller paused and then continued, quite beguilingly, "and, really, it does seem to me that people have been studying men for years."

Here, then, is another element in the appeal of Gilligan and others like her: the focus on women. Even if the title, *In a Different Voice,* may to some people imply that women are still to be seen as the contrast rather than the standard, the book itself does concentrate on women to the virtual exclusion of men. It may not be intellectually correct to make comparative statements after excluding fathers from the abortion study, but such a strategy certainly has emotional appeal.

More Evidence on Gender and Relationships: Negative Qualities

The quality of social interactions is determined by negative encounters as well as positive ones. Thus far we have looked only at the positive aspects of interaction—trust, intimacy, nurturance. What about the negative aspects? The evidence that we have just examined ought to relieve any juggler who has to or who wants to entrust her children to a man. It clearly shows men to be as relational as women. Will the sense of relief hold when we look at negative aspects of interaction? The most important negative quality is aggression, including sexual aggression.

Social scientists have for the most part agreed on a fairly limited definition of aggression; it is behavior performed with the intent of harming another or others. If Joe punches you, he acts aggressively. If Joe tries to punch you, but your manservant jumps from his hiding place and stays Joe's hand, Joe has behaved aggressively. If Josephine accidentally and unknowingly runs over you in her car when you have extended yourself across her driveway to get a worm's eye view of the herbaceous border, she has not behaved aggressively. The action, in other words, is judged by its intent. Foreseeable consequences, not actual ones, weigh heavily in the judgment.

Technically, hostility may or may not be a component in aggression. Anger, as author and psychologist Carol Tavris reminds us, is a misunderstood emotion, and social scientists have decided to separate the emotion of anger, conceptually, from the behaviors we classify as aggression.[60] If Ned presses the button that releases a bomb that kills 1,000 people because that is what his orders tell him to do, Ned may feel not a bit of anger—either consciously or unconsciously. But assuming that Ned foresees the effect of the bomb, his action of pressing the button is a very aggressive (although not hostile) one. Alternately, Ned may feel in an absolute fury at someone and yet exhibit no direct or displaced aggression whatsoever.

Aggression can be provoked or unprovoked. Provoked aggression occurs when there is an incident or set of circumstances that explain or justify the aggression. Fred insults Jane, and Jane slaps Fred. That is provoked aggression. Lucinda walks down the street, and Camille sticks her leg out just for the fun of watching a stranger take a spill. That is unprovoked aggression.

There have been many studies of aggression, and they have utilized a variety of measures—both verbal and physical—and a variety of research techniques, ranging from self-characterizations to direct observation by trained observers, for people in a variety of settings. Even dreams have been studied! Starting with babies and extending to old people, subjects at all ages have come under psychological scrutiny.

Maccoby and Jacklin assembled the evidence on gender differences in aggression that had accumulated up until about 1972. They classified and compared sixty-six publications reporting on ninety-four different studies. Their conclusion was that aggression might be the one social behavior to show a true sex difference. Men at all ages are more aggressive than women.[61]

Other researchers including Alice Eagly have conducted further analyses on the studies of aggression and have for the most part supported Maccoby and Jacklin's original conclusion. It is possible that men are more aggressive than women only when it is a question of unprovoked aggression and that the sex difference evaporates when we look only at provoked aggression. When provoked, a female is as aggressive as a male. But when no provocation has occurred, men may have a lower threshold than women for lashing out.[62]

The studies scrutinized by Maccoby and Jacklin look at nonsexual aggression. Aggression can be expressed sexually. Sexual harassment, rape, and incest have all, unfortunately, come to our attention in recent years. Men and boys rape. Women and girls are raped. Men and boys harass. Women and girls are harassed. Men and boys commit incest; girls suffer. In each instance the statistics are appalling.

Judith Herman, a leading expert on incest, estimates that between 4 and 13 percent of all American women have been the objects of sexual advances by members of their own families, including stepfamilies, before reaching the age of ten.[63] Intercourse is thought to have occurred in a small percentage of the cases. The scars of incest remain throughout a woman's life. The incest victim is prone to sexual dysfunction, depression, and even suicide.

One remarkable statistic is that mothers virtually never commit incest with their children, including their stepchildren. Women rarely force themselves on their children, biological or otherwise. Less than one-tenth of 1 percent of incest violators are female.

What accounts for men having cornered the market on sexual violence? First, there are the obvious anatomical differences. A man cannot, for example, have intercourse unless his penis is erect, and whatever else occurs in a man's emotional state during sexual arousal, an erect penis must certainly be a source of pleasure. The clitoris—erect or otherwise—is irrelevant to intromission (if not to lovemaking). A woman cannot automatically force herself on an unaroused other person. Also, the exterior, exposed nature of the male genitalia put men far more than women at the mercy of accidental stimulation. Accidental stimulation may not seem very consequential, but some authorities, noting that sexual fetishes exist much more among males than females, explain the male tendency toward fetish in terms of accidental stimulation.

It would seem improbable that accidental stimulation of the penis could account for more than a small amount of the huge sex difference in sexual aggression. Attitudes also matter. In the large and painstaking study of sexual harassment at the workplace, discussed in chapter 2, Barbara Gutek uncovered substantial differences in how the two sexes view their sexuality. Only 59 percent of the men, for example, as compared to 84 percent of the women in Gutek's survey thought that sexual touching at work constituted harassment. Two-thirds of the men, but less than one-fifth of the women in the study, claimed they would feel complimented if someone made a pass at them.[64]

Our culture is one that condones and promotes violence and that also emphasizes differences between the sexes. Not all cultures are as aggressive as ours. Given that rape is primarily an act of aggression rather than an expression of sexuality, our aggressive but sexually constricted society seems doomed to have special problems with rape, harassment, and incest. Rape is apparently a rare occurrence in hunting and gathering societies.[65] Not all men, in short, behave as badly as American men when it comes to sexual violence.

Given cultural variations in aggressive behavior, it seems plausible that men can curb their aggression. If men who are fathers can curb their aggression, then we need not fear that men are more likely than women to harm the children in their care. Add this to the observation of marriage and divorce counselors such as Lillian Messinger at Toronto's Clarke Institute of Psychiatry that "there is little doubt that fathers can be as loving and nurturant as mothers can be."[66] Conclusion? Parenting need not be restricted to mothering. Fathers can parent, too.

The Male Parent

Fatherhood has become fashionable. The popular television series, "The Cosby Show," has attracted millions and millions of viewers who obviously enjoy learning about the interactions in the home of a dual-professional family. How natural and appealing is the character of Dr. Huxtable, a man who is involved in the day-to-day details of his children's lives. That *Fatherhood* should be the title of an autobiographical book by Bill Cosby seems not at all surprising.[67]

The political correctness of involved fathering makes some researchers suspicious. "The discrepancy between the actual pace of change in men and the profusion of profathering imagery," says expert Joseph Pleck, "has led some to dismiss the image of the new, involved father as only media 'hype.' While this element clearly exists, it is also important to recognize that the new father is not all hype."[68]

Research does show that some men are spending a bit more time caring for house and children than before. A carefully conducted telephone interview of forty families each of whom included a husband, a wife, and a child aged one month to twenty-five months, found that the men in dual-earner families spent significantly more time than other men taking care of their children. More specifically, the men in dual-earner families performed twice as many child care tasks on their own (i.e., without the wife present) than the men in single-earner families.[69] A recent interview study of 141 single fathers documented how men on their own interacted with and took care of their preteen children. The sociologist conducting the study concludes: "[D]espite male sex role training, fathers respond to the nontraditional role of single parent with strategies stereotypically considered feminine."[70]

The new research on fathering behavior is also showing that men the world over are capable of spending significant amounts of time with children, and that children can benefit from involvement in the lives of their fathers. Especially interesting in this regard is a recent cross-cultural investigation by social scientist Wade Mackey.[71] Over a period of several years, Mackey and his team of researchers observed and recorded more than 49,000 instances of child-adult interaction in eighteen different samples. The research was conducted in fifteen countries on five continents. All of the research was conducted unobtrusively in public places.

Mackey's research allowed for some firm conclusions about men interacting with children in public. Around the world, found Mackey, children spend less time in public with adult men than with adult women; but men are often physically present in the child's world. In about one-fifth of the observations, on average, children associated exclusively with adult men. One-third of the time children were in the company of men and women. Half of the time children were in the exclusive company of women.

In the nature of the interactions—as opposed to the quantity of the interactions—men and women seemed indistinguishable. For instance, men touched the children as often as did women and in the same ways. Also, for men and women both, the age of the child produced important differences in adult behavior. Both men and women had more intensive involvement with young children (physically helping them, for example) than with other children. In contrast to age, the gender of the child made very little difference in how the adult men or women interacted.

Possible Costs

Armed with data of social and behavioral scientists, we must return to the old and terrifying question. We must ask again whether we expect children to pay the tab for what women derive from working outside the home. What harm do jugglers inflict on their children if they work in the paid labor force?

To personalize: What harm do I do my children, my teenager and my fifth grader, by pursuing my career? I do them the same harms as my husband does by pursuing his career. Sometimes I am not available when a child needs me; sometimes my husband is not available when a child needs him. Sometimes I am preoccupied with my work; sometimes he is preoccupied with his. Sometimes I make difficult demands on my children—like learning how to shake hands with strange adults or giving up their rooms to visiting scholars. So does my husband. And sometimes, too, my husband and I, separately or together ask enormous sacrifices of our children, sacrifices such as moving to a new town so that we can do our work.

I am not saying that my children make no sacrifices for my work. They do, of course. But they make no more sacrifices for their mother's work than for their father's work.

Ah, you say, the problem is not an either-or problem. The problem is one of accumulation. What sacrifices must a child make when both the mother and the father work? What happens to the kids when, as in the *New Yorker* cartoon, he shoots up to the New York office and she is whisked off to Denver? As long as we subscribe to the ideology of self-sufficiency, an ideology by which each family unit is supposed to be totally self-reliant, the family must absorb all demands.

When there is no expansion joint, increased pressure on one part of the system needs a compensatory decrease in pressure elsewhere or the system will burst. As long as the husband and the wife feel that they alone must take care of the children, either the woman decreases her involvement with her profession, say, when the man increases his or the children suffer.

The prevalent norm of the society is still that women's work is optional and men's essential. We still think of maternal, not paternal, neglect. The prevalent ethic is that it is necessary to condone maternal employment. Fathers, on the other hand, are expected to absent themselves from the home; they need excuses to stay home with the children.

Buttressing society's norm about maternal and paternal employment are our conceptions of female relatedness. If it is true, as Gilligan and similar theorists suggest, that the female self is essentially and distinctly bound to other people, then it surely seems natural to imagine that mothers, not fathers, must and should accommodate to the changing needs of various family members. To lose the responsiveness would seem somehow unnatural. The myth of the relational female, combined with the American ethic of individualism, makes it very hard for a woman to see that she is not to blame for all the family mishaps.

Yes, juggling is hard. Yes, some sacrifices need to be made. Accommodations and compromises must be fashioned. But we must recognize that we are not asking children to make sacrifices for their employed mothers any more than we are asking them to make sacrifices for their employed fathers. Because we think of women as the ones to safeguard the socioemotional life of the family, we tend to assume a competition between maternal employment and children's well-being. This assumption daily produces ten times its weight in guilt.

It is time to ease the guilt. Those who feel worried about the sacrifices that they are asking of their children as they juggle motherhood, work, marriage, friendship, and community involvement should remember these points: First, some sacrifices—like asking the ten year old to please sacrifice her social life for a minute so that you too can use the phone—are actually beneficial. A child who never needs to accommodate becomes a spoiled child.[72]

Second, when it comes to difficult sacrifices, the juggler may be the one literally to ask for the sacrifice without being the one to cause it. She might ask the child to be kind to the baby and mind Aunt Tilly while she is at an important business meeting because her husband is off in Hong Kong for a month. She asks, but it is his needs as well as hers that necessitate the sacrifices.

Parental job requirements are not the only elements of family life to which the children must bend. An older child might have to accommodate to, or make sacrifices for, a new sibling, for example. Or the baby might have to wait until the teenager arrives home before receiving a bath or dinner. Again, it is the woman, in her role as home manager, who usually arbitrates the conflicting needs and demands. But when she asks Jane to give John the bathroom for a while, she is only the go-between.

One final point to remember when the guilt builds up is that it is not just the woman, not just the couple, not just the family, but in fact the wider society that influences growth. Society can facilitate growth throughout childhood. So, too, can society make it hard for children to grow up well and healthy. Social conditions often render the juggling life harder than it need be.

Think, for example, about school lunches. I worked in Canada a few years ago. The professional women all hired nannies or rushed home at lunch time when the children came home from elementary school. When a working mother had to arrange for her child to eat lunch at the neighbor's house, she felt guilty. Society had conspired to pit the needs of children against the needs of working women. Children should not go hungry. They should not be asked to make their own lunches and to eat in solitude. But why wasn't it the responsibility of the Canadian schools to provide the children lunches? Few of the Canadian women stopped to ask such a question; they simply took the status quo for granted and bent themselves into pretzels trying to conform to impossible conditions.

The lesson is clear: The next time jugglers feel that they cause their children to make sacrifices, they should ask whether they are really causing the sacrifices. Perhaps they will make some useful discoveries.

The Benefits of Having an Employed Mother

Enough of sacrifices; enough of costs. Building on the earlier work of Lois Hoffman, researchers Sandra Scarr, Edward Zigler, and others have identified benefits that children reap from having a mother employed outside the home. To those benefits they mention I have added a few of my own. Here's the list generated more by life than by science.

1. Intimate contact with father and other family members besides mother

Men certainly do not do their share of the laundry, cooking, shopping, cleaning, and general household maintenance. They do not even do their share of child care. But (as we see in chapter 6) the child of a working mother has at least a little better chance than most children to see Dad in an apron. Such children may also have more opportunity than others to become intimately acquainted with Granny and Grandpa in Kansas City and Aunt Lucille in Berkeley.

When asked what effect their employment had on the father-child relationship, for example, 58 percent of the young mothers in a sample of middle-class Caucasians replied that the effect was unequivocally positive. Even a higher percentage of men in the sample agreed.[73] Another study, this time of Chicano families, found that maternal employment was strongly associated with a shift in the family toward egalitarian child-care patterns. When the mother worked, the father shed some of the trappings of patriarchy.[74]

2. Increased contact with the work world

Rigid separations between work and home are harder to maintain when mother works at the office as well as in the kitchen. When I was a child, I saw the inside of my father's office about twice a year. We did have a constant flow of his business associates through the house, and most dinners when he was home included conversations about the day at work. My mother was a helpmate to my father in his work and had no office of her own. Our children see the inside of my office several times a week. Tim's first trip to the office, in a little yellow jumpsuit, occurred when he was one week old. He has been coming to work with me ever since. In fact, the building where I currently work has a machine that dispenses chocolate milk, and Tim's comment when I told him about writing this book was: "Tell them about how the best part of your working is the chocolate milk."

That the children see my office more than my husband's office has to do, in our case, with the fact that his office is out of town—110 miles out of town. But even if we worked in the same location, the children might still know more about my work day than about his. Typically the children in two career families are drawn more into the work life of the mother than of the father. This, in any event, was what Lisa Silberstein found in her study of dual-career couples.[75]

3. Contact with other children and with care outside of the home

Sandra Scarr, Edward Zigler, Kathleen McCartney, and other researchers have found that children who attend high-quality child-care centers show benefits in their intellectual and emotional development as a result of contact with children and adults outside the family. Interpersonal resourcefulness and resilience are the hallmarks of some children in other care. Child care is a positive experience for many girls and boys. As high-quality centers increase, this becomes more frequently true.

4. Contact with new ideas and attitudes

Children can be very stereotyped in their thinking. One might expect some children to resent their mothers' involvement in a job or career. Yet, at least one study shows that children of jugglers are proud of them.[76] The question arises: Are the children of jugglers also more supple—less stereotyped in their thinking—than others?

A respectable amount of research has now accumulated on the sex-role attitudes of the children of housewives and of the children of employed women.[77] The research shows rather compellingly that children lose some of the rigidity of their sex-role stereotyping when they have mothers who play the provider role as well as the nurturer role. Employed mothers in two-parent families have children who are more egalitarian in terms of gender than are the children of other mothers. Less research has documented the effects of having a father who is involved in the day-to-day minutiae of family life; the little there is also suggests that children of men who are highly involved in child care retain less rigid sex-role ideologies than do other children.[78]

How you view a liberal sex-role ideology in your children is, of course, likely to depend on what you yourself believe. Twenty years ago the standard textbook on the sociology of the family contained

these grim words: "a child whose father performs the mothering functions both tangibly and emotionally while the mother is preoccupied
with her career can easily gain a distorted image of masculinity and
femininity."[79] Perhaps some people have retained such views, but
most parents today recognize the value of a flexible sex-role ideology.
Especially in view of the challenges presented to the contemporary
adolescent's sense of identity, children who are free of overly rigid and
confining sex-role stereotypes may be better equipped than other children to negotiate the traumas of teenage years. Most likely, too, flexible children are well equipped to confront the twenty-first century.

5. Positive self-regard and initiative

Learning how to get about in the world not only can make a child
more tolerant; it can increase his or her self-confidence. Some of the
classic investigations of "the achievement motive" demonstrated the
importance of graduated challenges. Without challenges, children did
not develop a striving for excellence. Children who faced tasks where
they had a good chance, but not a certainty, of succeeding developed
the need and capacity for achievement.[80]

Challenges must, of course, be at the right level. Challenges that are
too great stunt growth. There is nothing that disrupts emotional
growth so much as having inappropriate adult demands foisted on us
too early. Six year olds are not capable of carrying adult responsibilities. It is wrong of adults—whether or not the adults work outside the
home—to give children too much responsibility. Everyone needs a
childhood, and if you do not have one when you are young, you will
take one when you are older.

The woman who raised the question after my speech to the psychotherapists, has my agreement that those actions and responsibilities which foster self-confidence and boost self-esteem in the
adolescent can crush the younger child. I agree that the good parent
age grades the challenges he or she gives to the children. The parent
who is too busy or preoccupied to spend time fitting the challenge to
the child's development stage may do damage to her child.[81]

Where the woman and I part company is the point at which she
assumes that employed mothers are any less attentive to age grading
than at-home mothers. I know of no evidence whatsoever to support
such a view. Indeed, research invalidates her assumption. One intricate
study brought 100 mother and child pairs into the laboratory and
observed them as they played a cooperative game. The interactions

were coded on a number of dimensions. The researchers rated the mothers on the extent to which they were accepting, protective, indulgent, and ready to discipline the child. The employed mothers were just as warm in their interactive style as the at-home mothers.[82]

6. Money

The last major benefit—and it is, in my book, the most important—concerns finances. There are 12.5 million children in this country who live with a mother and no father. Many of these children depend entirely on their mother's income for survival. For these children, having a working mother allows them to have the basic necessities.

Even when there is a father in the family who brings in money, the mother's money also matters to children. Just as people are accustomed to thinking of men as babysitting for their own children, people are accustomed to thinking of women as helping out with family finances. Such a point of view has become quaint. Even as long ago as 1977, wives who were employed full time year around contributed about four dollars to the family coffers for every six dollars brought in by their husbands. Looking at all families at that time, wives' earnings accounted for one-quarter of family earnings.[83] In 1978, the average income of a family in which the husband was the sole earner leveled at just above $16,000. For the dual-earner families in that same year, average family income exceeded $22,000.[84] Two years later, the median income of a family in which both husband and wife earned money reached $27,700, about one-quarter higher than the median family income of the traditional family.[85] Recent government figures show that the wealthiest fifth of our citizens includes a disproportionately large number of dual-income families.[86]

Figures and facts change stereotypes and myths only slowly. Our tendency to discount the women's financial contribution to the family's welfare perpetuates maternal guilt. Why do we ask employed women how they can choose between their jobs and their children when we do not ask men the same question?

My friend Emily is married to a successful psychiatrist, Clark. Clark earns an astonishing amount of money each year. So does Emily, but Emily's astonishing earnings have held at about half the size of Clark's over the last decade. A few years ago Emily was offered a job in a city at a little distance from home. The job would have increased her earnings so that she would have earned 75 percent and not 50 percent of Clark's earning. Emily did not take the job. She claimed that her decision was financial.

"What I had to figure," said Emily, "was the tax angle. First, you have got to start with Clark's salary. He pushes us close to the top bracket. Then I push us over. So, an increase of X thousand dollars is really only an increase of one-half of X thousand. Then, of course, I subtract from that my transportation costs and added costs of the housekeeper for the extra hours I'm gone."

Emily was a feminist. She had written a book on women and working. Yet even she said, without batting an eyelash: "You've got to start with Clark's salary." Why? Why not start with hers and figure his as the add on? And why not charge the housekeeper, at least in part, to his long hours at work? Why only to hers?

It has taken me years to come to see myself as a financial provider, but I am glad to be at that point. So are my children. They are normal kids. They like the things money can buy—basics such as clothing, food, and shelter as well as extras, like chocolate milk from the machine.

Questioning Old Assumptions

Back in the days of June Cleaver, housewifely motherhood constituted the feminine ideal. Motherhood was assumed. Today labor force participation is taken as a given, and motherhood has become a question. Childlessness is on the increase. In the late 1970s, 2.7 million women were childless. In 1987, 4.5 million were.[87] Delayed childbearing is increasing, too. Among women who decide to have children, the desire for large families has all but vanished.[88] And, for fear of jeopardizing their careers, many bright-eyed young women today seem to opt, at least temporarily, to be child free.[89]

The ambitious young career women might appear to have values that differ dramatically from those of the family therapist who had asked, "What about the children?" In one fundamental way, however, they are agreed. Both doubt that a mother can work for money outside the home and simultaneously assume responsibility within. For both the frosty therapist and the career-track yuppies, the basic question is: Should a women juggle work and children or shouldn't she?

The should-she–shouldn't-she question has some curious aspects. While motivated in large part by a very legitimate concern for the health and well-being of growing children, it also assumes certain sexual scripts and precludes others. The same question is not asked of men. Presumably, then, no one really assumes a basic and immutable incompatibility between being a paid worker and being a parent. Apparently, people make the assumption of incompatibility in the case of female parents. This assumption is in turn tied to the belief—newly popular among those who hear women speaking in a different voice then men—that women are affiliative and men are not.

The should-she–shouldn't-she question strikes an odd note in another way as well: It derived from a limited vision and further impedes progress toward a larger view. Martha Minow has written: "The critics often repeat in new context versions of the old assumptions they set out to contest."[90] As long as we persist in asking whether she should or should not juggle, we will persevere in our old ways.

As the child-care debate shows, the time has arrived for new questions. Rather than ask simply whether she should or shouldn't, we must also ask: Given that she should and does combine roles, what are her strategies for maximizing the benefits and minimizing the costs? Benefits to children need to be enlarged; costs reduced.

There is final oddity about the should-she–shouldn't-she question. We frame the interrogative as if it were a question about role combination generally but we rarely ask about all the major life roles. Typically we concentrate on the conflict between paid labor and motherhood. What about marriage? It seems likely that we fail to question the mix of motherhood and marriage because we assume that they "go together like a horse and carriage." Perhaps—as we consider in the next chapter—we have it wrong. Perhaps marriage and employment mix poorly. Perhaps, in some cases, marriage clashes with motherhood even more dramatically than paid employment does.

The evidence reviewed in this chapter shows clearly that children are not the casualties of women's increased involvement in paid labor. The psychological benefits that women derive from combining different life roles are not paid for by their dependent young. Could it be that husbands are the ones most discomfited? Could it be that men, not children, create problems for today's juggler?

· 6 ·

Ah, Men

In her extended essay on juggling, *Enough Is Enough,* Carol Orsborn presents her readers with a satirical quiz to predict their level of superwomanitis. Near the middle occurs an item about the woman's love life. It reads:

> Your significant relationship . . .
>   *a.* is proud of your accomplishments.
>   *b.* is resentful of your schedule.
>   *c.* is pretty sure he would recognize you if he saw you on the street.[1]

The problem to which Orsborn alludes deserves attention. It is the problem of the male partner—often a husband—and how he fits, or does not fit, into the juggling life. How does any man react when his life partner takes on new life roles? How have men in general reacted to women's reentry into the paid labor market? How do men participate in the emerging American family? What have men lost and what might they gain from women's liberation?

The questions are basic. Women may change all they want; unless men undergo corresponding transformations, change will grind to a halt. Without the cooperation of men, women experience more and more stress as they seek to combine paid labor outside the home with domestic responsibilities. Without male cooperation, the contemporary juggler experiences conflict because her spouse role and her other life roles seem incompatible.[2] And if she is married to an unsupportive

146

husband, the juggler is also likely to find that her roles as mother and worker do not easily mesh.[3]

Husbands at Home

Contrary to some media images, jugglers are—as we have seen in previous chapters—doing well at work and doing well as mothers. While few commentators seem to notice, it is between spouses that the greatest trouble lies.[4] Some see husbands as primary victims of contemporary gender arrangements, as hapless but well-intentioned individuals who have had the rug pulled out from under them.[5] Others see husbands and husband-surrogates as villains rather than victims.[6] Male resistance to gender equality, according to the second line of reasoning, has been pervasive and persistent, and male obstructionism is clearest in the home.

My position lies somewhere in the middle. Research data force us to recognize that the typical American male has been less of a helpmate and friend to his wife than fairness would dictate. And yet, while men have perhaps typically been "brutes on the quiet," there is good reason to feel sympathy for their condition.[7] In the short run, the average husband has much to lose from women's liberation. It is only in the long run that women's gains are not bought at the expense of their husbands.

I argue, in other words, that men—and particularly husbands—have blocked progress. But I also enter a plea for compassion. Simply blaming men for the stresses of juggling does not decrease the stresses. For one thing, women have been coconspirators. As we have seen in the last chapter, for example, even some feminists have clung to sex-role stereotypes. For another thing, women can help men to change more effectively if we understand their situation rather than if we just decry it. Men's unhelpful behavior has resulted not from some quintessential testosterone-induced male personality, but rather from the circumstances of their lives.[8]

Husbands' Household Labor

In 1978, researchers at the University of Illinois telephoned nearly 700 American couples, representative of the nation's population. Husbands in single-earner families were asked: "How would you feel about your wife's working?" Husbands in dual-earner families were asked: "How do you feel about your wife's working?" Only 15 percent of the men admitted that they were or would be opposed to their wives' employment.[9] When it came to articulated beliefs, the typical American husband appeared to support his wife's employment outside the home.

Four years later, another researcher asked husbands of female clerical workers in banks on the East and West coasts their feelings about having a wife employed outside the home. The researcher, Rena Repetti, used a scale that ran from one (strongly in favor) to six (strongly opposed). For the twenty husbands in the study, the average response was about two, indicating that they were more than mildly in favor of the wife's employment.[10]

Again, if support were only a matter of what men said, all looked well. Even outside the protected environs of academe and of the other professions, men were not voicing opposition to their wives' decisions to work. It would appear that there were few Archie Bunkers in the 1980s.

What have husbands felt about facilitating their wives' employment? Would they be happy to vacuum the floors and share responsibility for the children so that their spouses could stay in the work force? Apparently men's feelings about housework and child care have been ambivalent. Three-quarters of those responding to a national survey in 1978 thought that household tasks should be shared equally if both partners in a marriage worked full time outside the home.[11] Yet as recently as 1983, half the men in another survey (this one conducted in Indianapolis) admitted to the researcher that they felt uncomfortable performing the stereotypically feminine tasks of child care. All the men in the Indianapolis study were involved in dual-career marriages, and all had at least one child under five. Despite their reluctance to do "women's work," they all professed support for the concept of women's employment and had, in fact, been selected for the sample because they were thought to be in the vanguard of social change![12]

When it has come to backing up egalitarian attitudes with action, men have accommodated to changing sex roles rather slowly. Between 1965 and 1975, for example, husbands across the nation increased the minutes they spent in housework from 81.4 per day, on average, to 82.5, on average. During a decade of rapid social change, in other words, men came to spend exactly 1.1 minute more each day on housework. That is 7.7 minutes per week—almost enough time to hard-boil an egg. Men decreased their child care and their paid work during the same decade so that in 1975 they spent a daily average of 14.3 minutes on child care and 380.9 minutes on paid labor.[13]

Since 1975, there has been some uneven progress. A national study in 1976 compared the amount of housework done by wives in single- and dual-earner families. Working wives continued to retain most of the responsibility for household chores.[14] Table 6.1 shows the percentages of women having sole responsibility for various domestic tasks in that study. Responsibility for other tasks was shared with men.

Shared responsibility might mean that the woman does 99 percent of the work while the man does 1 percent. To gain more precision, other investigators looked at the actual minutes spent by family members in single- and dual-earner families. One investigator in 1976 had 353 husbands keep diaries of how they spent their time. Men with employed wives spent four minutes more per day on household tasks than other men.[15] The next year, in the national Quality of Employment Survey similar figures emerged.[16] Three years later, in 1983, yet another investigator found that fathers in juggling families were likely to spend ten minutes per day more on child care than other fathers if they were white and sixteen more minutes if they were black.[17] The figures are mighty depressing.

Occasional rays of hope are visible. Among a small sample of highly educated people in Boston, husbands in single-earner professional families estimated that they spent fifty-one minutes per day on child care while those in dual-earner professional families estimated that they spent ninety-four minutes per day.[18] When you are putting in long hours yourself, the hour or hour and a half per day of child care spent by your husband may not seem very substantial—but 90 min-

TABLE 6.1
Percentage of Families in Which Wife Has Sole Responsibility for the Chore

	Employed	Housewife
Child care	39%	56%
Cleaning house	41	57
Cooking	65	81
Grocery shopping	64	68
Washing clothes	66	79
Washing dishes	34	49

Adapted from table 1 in Elizabeth Maret and Barbara Finlay (1984), "The Distribution of Household Labor among Women in Dual-Career Families," *Journal of Marriage and the Family* 46, 357–64.

utes compares very favorably to the 14.3 minutes put in each day by the average American husband in 1975.

Perhaps the critical comparison is not between single-earner husbands and dual-earner husbands but rather between women and men in dual-earner families. Perhaps when a wife stays at home, she dawdles and does her work inefficiently. Possibly the juggler is a more efficient domestic worker than her at-home counterpart. If so, the juggler's husband may do his fair share (50 percent, let's say) and still do only a few minutes more housework than the traditional husband. Perhaps the most telling question is: How do employed husbands compare to employed wives in the systematic studies and surveys conducted since 1975?

If the question is telling, so is the answer. One of the previously cited studies also reported that in 1976 men in dual-earner families were spending four minutes per day more on domestic labor than men in single-earner families. Meanwhile, wives exceeded their husbands' domestic labor per day by three hours. (That is 180 minutes!)[19] Similarly, the 1977 Quality of Employment Survey revealed that married working mothers around the nation spent 4.3 hours per day in housework (which was twice as much as their husbands) and 2.7 in child care (which was one and a half times as much as their husbands).[20]

Local studies show more diverse patterns. On the one hand are data that indicate little change in the stereotypic male disdain of domestic work. In an observational investigation of parents of babies, mothers exceeded fathers in the time devoted to every caretaking task except reading and watching TV. For reading, the differences between mothers and fathers were trivial—probably because the amount of time spent reading was itself trivial. Only when the category was "watching TV with child" did the father put in more time than the mothers. One has to wonder, further, what it means to watch TV with a child, especially given that the ages of the babies in the study ranged from one month to nine months.[21] Meanwhile, questionnaires in Austin, Texas, completed by the parents of local second-graders also showed the persistence of the traditional divisions of labor in the home, so that she does almost all and he does almost none.[22] And in Columbus, Ohio, among attorneys, social workers, high school teachers, and college professors, employed mothers devoted twenty-eight hours per week on average to child care while employed fathers devoted one-third that time.[23]

On the other hand, there are also data giving a glimpse of the fabled "new male." In three careful studies, investigators were able to locate small numbers of highly involved fathers.[24] Younger men seemed especially capable of change. Yet a survey included quite a few men who were less likely than their juggling wives to think that the woman's attempts to balance career, marriage, and motherhood caused problems. Husbands in this third study appeared less critical of their wives than the wives were of themselves.[25]

A recent poll by the *New York Times* targeted wives working full time with children under 18. Pollsters asked who did most of the domestic labor in their homes. In 65 percent of the homes, the juggler did most of the housecleaning. For other tasks, the numbers read:

64 percent of the cooking
62 percent of the food shopping
61 percent of the check writing and bill paying
56 percent of the child care
22 percent of the household repairs.[26]

The importance of such figures depends in part on the context in which they are seen. Compared with women in the post–World War II era, contemporary women appear to have made progress. Compared with contemporary women in some other countries, furthermore, American women appear to be doing well.[27] But in view of the contemporary rhetoric about gender symmetry, rhetoric that men themselves are spouting, the picture seems oddly imbalanced.

Conflict and Support

How we interpret the published figures depends on several other factors as well. Clock time may be quite different from experienced time.[28] Jugglers who have had to remind reluctant spouses to wash up after dinner or had to instruct them (repeatedly) about how to run the washing machine, may look with a jaundiced eye at figures on the division of domestic labor. When is an hour of work not really an hour? Many women might tell you: when you have to nag and plead to get it. In the words of one research participant who was keeping a log of her time for one week: "I wish there were some accurate way to record and describe how much work it is to get others to do their work."[29]

Having to nag is bad enough. Also discouraging is the need to accept labor at times that are inconvenient. You do not have to be a highly trained investigator to overhear householders talking about the difficulties of undertaking home repairs and improvements. The annoyance of waiting for the plumber, carpenter, or electrician who fails to appear on schedule is a common complaint among anyone who is not a handyperson. Less often discussed, but no less draining, is the issue that many wives have to face—the husband who contributes his portion too late to be of real use.[30] The timing of her spouse's household labor was a source of irritation to Janice, a professional woman in her forties. Describing how her husband would passively resist her scheduling needs, Janice said:

> After we had a child, it was clear that I could not do all the work at home. John's jobs included vacuuming, dusting, and doing dishes. He would do the dishes usually right after dinner. But vacuuming and dusting was a problem. If we were going to have people over, I wanted the place to look okay. I would mention to John well in advance of a party or gathering about, say, the living room. But somehow he would never manage to do the cleaning up before the guests were coming. Often I would have to rush around myself at the last minute to get things presentable. His point was, "Hey, I would have done it tomorrow." But tomorrow would not have been the same. It made me furious, especially because I was the one who ended up looking like the nag.

Timing proved critical in the marriage of another juggler, Kim Ross. Kim married Ted in 1979 while they were both in graduate school. A few years later Kim and Ted had their first child. Kim's mother babysat for little Jessica while Kim worked her way up as a researcher and Ted began his career as a consultant. For a while and on the surface, the Rosses seemed to lead a charmed life. Kim and Ted both advanced in their professions, and Jessica thrived. The Rosses bought a home and divided the housework in half. The only problem, it seemed, was that Ted never remembered to do his chores and Kim had to constantly remind him. Without anyone saying anything out loud, it came to be understood that the timing of help was vital, that help given when it was needed was not at all the same as help given at another time, and that an extremely effective way to sabotage the partner was to to do the right thing at the wrong time.

When Jessica was five, a sister was born. The next year Kim—who had not taken time off for either child—received a huge promotion. She was looking like superwoman, and Ted began to sulk in very subtle ways. Battles over the timing of vacations began to occur, and sniping over the timing of housework increased. In March of 1988, events took a sudden turn for the worse. Ted concocted a big surprise for Kim's 35th birthday. Ted arranged for Kim's mother to take the children while he took Kim to New York for the weekend. To the world, Ted looked like a modern Prince Charming—wining and dining his lovely wife, providing a romantic escape from the work a day world.

To Kim, however, Ted's surprise gift looked like an act of extremely subtle but unquestionable hostility. Kim had counted on using the weekend before her birthday to prepare an important grant application. She had cleared the weekend with Ted far in advance and had only recently repeated her request for a weekend to bury herself in her work. The deadline for the grant occurred ten days after her birthday and if she could meet it, Kim stood a chance of obtaining excellent funding. Ted knew how important the grant was. What appeared overtly to others as affection may in fact have been covert sabotage.

Kim confronted Ted on his motives and became convinced that he had in fact known at some level that his grand act had less to do with saving Cinderella from the toil of her work than it had to do with reducing Kim's career aspirations to ashes. Six months later they had separated. Today Kim is living her life without Ted and finding that it is much easier to raise the children and to excel at her career without having to engage in a constant subterranean power struggle.

Kim's story is both unusual and common. Kim is out of the ordinary in her willingness to confront her spouse. There seem to be only a small number of women who are willing or able to bring into open discussion with their partners the power dynamics inherent in arranging family work and play. Such is the implication of a beautifully designed study by psychologist Lucia Albino Gilbert. Gilbert contacted fifty men married to professional women. These men were, by and large, very liberated. One-half of them claimed to see their wives' careers as equal to their own in importance and many of the men spontaneously reported that their colleagues admired them for their marriages. Some men in the study even took a large proportion of the responsibility for domestic chores. Yet, not one man in Gilbert's sample had discussed with his wife how household tasks were to be handled or divided. Silence—not confrontation, or even open discussion—was the order of the day. "The lack of discussion in this area," observed Gilbert wryly, "is noteworthy given the difficulty most couples have in establishing satisfactory arrangements for sharing household responsibilities."[31]

Aside from the confrontation, Kim's story seems to all too common. The majority of women with whom I have spoken over the last years about juggling have acknowledged that scheduling issues, including the scheduling of domestic work and play, often become power issues within the marriage. And the majority have realized that men do not resist or resent their wife's professional commitment until they have children.

It is with the arrival of children that domestic struggles proliferate. As any sociology textbook will tell you, the birth of a child—especially the first one—is usually accompanied by a dramatic decrease in marital satisfaction.[32] One book offering advice to working mothers states: "Having children is both the most uniting and the most divisive experience you and your husband can undergo. Alongside all the joy that children bring, many couples will also date their children's arrival as the beginning of the greatest strains in their marriage."[33]

There are many reasons why babies and young children produce marital strife; certainly one very great source of conflict in many families is the shortage of time and energy to complete all the jobs that babies and small children generate. To attend to all the needs of a baby, one might spend twelve to fourteen hours a day on the task. To find an extra twelve or fourteen hours each day is no trivial matter, even when one does not work for money eight hours a day. Disagreements about which tasks to perform and when to perform them stand some chance of arising when two tired parents try to cope with careers and home. And when the parents come from different cultural or ethnic backgrounds, disagreements are sure to develop.

Marital disagreements take on a special urgency, furthermore, when the family includes a young child. Instructive in this regard is the case of Barbara, an accomplished potter, and her husband Turan. Barbara is a Connecticut Episcopalian by birth and breeding, with china blue eyes and a way of smiling that communicates a perfect mixture of entitlement and warmth. Turan is of Turkish descent, very worldly and charming and suspicious of anyone who is addicted to work.

Before Barbara and Turan adopted their child, Joey, Barbara would sometimes express impatience about the marriage of her sister-in-law Harriet. If Harriet seemed upset about something in her married life or fought with her husband, it was usually because of a disagreement over the children. Alone in the kitchen with Harriet, Barbara would comment: "So maybe he's a dope. Or maybe you are the dope for staying with him. Why don't you just leave him?" Barbara was pretty sure that if Turan ever acted like such a bore, she would leave him in a minute.

Two weeks after the actual adoption, Barbara, Turan, and Joey visited Harriet and her family for a weekend. On the morning of the second day, Barbara pulled Harriet into the dining room and hissed:

"Turan has become a total idiot. It's incredible. We disagree about everything. But I want you to know that I understand now, and I want to apologize for my running commentaries. With a child, and one we both love so much, it is impossible even to think of divorcing Turan and impossible not to want to."

For Barbara, and for so many women with whom I have spoken in the last four years, there is very little emotional pull between the worker role and the mother role but a strong tug between the spouse role and the other life roles.[34] The stresses are rarely delineated. They remain all the more potent for their lack of recognition.

Consistent with the stories I have heard from women is a fascinating pattern of findings that emerged in one statistically oriented study of work-family conflict. Among a sample of employees at a large university, two psychologists measured people's psychological involvement in their jobs, in their marriages, and in the parenting role. The researchers had predicted that women and men who were very invested in their work and very invested in their children would experience inter-role conflict. This is not what they discovered. Being involved with work did not conflict with parental involvement. But investment in work did create conflicts among those with a psychological investment in being a good spouse.[35]

Of course, the flip side is also true. If a resistant husband interferes with a woman's career, a truly supportive one can help it. Looking at families in Israel in which both parents are physicians, researchers at Bar-Ilan University identified a few couples in which the wife earned more than her husband. Among such couples, but not among others, the husbands did an equal share of child care and housework.[36] No one can say for sure which comes first, the wife's professional success or the husband's domestic involvement. The head of the research team, Dafna Izraeli, believes the process to be a cyclical one in which encouragement facilitates success which, in turn, leads to more encouragement and support. Izraeli would agree with French physicist Henriette Faraggi that, "You must be lucky to have a good husband who is able to understand and help you, even with the children. And let you go and spend the night at the machine. If this is not achieved, I do not think you can do good work."[37]

In sum, if a juggler's husband is one of the new breed of men who truly involves himself in the household, then she is in a small minority. Probably her spouse does not declare himself opposed to participating in household work. But probably, too, her husband's lip service to gender equity far exceeds his actual input.

Understanding and Forgiving Men's Reactions

On reading portions of the working draft of this book, a friend of mine asked: "What do you do with the anger?" She, for one, was not glad to be in good company. The statistics on marital inequities did not reassure her at all; she was not relieved to know that her marriage was no more out of kilter than any other. On the contrary, she was furious. "I love men, of course," she insisted, "but I am so damn mad at them." Said another woman: "Individually, they're fine; it's collectively that they are a problem."

For me, too, there have been moments of anger. Back when I could bend my knees without noticing, back before age had left its mark on my thighs, back when I thought that someday I would die all of a sudden instead of deteriorating a little bit more each day, back before either of my sons had become a man-child, I was capable of being angry at men for days and even weeks at a time. But I seem to have lost the knack. Forgiveness seems much more suitable, even for those men who do not yet understand that they need to be forgiven.

For women who, like my friend, wonder what to do with the anger they feel toward men, my advice is to package it up and post it away. There are at least three reasons why it would be unfair as well as unwise to remain very angry at husbands:

✦ First, we women have been co-conspirators in creating and maintaining gender imbalances.
✦ Second, men's lack of cooperation in social change usually comes from insensitivity rather than from malice.
✦ Third, and most importantly, when men put on aprons, they incur several immediate losses. Anyone who had to sustain such losses would prove resistant to change.

Women as Co-Conspirators

Wifely complicity occurs at two levels. At a basic level, many women have the habit of keeping family squabbles private so that, without any one planning it, each woman comes to think of the natural conflicts and difficulties of daily living as a mark of special personal failure on her part—or on the part of her husband. At a deeper level, some women weave an intricate web of half-truths and shared delusions so that they—as well as everyone else in the family—can maintain the comfortable fictions of a new era in gender relations. Fiction can be more palatable than reality.

There are times when an individual's silence informs others about her experiences and opinions. Imagine that a group of middle-class wives is discussing the circumstances of those women on welfare and that the newcomer to the group does not speak up and say, "now wait just a minute; did you know that I've been on welfare?" The new woman's silence—her lack of objection to a particular manner of speaking—would most likely give the signal that she shares the opinions and experiences of the other women in the group.

More frequently, perhaps silences misinform or mislead others. When Jane tells Francine that Harry insults her, and Francine listens but never says that her husband, Mark, insults her, too, poor Jane may readily assume that she alone has to deal with a cranky husband. And yet the truth may be just the opposite.

Why don't we disclose more about our domestic struggles? We don't disclose much, I believe, because of our wish to protect others as well as ourselves. As important as our own image is the image that we present to the world of our loved one. To divulge information about any person can seem disloyal unless we know that the information will be well received.

The issue of disclosure presented itself to me last year during an interchange with a young woman named Lilly who was attending Stanford Law School. Several years before, Lilly had been a student of my husband, Travis, at Wheaton College. Because Travis helped Lilly blossom at Wheaton, he now has a special place in Lilly's heart. Like other young people who have benefited from the care and attention of a college teacher, Lilly has continued to turn to Travis for advice in moments of crisis.

When Lilly phoned to speak with Travis, he was at a dusty library some three thousand miles away. I sensed in Lilly's voice a need to talk and tried to "bring her out." Soon Lilly was telling me her big news and also confiding her hopes and fears. After telling me about her current relationship and her marriage plans, Lilly told me about some problems she had experienced in a previous relationship. Somewhere in the exchange, I uttered something pious about how every relationship has its ups and downs and about how a good marriage is marked not so much by the total absence of overt conflict but rather by the ability to resolve conflict. And then I mumbled something like, "Well, you know, in nearly twenty years of marriage, Travis and I have not always been in total agreement about everything, and . . ."

"That really surprises me," interjected Lilly. She was completely serious, without a shred of irony in her voice.

All of a sudden I felt like a terrible traitor. I felt as if I had made a horrible, unforgivable revelation about Travis to a younger person who liked and admired him. Of course, I had revealed a lot about myself in the same statement. But I am free to make revelations about myself. I had intended to say something about how skilled we have become at conflict resolution and here, without warning, I was feeling as if I had just said something very revealing and self-damning. I was aware in a flash of how infrequently I talk about conflict in my marriage.

It is a self-perpetuating problem. Lilly, overtly, and I, much more covertly, apparently share the myth that conflict in marriage is a sign of personal inadequacy. As long as we believe the myth, there is no way to combat it, for to tell someone about domestic squabbles is to confess not only our own inadequacies but also those of our mates. And no one likes to think of herself as a tattletale. Yet, it is only by learning that everyone fights in marriage that we can learn that not all normal American families are like the ones we see in television situation comedies.

Until jugglers learn that everyone, including me, fights with her life partner, they may wonder what is wrong with them or mistakenly think that their partners are somehow inadequate. A juggler may further assume that his inadequacy somehow springs from her own failures—failures to provide love and support, to be understanding, to be attractive and motivating. All across America, families daily struggle with the new egalitarian rhetoric and the persistent old inequities.[38] And across the land, a silence enshrouds the struggle.

The fact that many couples experience strain ought to convince us that there is something wrong in the system, not in the individuals caught within the system. One major structural problem is the ideal of self-sufficiency for each separate family. The impetus toward autonomy contributes to the silence.

Given how difficult it is to discuss with anyone the disappointments and conflicts that arise when old habits clash with new rhetoric, it should not surprise us that some women convince themselves that life is much better and fairer than ever before. Some wives conspire in the perpetuation of gender inequities by deluding themselves about the true nature of their relationships. Consider Nancy and Evan Holt, a couple whom Arlie Hochschild and Anne Machung describe in their study of dual-earner families, *The Second Shift*. Reviewing the book, Robert Kuttner summarized the case:

> Nancy describes herself as an egalitarian, and Evan professes support for sharing the responsibilities of parenting and housework. But in practice Evan doggedly resists. When he is on duty, domestic chores somehow don't get done. . . . Eventually, after several failed attempts to schedule equal sharing of domestic life, the couple agree to a bargain in which Nancy is responsible for "upstairs" and Evan for "downstairs." This turns out to mean that Nancy shops, cooks, cleans, pays the bills, does the laundry and most of the work of raising the child, while Evan deals with the car, the garage, his hobby workshop, and the family dog. Most poignantly to the observer, the two have convinced themselves that this arrangement is fair.[39]

Both Hochschild and the reviewer point out the discrepancy between the cover story and the real story. Such discrepancies can put the juggler with a resistant husband in a no-win situation. Either she tries to ignore the reality of her situation and thus allows inequities to continue or she attempts to confront explicitly the implicit power struggles and thus risks appearing shrewish, selfish, and ungrateful.[40]

If the lives of jugglers and their families are to keep changing, we need more openness. Open and honest commentators such as Katha Pollitt, Letty Pogrebin, Phyllis Rose, and Maggie Scarf who have written for the "Hers" column in the *New York Times* have contributed a great deal.[41] So have women like Anna Quindlen, who wrote the column, "Life in the 30s" and describes herself as a reporter: "Since I reached puberty, I have been a reporter. Most recently, however, I have been a reporter of my own life. Half of me has lived—thoughts, opinions, marriage, motherhood, friendship, doubts—and the other half has watched me live, notebook in head." Fortunately, she is a reporter with a sense of humor and a willingness to tweak the standing gender arrangements. How cleverly she invites the reader to sympathize with one and all when she writes: " 'Could you get up and get me a beer,' my husband said one night, 'without writing about it?' "[42]

Insensitivity, Not Malice

If women—even the brave and witty ones who are paid to examine their own lives in magazines and newspapers—have difficulty facing the complicated truth, should we expect men to have an easier time?

Clearly, we should not. This brings me to the second reason why I cannot sustain a sense of righteous indignation when I think of how husbands can undermine their juggling wives. Men are not necessarily malicious. Nor are they always callous and uncaring. Often, it is ignorance, rather than evil, that accounts for the unhelpful and brutish behavior of husbands.

Most husbands underestimate the amount of hours that their wives—working or otherwise—devote to domestic labor.[43] And being documentably happier in the spouse role than are women,[44] husbands tend to underestimate the discontent that their wives experience with domestic arrangements.[45] One man whose marriage ended suddenly and who later participated in a study that I conducted about divorce and the corporation seemed to sum up the situation of many marriages. Reflecting on his wife's growing disenchantment with their marital arrangements, he said, in effect: "For several years, I was ignorant but content and she was furious but silent." This man was truly bewildered when his wife complained about his lack of involvement in the home. He had thought of himself as a good family man and had imagined that he was doing his fair share.

Bewilderment is a common reaction among men who think their wives ungrateful when they help around the house and when they help with the woman's career. This is one conclusion of a recently completed ground-breaking study by Robert S. Weiss, a sociologist who has been studying and writing about close relationships since 1954.

Weiss interviewed seventy men between the ages of thirty-five and fifty-five living in an upper-income suburb of Boston. Other than age and residence, the only requirement for inclusion in the sample was that the man occupy a prestigious position in business or administration. About 60 percent of the men Weiss contacted agreed to participate in the study. The men in the study were interviewed for six to twelve hours each. Weiss also conducted lengthy interviews with the wives of twenty of the men.

Among other things, Weiss wished to know how the men made sense of their wives' employment. The majority of the married men in the sample had wives who earned some money outside the home. Although none of the wives earned as much as her husband, some women in the sample had well-paying jobs or careers. Given the ages and social classes of the women and men who participated in Weiss's study, there were hardly any couples in which the wife had worked continuously and only a few couples in which the husband had not.

A few of the men in the study actively and bitterly resented their wives' employment. The great majority of husbands of employed women saw themselves as supportive of their wives' desire to work outside their homes. The men were reluctant to help out at home, but they were quite often eager to encourage the wife to develop herself. Typical—or in any case highly quotable—was Mr. Foster. A few years earlier, Mrs. Foster, at home with three little Fosters, had begun to display signs of discontent. She was restless. She woke up in the middle of the night crying. "We never got to the point of having any [psychological] help," said Mr. Foster,

> But it sure was difficult. . . . And what we did, she went back to school. I was absolutely supportive. I pushed it. Because, why the hell shouldn't she? Why should she stay home? It's ridiculous. Her working, I don't think, has affected me very much at all. I've done just about what I would have done before. I did the dishes before. . . . I don't want to get waited on.[46]

Immediately after stating that his wife's employment did not affect him, Mr. Foster expressed some resentment about having to entertain less frequently at home.

Like many of the men in Weiss's study, Mr. Foster expressed his resentments frequently but indirectly. He was baffled about what he experienced as a lack of appreciation. Because he saw his wife's career as something she did for herself, he felt that his wife should give him recognition and thanks whenever he took care of some domestic matter in the service of her professional life. The reverse, of course, did not obtain. Assuming that his own career was something he did for the family, Mr. Foster did not imagine that he ought to express gratitude for the ways in which Mrs. Foster supported him. The Fosters, in part because of their mutual respect for each other, were able to resolve or overlook these differences, but in many of the couples there developed an undercover war of misunderstandings, hurt feelings, and mistrust.

According to Robert Weiss, "men's traditional understandings of marriage are in no way modified by wives working, even if the wives have significant careers." The men continue to see themselves as the sole providers for the family and to interpret their wives' earning as helping out (just as the men help out at home) or as something the wife does for herself. Any support that they give to their wives' work, these men understand as "one of the ways they discharge their responsibility to support their wives' well-being, albeit at some cost to themselves."[47] Wifely support of their work, in contrast, is taken totally for granted.

One might wonder why the men in the Weiss study, all of whom are highly educated, would have trouble understanding that their wives are not just helping out and are not simply working for their own self-development. Like the Dutch feminist, Aafke Komter, one may see ignorance and misunderstanding as strategies for maintaining the patriarchal status quo within the family,[48] or may even see husbands' bafflement as evidence of some fundamentally male inability to relate to other people.[49]

Or one might, like May Sarton, analyze men's blindness in terms of their privilege. Sarton reflected on the enhanced vision of the under-dog after watching a televised episode of *Roots*. Her journal entry read:

> [T]he most powerful moment last night was when the upright black father of the clan . . . runs into the white colonel who has betrayed his formerly liberal position. . . . The colonel does have a conscience and is eaten up by it, and as he rides by the black man he stops to say, "You and I understand each other. I've always known what you were think-ing and you've always known what I was thinking." The black man (this episode comes shortly after a lynching) doesn't smile or bow, but looks the colonel straight in the eye and says, "No, I've always known what you were thinking, but you have never known what I was thinking."[50]

Privilege can simultaneously blind people and convince them that they are not blind.

Privilege operates in the same fashion for women and for men. The second reason that jugglers should not become angered at men's ob-structionist tactics, then, is that women would surely behave no better than they were we to enjoy the kinds of privileges men have enjoyed. Because there is little that is intentional or even conscious about male resistance to women's progress, anger is hardly the most appropriate response.

Men's Lost Helpmate

It is, of course, entirely possible that men (or anyone who is rela-tively privileged) are most defensive, most obstinate and unseeing when they are worried about losing their privileges. Fear can close even the most open mind; and vague, ill-defined fears can make us all mulish. In the reactions of husbands, I detect a haunting worry about what they will lose when true gender equality arrives.

There is cause for concern. When a woman combines family life and paid labor, her husband can pay the emotional price. I do not mean that he must endure drudgery at home. As we have already seen, the time he spends on domestic labor increases only a tiny amount; and so, at first, the proposition that husbands suffer when wives gain may appear ridiculous. But men do suffer at least four identifiable losses: First, husbands of jugglers lose helpmates for their professional lives. Second, they lose exclusive rights to their provider roles. Third, they lose some of their authority at home. Finally, they lose the assurance of intimacy.

Taking first things first, reflect on how wives help men in their careers. The traditional American husband was able to count on his wife to help him manage his work life. Whether he was a construction worker or a top-ranking executive, he expected that "the wife" would make his lunch or pack his overnight bag. The traditional working man with a supportive wife did not have to devote energies to the time-consuming tasks of feeding or clothing himself.[51]

And, if he had a profession, the traditional man could generally count on his wife for direct work-relevant support. The first Mrs. Spock, according to her obituary, "assisted" her husband in "the research and writing of *Dr. Spock's Baby and Child Care*."[52] Samuel Beckett's wife found him a publisher. And the first Mrs. Einstein helped Albert develop his theory of relativity.[53]

Contemporary husbands are left to take care of many more details themselves. When I taught at Yale, for example, I noticed a split in life-style between the older, traditional men and the younger men. A number of the senior men employed their wives as research assistants and typists. Sometimes, but not always, the wife received pay for her services. My junior male colleagues—being of the same generation as I, more or less—had a much rougher row to hoe. Most of their wives had careers of their own, and were not available to search the library stacks or to file and type. They were still available to cook and clean, as far as I could tell. But even though a man who is rushing to submit a large grant proposal benefits from having someone else prepare his meals and keep his house and his clothes neat and tidy, when the young male professor is up until three in the morning typing in last-minute revisions himself, he may long for the traditional academic wife.

The relative unavailability of the employed wife as staff for the husband's career makes it impossible for the man to play the hero at work.[54] Heroics tend to require an invisible staff. Superman appears to fly—but only when the hands that prop him up do not show on the screen. In our meritocratic society, the unseen but sustaining labor of a wife helps a husband maintain the image of personal merit on the job.[55] Without the invisible helping hands of his (house)wife, the employed man risks problems with his image.

The ways in which women have contributed to the professional image of their husbands and how they have done so in largely unnoticed ways is documented in a peppery and wise book by Martha Fowlkes. In 1980, Fowlkes interviewed twenty women married to physicians and twenty women married to academics as the basis for her book, *Behind Every Successful Man*. Medicine, according to Fowlkes and others, constitutes the male profession par excellence. It is hierarchical, with nurses and paramedical staff ministering to patients under strict control of the physician who, in turn, can heal or harm the patients in his care. The physician, who until recently has worked independently of peers, exercises more complete authority over his staff and over his charges than does virtually any other civilian professional. An air of drama pervades the proceedings, too. One person, and one person alone, possesses most of the knowledge, often knowledge that makes a critical difference in someone's life. Research and teaching are less dramatic. Students die of boredom only metaphorically. Physicians may be more accustomed to a hierarchical world then are professors.

Given the differences between the two professions, at least in 1980, it did not surprise Fowlkes to uncover differences between the medical and the academic marriages. Typically, the medical marriages were more hierarchical than the academic marriages. None of the doctors' wives worked outside their homes, but some of the academic wives did—albeit more often in jobs than in careers.

More surprising, at first blush, were the similarities. For both types of marriage, the wives played "double-duty roles as parents, homemakers, and directors of family life."[56] Fowlkes expressed difficulty imagining either the professors or the physicians in her study "living the kinds of professional lives to which they are accustomed if they were also responsible for grocery lists, kindergarten car pools, after-school play groups and birthday parties, dentist appointments, sick children, and the evening roast and so on."[57]

The professors, no less than the physicians, had "made compliance with career structures" a priority.[58] Career-free wives allowed the men the flexibility they needed to excel at their careers.

We jugglers ask our husbands to sustain both obvious and hidden career costs. When our job demands increase, we stay available to our children, but we diminish the quantity of our staffwork for our husbands.[59] Without women there to function as the booster jets on their sneakers, the gallant men have a hard time playing the idealized hero who leaps professional hurdles in a single bound. That is why men in dual-professional families experience dissatisfaction or relative deprivation when they compare themselves to husbands who play the role of sole professional.[60]

Men's Lost Provider Roles

Projecting a good image to the world at large is only one way of being a hero. Equally satisfying is the role of hero to those at home, a role well documented in popular movies and children's stories.

Take, for example, Roald Dahl's *Fantastic Mr. Fox,* a book that appeals to elementary school children and their parents. The story line revolves around the adventures of the Fox family as three despicable farmers try to capture and kill Mr. Fox. Repeatedly and delightfully, Mr. Fox outwits the farmers, thereby saving his family and himself. Mr. Fox acts the general throughout and Mrs. Fox and the four little Foxes loyally follow his commands.

At one point in the story, the farmers come after the foxes with bulldozers. Mr. Fox has the idea to elude the enemy by digging deep into the earth. Together, the family digs fast and furiously until "gradually the scrunching and scraping of the shovels became fainter and fainter" and after a short while:

> they all sat down, panting for breath, and Mrs. Fox said to her children, "I should like you to know that if it weren't for your father, we would all be dead by now. Your father is a fantastic fox."
>
> Mr. Fox looked at his wife and he smiled. He loved her more than ever when she said things like that.[61]

Mr. Fox is clever as well as brave: more than once he steals foods from the larders of the men whom he outsmarts. Not only does Mr. Fox save his darlings and his friends; he also provides great feasts for them. It is because he is a quartermaster—and not only a general—that Mr. Fox wins the hearts of his readers as well as of his family.

So too for the traditional American husband: fantastic Mr. Dad provides handsomely for his dependents. Indeed, as social scientists have noted, the traditional American family man has been, first and foremost, a good provider.[62] And a "good provider, not only provides money to pay for the family's goods and services, but provides in sufficient abundance that the other family members do not have to supply any money, and, in fact, can donate a considerable amount of time to spending the money brought home by the good provider."[63]

The centrality of the provider role is not visible only to social scientists. Men themselves speak clearly of how important it is for their sense of self to provide well for their families. Many young men in college today admit that they would like to provide well for their families.[64] Young fathers enjoy being providers. In one study of 400 fathers, for example, about half of the young men explicitly mentioned how positive they felt about acting as bread winners for their children.[65]

Most men grieve if they lose their bread-winner roles, especially through death or divorce. This was one of my findings in a study of women and men going through divorce. Many qualified without reservation for the label workaholic.[66] They would sometimes rise early and be gone from the house before the children were awake. Often they would return in the evening with time only for ritualized short exchanges with the children. For the men in my sample, their wives managed the children throughout the day.

Yet, even the workaholic men in the study were devastated when the family came apart. Actual time spent with the family may have been short, but psychological time was long indeed. Almost without exception, the men carried around all day, everyday, an internalized image of the family. In their own minds, the men were not working only or even primarily for their own glory; they were working for the family. Several research participants commented that losing their families meant that their careers lost their significance. Said one man: "After a separation, work becomes 'what the hell is the sense of this?' You have no one to share it with. So you don't keep achieving. You just feel sorry for yourself."

Divorce and death are not the only events that can threaten a man's claim to the provider role. Women's employment can, too. Some men see their wives' entry into the paid labor force as an indication of their own inadequacy as providers. When this happens, the men come to dislike their jobs.[67] Other men remain unthreatened until the women begin to earn as much as they. The number of women who earn more than their husbands has been estimated to be between 5 and 10 percent nationally; but many more women are beginning to close the salary gap.[68] Writing about the provider role, psychiatrist Robert Gould notes that:

[T]he situation becomes . . . complicated when the "head of the house" is competing against his wife's paycheck as well as his own expectations. . . . Given current salary inequities, it is unlikely that she will threaten his place as number-one bread winner. But if she does, if she can make real money, she is co-opting the man's passport to masculinity . . . and he is effectively castrated.[69]

When a woman begins to take her job seriously, whether she is a Madison Avenue executive, a secretary, or a welder, she comes to think of the job as integral to the family as well as important for her own ego. She begins to play the provider role. Sharing this role, especially if it is his major one in family life, can easily be construed as loss by even the most liberated husband.

Claudine's husband, Eric, appeared liberated in many ways. But he never accommodated to Claudine's professional successes. When he had to share the provider role with Claudine, Eric became defensive. If Claudine invited her colleagues to dinner, for example, Eric would spend the evening trying to belittle her. After several years of marriage, an incident involving Eric, Claudine, and their young child made Claudine see the light. According to Claudine:

> Our daughter had measles and was very ill. We were all supposed to go on vacation in Maine, and Eric said, "Well, it looks like she has a little problem. You stay home with her, and I'll go on vacation. I need a break." By this time I'd decided to leave him. So he went, and she got much worse and had to go to the hospital. He was in a situation of having gone off and left us. So, in August one day I said, "Eric, I want to leave you." He was very upset, very upset. He got sort of violent, for the only time in our whole relationship.

In hindsight, Claudine saw that Eric had never been comfortable with her attempts to juggle mothering and working. There was, and always had been, an "unspoken contract that his work took precedence." When Claudine was excited about her work, Eric's response was jealousy. When he received a large increase in salary, he became—in Claudine's words—"delighted to be earning more than me" and "renewed his pressure for me to quit."

Even men with a highly developed sense of self-worth can feel upset when their wives receive occupational rewards. When one woman whom I interviewed finished her graduate work and accepted a well-paying job in banking, her husband sulked around the house for days. The problem was definitely not that he was jealous of her success; no matter how successful she was, she would never catch up to him in salary or occupational prestige. The issue went deeper. He felt his wife was encroaching on his territory. "Look," he finally blurted out, "you've always been good at supervising the children and managing the house. Now you're also good at earning money. What part is left for me in the family?"

In sum, the traditional American husband and father had the responsibilities—and the privileges—of playing the role of primary provider. Sharing that role is not easy. To yield exclusive access to the role is to surrender some of the potential for fulfilling the hero fantasy—a fantasy that appeals to us all. The loss is far from trivial.

Men's Lost Authority

Men's third loss, although also substantial, excites less sympathy in me. The contemporary husband whose wife works for more than pin money or self-fulfillment has less control of family decisions than the man in a one-earner family. It is no coincidence that the census bureau has always classified most American households as "husband headed households" because since its inception men have earned the major proportion of family income. As Virginia Woolf so beautifully noted, independent income provides the surest means to moral and psychological independence.[70] If a woman is to have a room that is truly her own, she must pay the rent herself, with, as it were, her own "three guineas."

Woolf's view was validated in a massive telephone interview study conducted by Joan Huber and Glenna Spitze. In 1978 a team of researchers interviewed more than 2,000 people who constituted a representative national sample. Among the host of interesting findings was one of special relevance to the issue of authority: Husbands of employed women more than other husbands reported that their wives played a great role in decision making.[71]

Knowing that the mere fact of a paycheck influenced the balance of power in marital decisions, another group of researchers wondered if power would also be linked to the relative size of a wife's earnings. In 1980 an organization named Catalyst collected information from 815 dual-professional couples. One question in their six-page questionnaire asked about earnings; from the answers, researchers Janice Steil and Beth Turetsky calculated the gap between the husband's and the wife's earnings. Another question asked the individual to rate the importance of her or his own career and of the spouse's career. The couples were divided into three categories: (1) those who thought both careers of equal importance; (2) those who thought the husband's career more important; and (3) those who thought the wife's career more important. For couples in the study, the more equal the careers, the greater the equality of decision making. The greater the economic and psychological value of the wife's career, in other words, the more power she exercised in decisions such as where to take a vacation.[72]

Decisions are not always made without disagreement. One indirect way to assess the importance of a woman's working is to examine marital disputes. Disputes about the division of labor are more common in dual-worker than in single-earner families, but there is little evidence that one type of family has more or less conflict overall than any other type.[73] What is clear, however, is that women win a greater percentage of the disagreements with their husbands if they are employed outside the home. A study of married couples in a large metropolitan area found that housewives win a quarter of their fights while working women win over half.[74] In this instance, to be sure, her gain is his loss.

Some men are so threatened by the potential loss of authority in the home that they actively oppose their wives' employment. Jane was a middle-aged mother before she returned to work. When my associate Ann Cameron asked Jane about how her husband reacted to her return to employment, she said:

> Not good. He wasn't at all happy about it. He made it very difficult for me. We had been kind of growing apart at that time anyhow. I had a chance to go back to the company at nights. The money was excellent. It was perfect hours. And he was wicked, wicked. He wouldn't babysit; he wouldn't cooperate; it was terrible. He didn't want me to leave that house. Now that I look back on it, it was all part of the tactics; that he must have been threatened by me. He didn't want me to work because he didn't want me to get any power.

Sometimes when a man continues to horde the power, his employed wife finds herself forced to make a choice between marriage and work. Such was the choice faced by Colleen, a manager interviewed by educator and therapist Sue Freeman. Colleen described her marriage: "he always felt that he made the decisions for the family. Consequently, his decisions were the right ones and the good ones. And if I requested something or I felt something should be done, that was selfish on my part."[75] Colleen always had "a gut feeling" that the situation was unfair, but it was not until she began to develop her career that she found the courage to change the status quo.

The late psychologist B. F. Skinner distinguished between two basic types of freedom: freedom *from* and freedom *to*.[76] The traditional husband and father enjoyed freedom from domestic labors; when the woman juggles, she may erode a little of the man's freedom *from* house chores. The traditional husband and father also enjoyed freedom *to* make many decisions; when he is married to a woman with some financial independence, the man loses a portion of his freedom to make decisions as he pleases. Even as we are glad about the reduction of patriarchal power, we can see that any loss of freedom and privilege must, at first, feel somewhat frightening to men.

Men's Lost Listeners

Much more frightening, and legitimately so, is the potential loss of family intimacy. When the woman in the family juggles, her ability to respond instantly to everyone's needs is put in jeopardy. And it was this ability that was the best assurance, in years gone by, that everyone would feel intimate and cozy.

When you feel intimate with someone, feel love, feel that you are close friends, then you feel that the other person would understand and sympathize with you in times of trouble and would laugh with you in times of joy.[77] You feel that you could talk when you wish and remain silent—be given privacy—when you wish. You feel that you could invite the other person to engage in some activity—going to a baseball game or going to the opera—and have your invitation be accepted with genuine pleasure. And you feel that the reverse would happen too, that some invitation extended to you would please you. In other words, when you have an intimate friend, you feel *in synchrony* with the person.

What makes people feel in synchrony? Sometimes verbal disclosures are important; sometimes not.[78] Sometimes there is a specific incident that moves the relationship to a new level of intimacy and trust, sustains the current level, or causes disappointment. Sometimes, there is a slow accretion of small moments, none exciting special attention, but all of them together essential to the feeling that emotions match. A lasting relationship usually contains a mix of many small moments and one or two specific incidents that then become emblematic of synchrony or a lack thereof.

I have been lucky enough to experience some long-lasting and deep friendships; and in each intimate friendship, some critical event has occurred that remains encapsulated in my memory. The memories always symbolize to me synchronicity—a moment when one person in the pair was especially attuned to the other's needs and wishes.

There was a day in late April 1985, for example, when my longtime friend and neighbor Meredith seemed to know instinctively my needs and rearranged her day to help meet them. My schedule, on the day in question, left "no time for repairs" as they say in the *New Yorker* advertisements for facial makeup. In fact, there was no time for makeup, repaired or not. I was logging in a twelve-hour day that included, among others, these items in New Haven:

7:30 A.M.	Put Matt on bus for sixth grade.
8:00 A.M.	Shovel self and Tim into car.
8:15 A.M.	Drop off Tim at child care.
8:30 A.M.	Start series of appointments with students and research assistants.
noon	Telephone physician per prior arrangement: learn results of a particularly distasteful medical procedure.
12:35 P.M.	Collect Tim from child care.
12:45 P.M.	Collect Matt from school.
12:50 P.M.	Start out for Northampton.

and then in Northampton, 90 or 100 minutes up the road:

2:30 P.M.	Look over house to sublet next year; meet current tenants.
4:00 P.M.	Meet with a member of my new department.
5:30 P.M.	Start back for New Haven.

Meredith had known of the medical exam and knew that I would be hearing the results and then rushing with my boys to Northampton. She knew too that there was more than a minuscule possibility that the test results might indicate cancer. Neither Meredith's family nor mine was a stranger to cancer. So, while the thought that I might need treatment evoked no panic, it did create some realistic dread.

At 12:42, bang on schedule, I swung the car onto the street of Matt's school. Tim was strapped in his car seat in the back, already munching his car picnic lunch. Matt was waiting for me at the school entrance. And so was Meredith—sitting right there on the parapet next to Matt. Without any fuss or fanfare, Meredith had simply arranged to make herself available in case I needed some support.

"Hi cutie," she called. Meredith calls all her friends cutie, sweetie, and dearie. "What news?"

"It's okay," I replied truthfully.

"So you're off to see the house in Northampton?"

"Yep."

"Well, that's good then. See you soon. Fill me in on the details when you get a chance."

John Wayne could not have been less loquacious. But in five or six sentences, Meredith communicated worlds. Of course, Meredith and I are not always so understated. Other times and places, Meredith and I have talked and talked. Indeed, if words were water, we would by now have filled the Grand Canyon twice over. But that day in April was not an occasion for words. It was a time just to see a friendly face and to know that someone was thinking of me and ready to help. And to a degree that no amount of discussion could have achieved, Meredith's action, so synchronous with my needs, helped solidify and deepen an already loving friendship.

How do people get in synch with each other? Sometimes, especially when people are in love, the matching of tastes and desires seems to happen spontaneously. More often, synchrony occurs because people work at making it occur, because at least one person intentionally interrupts her or his day to become available to another. This is what Meredith did for me. Friends take turns matching or following each others' moods, alternating who is available to whom. Parents make themselves available to their children; and as children age, they increasingly assume the role of emotional mirror or enabler.

Spouses, in theory, make themselves available to each other, each ready to march in step with the other. But theory and fact do not always coincide. In fact, when each spouse marches to the beat of his or her own professional drummer, it is hard for them to keep in step with each other. In contemporary dual-professional families, schedules can be out of phase with each other.[79] Mr. Jones comes home tired and embattled, but Ms. Jones hands him the skillet and ketchup as she rushes out the door for her tour of duty at the emergency room. Ms. Smith comes home exhausted, but Mr. Smith wants to celebrate passing the bar exam. Mr. White is ready for some gaiety and heel kicking, but Ms. White needs to stay up all night to slave over the facts of the such-and-such merger proposal that she will present the next day to the vice-presidents.

Emotional intimacy is a casualty. Can the man put his needs on hold until both work histories have sorted themselves out and the children are in college? And why, he muses, should he? He can remember the families of his youth. In those families, the wife made herself available to her husband, helping him to respond to the dictates of the world outside the family. As one male lawyer in Lisa Silberstein's study of dual-career couples mused: "My dad would come home at 7:30 or 8:00, with the kids in bed or doing homework, and my mother would have dinner prepared. He was a wonderful man, but in a nutshell, he didn't have to do any shitwork, and that makes a big difference to one's feeling of harassment."[80]

The man regretted that his own wife, through no fault of her own, was not available to him in the same ways that his mother had been available to his father. He experienced a loss because he remembered— or imagined that he remembered—the days of mirrored feelings and emotional synchrony.

He, and other men in Silberstein's sample, also remembered when his wife had time for sex. Sexual intimacy constitutes an important element of many adult relationships, even marriage. Eighty percent of Silberstein's sample believed that their sex lives were impeded by work. Fatigue, depression, anxiety, and preoccupation were among the ways in which work intruded into the conjugal bedroom.

Of the thirty-two people in Silberstein's study who believed that work interfered with their sex lives, fourteen thought his work and hers interfered equally. The other eighteen people expressed the belief that her work interfered with their marital sex lives more than his did. One man said that when he experienced pressures at the office: "I'm snappy and irritable when I first get home, but then by bedtime it's out of my system. She doesn't get rid of it so fast, and then doesn't want sex."[81] Said another man: "The way I feel about it is when you're down, sex cheers you up, and when you're up, sex cheers you up. The way my wife feels about it is when you're up, sex is fun, but when you're not so up, it's not that much fun. So my ups and downs at work don't affect my interest in sex, whereas hers do."[82]

To summarize: The husband of the juggler is justifiably afraid of losing intimacy. As Robert Weiss observed, "Men need their wives' accessibility—emotional as well as physical—to feel entirely secure."[83] Sex is part, but only part, of the issue. Also at stake is a more pervasive question of rhythms and how, in the midst of massive scheduling and split-second timing, there are to be the sustaining moments of connections.

Husbands' Well-Being

If men experience as much loss as I claim, they should register the loss psychologically. One might expect to find that the husbands of jugglers are in worse shape psychologically than other husbands. At least, that is what I expected only to discover that there is virtually no good current information on the issue. Some studies contrast the well-being, self-esteem, life satisfaction, job satisfaction, or marital satisfaction of husbands in dual-income and single-income families; but hardly any of the studies take children into account. Surely, the mental health of a man whose wife works could depend on whether or not he and his wife have children. Perhaps the lack of attention to children is one reason why the research has proven inconclusive and contradictory.[84]

One ingenious study broke with tradition and turned up some fascinating results. In 1980 and 1981 Rosalind Barnett and the late Grace Baruch of the Wellesley Center for Research on Women went into the elementary school system of a Boston suburb.[85] The population there was basically white and middle class, and Barnett and Baruch restricted their sample to white middle-class families with at least one child in kindergarten through fourth grade. If the mother worked at least 17.5 hours per week outside the home for pay, Barnett and Baruch classified her as an employed mother. Other mothers they classified as nonemployed. Altogether, the study included eighty families with an employed mother and eighty with a nonemployed mother.

From interviews with each family, Barnett and Baruch found few major differences between the husbands of employed mothers and the husbands of nonemployed mothers. On average, both groups of men exhibited low levels of role strain and high levels of well-being. Neither group was distinctively happy or unhappy.

Barnett and Baruch also looked at the associations between well-being and role strain, on the one hand, and female participation in child care, on the other. Among the women there was virtually no connection between the amount of child care a woman did and how much role strain she experienced or how well she felt. Typically, jugglers who did a small amount of child care felt good; and so did jugglers who did a large amount of child care.

Among the men it was a different story. Husbands' feelings were strongly influenced by how much child care the wife performed! For the families that included a juggler, as the woman's involvement in child care increased, the husband experienced less role strain, felt more benefited in the marriage, but felt less competent as a parent. The fewer hours the wife spent with the children, the more strain the husband experienced—even though his own hours did not increase.

Why should men experience strain? My guess is that expectations are an important aspect of the resistance that men have shown to changing sex roles. Men over forty and perhaps even men over thirty have entered their adulthood with certain unquestioned assumptions about how life proceeds in the family. Current arrangements challenge the old vision—even when the arrangements do not entail much extra work for the father. In the words of one professional man interviewed by Lisa Silberstein:

> I remember saying to [my wife] Jane ten years into the marriage that I felt like the game rules had been changed on me. I hadn't changed, but society had. And now I was being asked, or rather told, that I needed to be different. I married with an expectation that I would come home and find dinner on the table and that I would provide the money. My wife's end of the bargain was to take care of the house and kids. So it's been hard. I felt like the rug was swept out from under me.[86]

Even when a man did not have a firm preconception of what family life would (and should) entail, he may not have anticipated the challenges of contemporary family life and so may feel tired and inconvenienced. Jack and Sophia, a couple studied by writer and activist Lisa Wenner, typify the new family in which everyone intended to cooperate but nobody had envisioned how difficult cooperation would be. Said Wenner in a case history:

> Arrangements can be and, in fact, usually are quite complicated, tedious, and constantly in need of revision as the child's and parents' needs change.
>   Sophia and Jack's household became more complex as their family grew. Jack says, "We got better at negotiating, but all the time new balls were being added to the ones that we were already juggling. So as soon as we got good at juggling three balls another one would be added. Pretty soon you have ten balls in the air. So, you get better, but if you drop ten balls. . . . [Neither Jack nor Sophia anticipated how] in order to coparent you have to sit down once a week; we did it every Sunday night for four years with our schedule books. The questions were: Where were we? Where was the baby? Where was the car?"[87]

A Sense of Discomfort

Amassing and reviewing the materials for this chapter, I have had a strong sense of discomfort. In the materials I have read, the interviews I have conducted, and the conversations I have had, I have repeatedly encountered negative emotions. Women have expanded their roles, taking on occupational as well as domestic responsibilities. But their partners, professing support and promising implicitly or explicitly to join in the struggle for a new social order, have really changed little. Complaints and recriminations are everywhere in evidence, and both sides in the drama seem disillusioned and resentful.

These impressions worry me. At one level, I am concerned that my own personal history and the histories of my close friends have unduly influenced my view of men and women in America. Married in 1970, my husband and I originally aspired to the sort of academic marriage that Martha Fowlkes has analyzed. Unacknowledged as well as obvious asymmetries abounded for I had chosen to play the role of the wife behind the successful man. What a lot of changes there have been in twenty years, and what a lot of heartache. Does my portrayal of male resistance come only from my own disappointments and confusions? Am I, like journalist Anna Quindlen, simply writing (publicly) about the husband who asked (in private) if I could get him a beer, or fold his socks, or drive him to the station without writing about it?

Deepening my dilemma is the fact that much of the evidence about male resistance, like male resistance itself, is elusive. To be sure, there are the bald statements of opposition to gender equality, some of which I have recorded already on these pages. But far more pernicious than frank confrontations and oppositions are the subtle and pervasive tactics. When he punches her and says that "no wife of his" will work outside the home, there is at least an identifiable enemy; but when he lies in bed at 6:30 A.M. and announces in a whiny voice, "I have no socks," she can feel that she is boxing shadows.

Some hard facts and figures about the supposed new man speak forcefully of men's failure to support their working wives in deed as well as word, including for example, the time-use studies that I reported earlier. Added to the stark figures are other, more indirect findings that corroborate the presence of male resistance. There is, for example, a research report stating that in "high-quality marriages" husbands and wives agree about the greater importance of the husband's career relative to the wife's while in low-quality marriages they do not.[88] Or there is Lucia Gilbert's data-based observation that the men who make no pretense about believing that their own careers are more important than their wives' careers are most "free to support their wives' career pursuits."[89]

Definitive studies have not yet been done. Only a few studies have been designed in a way that would lead to complete answers.[90] Why?

The paucity of adequate research is related to our cultural biases.[91] Social scientists, like everyone else, assumed for a long time that raising children was a job for each married woman to carry out within the privacy of her own home. Until social scientists stopped assuming that the post–World War II nuclear American family represented the healthy ideal, they were unprepared to examine power functions within the family unit.

Trying to decide on the most appropriate reaction to male resistance only increases my discomfort. Anger, as I said earlier, no longer seems correct. Recognizing what men have lost allows me to sympathize with the man who feels threatened by changing sex roles. Yet sometimes I feel impatient to the point of anger.

Men Gain, Too

However much or little we sympathize with men's losses, we need to keep in view what men gain from women's freedom to juggle life roles. Surely, there are some very important benefits to men, but hardly anyone has done any empirical investigations, and very few have even theorized about the gains. So I hereby offer for consideration a list of benefits that a husband can gain from his wife's employment while there are children in the home. Let us start with the least important.

1: Developing Domestic Skills

The man with an employed wife may acquire domestic competencies that give him pleasure and a sense of accomplishment. It was pretty chic, for a while, for the host at a dinner party to produce the Moo Sue Pork or some other equally esoteric specialty. What man would not like to have his culinary accomplishments applauded by the assembled dinner guests?

Some skills, in and out of the kitchen, probably provide more than a chance to be admired; some offer intrinsic pleasure. Cleaning and mending are probably not as much fun, for most people, as cooking. But even so, some sense of satisfaction may be gleaned from keeping a well-ordered house.

2: Enhancing the Marriage

If the scheduling logistics of the juggling family interfere with the woman's availability to her husband, the independence and sense of self that a wife and mother gains from employment outside the home can also make her a better companion, in the long run, to her husband. Comradeship may be an important benefit of the symmetrical family in which family responsibilities are not as specialized and as divided along gender lines as in the past.[92] Even as synchrony is harder to achieve, mutuality may be more likely.

The traditional housewife might have enjoyed access to the adult world through her neighborhood, church or synagogue, and volunteer activities. But she also had to rely heavily on her husband for news of the larger world. Today's housewife may be even more isolated: With so many of her contemporaries in the paid labor market, she may experience difficulty creating a life of her own over the back fence and in women's volunteer groups.

When one adult member in a partnership is isolated from society while the other is not, trouble brews. Certainly, isolation was part of the problem that drove Mr. and Mrs. Foster, in Robert Weiss's sample, to seek change. Isolation tends to create dependency and resentment.[93] The man who is married to a housewife may come to experience the woman as a emotional anchor in more than one sense.

And the man who is married to a juggler may come to experience his wife as a buoy. Three-quarters of the women faculty who took part in Sara Yogev's study believed that their careers had improved their marriages. Independence and mutual respect were among the reasons why. In the words of one respondent: "We are not dependent on each other; we have things we enjoy together as well as separately. We also have more respect for each other."[94]

Similar sentiments were expressed by both husbands and wives in Rosanna Hertz's in-depth investigation. One woman described how similar employment experiences freed each partner from resentments that might otherwise have developed: "Another aspect of my traveling and his traveling is that each of us understands what travel is to the other, and it's not sitting at home thinking that it's glamorous or exciting and that I'm being left out, as a lot of wives do who are very resentful of their husbands' traveling."[95]

The participants in Hertz's study also note the closeness that can come from discussing matters of mutual professional interest. One man articulated his appreciation for his wife's professional advice:

I listen to her, and I weigh her judgment. I make my decision, and sometimes it is very much in line with her ideas and sometimes it is not. What we discuss are business relationships: What am I going to say to person X in regard to a disagreement about something, or how am I going to handle the fact that I am angry about a decision? The same kinds of issues come up in Jill's business, so she understands.[96]

Hertz' respondents were not the only people to express such feelings. So did the men and women in Lisa Silberstein's study of dual-professional couples and the lawyers with whom Cynthia Epstein has spoken over the years.[97] A man who is a lawyer and who is married to a lawyer can experience a special kind of mutuality that other male lawyers lack.

3: Increasing Money

Many of the benefits of money are obvious. Even a pedantic academic does not need to dwell on how helpful cold cash is to the achieving and maintaining of a decent life-style. Money buys the same amount, no matter who earns it.

Less obvious perhaps, but no less important, is the psychological boost that occurs when a man is liberated from the pressure to provide. While threats to self-esteem are (as we have seen) real and immediate when a husband first contemplates sharing the provider role, the long-term benefits can be great indeed. More than half of the fifty dual-career husbands interviewed by Lucia Gilbert, for example, said that they felt their careers had been enriched by the decrease in financial pressure. The men felt free to take risks and to explore options and opportunities that they might have desired but not dared to take when an entire family depended on them solely or mostly for financial security.[98]

A good example occurred within my own extended family. My brother-in-law, Tom, had worked for the same corporation since earning his master's degree in electrical engineering. Mid-life came, and Tom wanted to try something new. He joined a little high-tech company that some friends of his, having resigned from the big corporation, had started. At the time Tom joined the company, he knew it would be a risk. Maybe they would all make a million. Maybe the company would fizzle, as 90 percent of new businesses do. Only one thing was certain: Tom would have to forgo a salary for at least six months until the company got started.

Tom discussed the matter with my sister. "Okay," she said, "take your time and try this out. After all, you did put me through medical school. It's about time I carried the family alone for a while."

The new company did go under, but the story has a happy ending. Tom's old corporation realized how much they valued him, and they hired him back—with an enormous raise in salary. And Tom had the fun of sowing his wild professional oats.

Even when there are no dramatic risks beckoning, men can feel less constricted in their professional lives if they are not the sole family providers. The liberating effects for a professional man of having an employed wife were documented by Harvard researchers Samuel Osherson and Diana Dill.[99] In 1978 Osherson and Dill collected information from over 350 men aged thirty-five to thirty-eight. The men had been interviewed at various times over the years. The sample was highly educated—40 percent of them had obtained doctorates or the equivalent and another 45 percent had some professional or academic training after graduating from college. They earned relatively high salaries, on average, and some of the men earned enormous salaries.

Osherson and Dill asked the men, in a questionnaire, about the satisfactions they derived from working. Two basic types of satisfaction emerged from the statistical analysis of the men's answers. First, work could be rewarding because it allowed an opportunity for self-discovery and personal growth. Second, work could be rewarding because it made a person feel valued and powerful in the eyes of other people. Men who enjoyed their work primarily because of the first satisfaction we can think of as self-actualizers. Men who enjoyed their work primarily because of the second reason appear more driven by competition.

Osherson and Dill discovered that self-actualizers tended to have working wives while the more competitive men tended to have housewives. Two-thirds of the sample were fathers. Among the fathers, those with working wives derived more pleasure from self-discovery at work than those with wives at home, and fathers in dual-career marriages did not feel less successful, in a competitive sense, than other men.

4: Spending Time with Children

One must not romanticize parenthood; we are all aware of the stresses. Indeed, anyone who sees me in the grocery store at 6:00 P.M. probably finds me locked in serious conflict with one or both of my children. And there have been times, strapped by finances and hemmed in by asphalt, that I felt a shocking recognition of the child abuser that may be deep inside all of us.

There are, of course, many advantages of parenthood. Having an opportunity to interact with children on a day-to-day basis, to have children as part of the daily interweave is a great privilege in our age-segregated society. To spend time on the details of life with his dependent children can be extremely rewarding to any man. Although men in traditional families can have intimate daily contact with their children, the men in dual-earner families may have the most opportunities for it.[100] Time with children is perhaps the biggest reward of having a wife who juggles.

The special circumstances of men in dual-career families have not escaped everyone's notice. One man in Silberstein's sample reflected:

> I remember my sister saying to my mother, "Gee sometimes it seems like Dad is a guest in our house." I doubt my children would ever say that about me. My father—we didn't have an intimate association with him. And he didn't have a full sense of us, from day-to-day dealing with us. I could have this relationship with my kids without being part of a dual-career couple. But because I am part of one, I don't have any choice, and I think I do better when I don't have a choice. And sometimes the more difficult the things are the most satisfying.[101]

Satisfaction with a job well done is rewarding for many fathers involved in coparenting their young children. In the study of dual-professional families in Indianapolis mentioned earlier, 47 of the 50 men in the sample reported that they were quite satisfied with their participation in child rearing.[102] Many of the fathers wished they had more time to spend with their children, but virtually none of the fathers thought they somehow floundered in the time they did spend.

Also satisfying is the opportunity to bond with sons and daughters. A 30-year-old businessman in what Lucia Gilbert calls a role-sharing marriage admitted, "It warms my heart and melts it when my son snuggles up to me."[103] The testimonies of fathers to California researcher, Diane Ehrensaft, were equally glowing.

> I'm absolutely in love with her. Just passionately in love with her.

> There's something wonderful looking in his eyes. There's this person there—he's intelligent, he loves you.

> It was at that moment that I realized Ruthie was the person I was most honest with and who understands me, and was able to look at the lines on my forehead and say, "What are you worried about?"

Ehrensaft notes that such comments were the norm, not the exception, in her study and comments: "There was an intensity and effusiveness to the men's expression of their emotional reactions to their children that neither the fathers, the mothers, nor the 'informed' interviewer was capable of predicting. The men, in short, ended up 'falling in love' with their children."[104] Falling in love is not an insignificant gain.

Summing Up

As soon as we think about marriage, the account of juggling takes on some peculiarities. Changes in sex roles have been for the good. When the changes occur in fact, and are not simply given lip service, women benefit. So do children. For men, the benefits will come too, but at some delay and with costs attached.

Men's defensiveness, their reluctance to pay the emotional costs, their resistance to change when the changes will profit them only in the future have led many feminists to express impatience. Sides are taken in the battle, and each side feels abused and undervalued. When it comes to relations between the sexes, ours seems a particularly confused time, full of contradictions, uncertainties, and misunderstandings.

It is also a time of hope. Perhaps we are currently rewriting the rules so that family life will be easier for both men and women in the generations to come. Let us hope, along with activist and writer Barbara Ehrenreich:

> [T]hat a reconciliation between the sexes is still possible . . . as long as we have sons as well as daughters, it will have to happen. . . . But what would be the terms of such a reconciliation? . . . I can see no other ethical basis for a reconciliation than the feminist principle—so often repeated—that women are also persons, with the same needs for respect, for satisfying work, for love and pleasure—as men. . . .
>
> Then, finally I would hope that we might meet as rebels together—not against each other but against a social order that condemns so many of us to meaningless or degrading work in return for a glimpse of commodified pleasures and condemns all of us to the prospect of mass annihilation.[105]

· 7 ·

The Metaphors
Deconstructed

A long-legged blond descends the stairs of the aircraft. She has a beautiful figure and the kind of rich, full-bodied hair that makes you want to gather it up in your fingers. Here, we think, is a woman with no unmet needs. Her children never wipe their runny noses on her business suit or throw up on her fun fur. Her husband never complains about his socks. Her boss never faults her work. She is an advertiser's image of a juggler, ever successful, ever fulfilled.

In stark contrast is another media image: the bedraggled juggler, overwhelmed by life's responsibilities. The latter vision has bags under her eyes. Her nails are ragged, and she exudes an air of desperation.

Neither view is very encouraging. Both suggest to the flesh-and-blood woman that she should not try to combine real work outside the home and real work within it. The bedraggled picture can make a woman think that she ought not to try because, after all, everyone fails sooner or later. And the image of the unwrinkled juggling bombshell makes the real woman, with her extra roll of skin and her unpressed skirt, feel downright inadequate.

From my interviews with women, I have the strong impression that contemporary middle-class women do seem prone to feelings of inadequacy. We worry that we do not measure up to some undefined level, some mythical idealized female standard. When we see some women juggling with apparent ease, we suspect that we are grossly inadequate for our own obvious struggles.

183

In April 1990, for example, a professor of theater at Smith College wrote an open invitation to her colleagues to attend a reading of the letters of a turn-of-the-century professional woman named Ludella Peck. The letter from the Smith theater professor began:

> I sometimes feel that teaching theatre at Smith, wonderful as it is, is a life-devouring proposition. About mid-April of every year I find myself wondering why I got myself into this. I imagine that other, wiser people still read novels, watch movies, have sex, eat strawberries in bed on a Sunday morning, live without datebooks. I wonder if it's my fault that I live as I do; if I manage my life badly, if I'm inefficient, if there's a better way to do this and I'm just too stupid to figure it out. I note my privilege, and I feel that I ought to be happy; I'm just too tired.

Kendall, the theater professor, is not the only woman who feels that she ought to be happier, or at least more superficially cheerful than she is.

"Why," asks Naomi, of the Chinese restaurant, "can't I manage better?"

"How," asks Dana, helping me arrange a hectic conference, "am I to listen to other women recounting their achievements at work and at home without feeling that I ought to be achieving more myself?"

"What," asks Faye, "have I accomplished of any value today?"

To test my hunch that insecurity underlies some of women's fascination with juggling, I asked my friend Nancy if she would be willing to be interviewed, in a formal and methodical way, about the issues of juggling. A full-time mother, part-time dancer, and self-employed artist, Nancy sees herself as someone who is "trying to find what works for me." She admits that media attention to glamorized jugglers makes her reflect less on the benefits of multiple roles than on the multiple ways in which a woman, any woman, can be made to feel not quite up to par. She resents the current fashion of seeing housewives and other non-career-oriented women as "a sort of lower form of life, you know, unevolved." Steaming up, Nancy agreed to the interview.

Two months later, when we manage to squeeze the interview into our schedules, my hunch proves partially correct. My first question, "Do you still feel that the image of the successful juggler can make the average woman feel unsuccessful?" drew this long reply:

> The more I think about it, I come back to a very personal answer . . . I don't have to work for money . . . I have a choice to juggle as much as I want. . . . Recently I was talking to this woman who was studying

for her Ph.D. . . . She turned to me and said, "You've really had it easy."
Well! I was home with a three year old and an infant! . . . Hers was very
much a personal career choice—you know, the Ph.D. meant a lot to
her. . . . But she got it at a time that stressed her out, stressed out her
family and made her . . . turn to me and say in a nasty voice, "Well, you
had it easy." I think that in some ways I am fighting that view. . . . I am
trying to find out how much stuff I want to do, whether I need those
[professional] degrees, how much I want to enter the public arena.

Growing up when I did, I am really on the borderline of change. My
mother was a housewife with five children and very passive. My father
did all the decision making. She did all the children. . . . All money
decisions were his. So I was raised with that and then I went to college
and ran into the women's movement. Now in some ways I didn't just
run into it. I think I was waiting for it, too. . . . Going through school
and being encouraged to make *A*'s and then encouraged to go to an Ivy
League college, it was hard to get all those rewards and then be expected to stay home.

As I found out when I did stay home, the outside world doesn't
come in and say, "Good job, Nancy. You get an *A*." So there was always
that dichotomy for me—that I do want to get out there and get the
respect but unfortunately for me and women like me, I'm not sure of
how to be a respected adult. I can understand why Sharon went for that
Ph.D. when it was such a hard thing for her to do. Without it, I think
she doesn't feel important enough, respected enough, adult enough.

Toward the end of the two-hour interview I asked Nancy what her
perfect life would look like. She replied:

I think I'd like exactly what I have plus self-esteem. I just wish I could
get off my case a little bit. . . . What I need is a sense of peace. Sometimes I wonder if other people manage to have it. . . . I want to be
respected, and just to get that respect, you need degrees or you need to
make money. Without those, I'll be only [she paused, searching for the
right phrase]—*only a woman,* only somebody who raises kids, only
somebody who greases the wheels of other people, who sends her
children and her husband out into the world.

I should like to take my life as it is and somehow shut out that voice
that wants the *A*. It's a useless voice for me. It doesn't drive me to finer
things, or peace and happiness. Instead, all it does is drive me. No, it
doesn't even drive me. It's more like all it does is depress me.

Nancy had put her finger on it. For her, and no doubt for most of us,
our curiosity about whether other women are managing well occurs in
part because we lack "a sense of peace."

And why are we not at peace? Why are we insecure? Part of the problem comes, as Nancy notes, from the rapid changes in sex-roles. Because we do not quite know what is expected of us, we do not know if we are doing what we ought.[1] Our wish to do what is right for others, coupled with a lack of certainty about how to know what is right and what isn't, keeps us mulling and ruminating. And, as Rosalind Barnett and Grace Baruch have pointed out, the problem is compounded by the cultural taboo against admitting how difficult it is to be a good mother and wife. Even though many women find family roles less conducive than work roles to self-fulfillment,[2] "to admit stress is tantamount to admitting failure as a woman."[3]

At the base of the insecurity is, I believe, the apprehension that has more to do with continuity than with change in sex-role stereotyping. It is the sometimes unconscious worry that whatever we do, however much we accomplish, however hard we try, we cannot escape the judgment that in the final count each of us remains, in Nancy's words, "only a woman."

Sexism

That women are undervalued in our society must come as no surprise. Since the first days of feminism, the entire nation seems to have noticed our culture's strong, pervasive, and unfounded bias in favor of males. There have been, as we have seen in chapters 2 and 5, obvious shifts in public opinion regarding women and men. It is no longer fashionable, or even permissible in most middle-class and professional circles, to declare that men are good and women are bad.[4] Sexism is no longer so overt and simplistic. And it is in style to be a feminist. In 1988, for example, six out of ten young women graduating from colleges in the New Haven area labeled themselves feminists.[5]

Yet, blatant gender imbalances persist. At work women are paid less than men for comparable work. At home every hour that a man devotes to domestic labor and child care is matched by two or three hours of labor from his wife—even if she works full time outside the home.[6] Sexism is one reason for the persistence of gender imbalances.

Perhaps more worrisome than the old, blatant sexism is the subtle, covert sexism. The latter was reflected in a series of articles, "Managing Motherhood," a few years ago in the *Wall Street Journal*. Initially the message appeared to be: "We care about the plight of women." But then the message transformed itself insidiously into "We are sorry that it is so hard for women to juggle" and finally, destructively, into the misogynist message: "We are sorry that it is so hard for women to juggle that they constantly are on the verge of bungling their professional responsibilities." Given that the *Wall Street Journal* both influences and reflects the opinions of its readership, such a message is dangerous as well as wrong minded.

In other places, too, the captains of industry give double messages. The various professional schools of a prestigious university recently held a conference for educational, civic, and business leaders. At the meeting, a president of a major multinational firm spoke about all that his corporation has done to help women break through the glass ceiling that usually keeps women out of top management.

> We have a young woman who is extraordinarily important to the launching of a major new product. We will be talking about it next Tuesday in its first worldwide introduction. She has arranged to have her Caesarean yesterday in order to be prepared for this event. We have insisted that she stay home and this is going to be televised in a closed circuit television, so we're having this done by TV for her, and she is staying home three months, and we are finding ways of filling in to create this void for us because we think it's an important thing for her to do.

To his own ears and probably to the ears of most of the people attending the conference, the bank president must have sounded full of understanding and wisdom. But to the ears of Joanne Martin, a professor at Stanford University School of Business Administration, a troubling theme was audible. "Beneath the surface of the company's apparently benign concern with the employee's well-being are a series of silences, discomforts, and contradictions," said Martin.[7] Whose welfare is being sought? The woman's or the company's? The president acts as if the company were doing the woman a great favor to have her (re)schedule a crucial life event and then to bring television cameras into her bedroom a few days after a major operation. Would he make the same assumption if the employee were a man needing a coronary bypass? How silly the president would look saying, in effect, "We are so kind that we have consented to allow the young man to keep our profits up rather than letting his heart heal."[8]

Of course, most instances are not as dramatic as the one Joanne Martin describes. I myself have seen at close range a fair amount of subtle sexism. A few years ago, for example, a very talented young woman was about to defend her doctoral dissertation before a panel of Yale professors. One of the older men in the room, reputed to be a "great supporter of women" decided magnanimously to put the young woman at her ease by engaging the assembled high brows in a little chitchat until the time for the oral examination. There was only one slight problem. The man's chitchat consisted of a monologue on how he had read in a pediatrics journal of the high rates of infant mortality in the United States. The young woman who was defending her doctoral work was eight and a half months pregnant. None of the men in the room—and certainly not the speaker—showed any awareness of how bizarre and insensitive was the monologue.

Sexist notions about gender and paid labor exist among men at all levels of organizations and not just at the upper levels. Motormen and conductors in a major rapid transit system, for example, have had trouble accommodating to the entry of women into their ranks. Drawing on four years of experience as a participant-observer, Marian Swerdlow—subway conductor turned college professor—has outlined the strategies used by male drivers and conductors to preserve their self-esteem when "their deeply held belief in male superiority was challenged by the increasing evidence that women could perform their jobs competently."[9] One common strategy was to sexualize encounters with women coworkers. Ms. Swerdlow and the other women in the system were so often propositioned that they eventually joked about requesting an application fee. Another way the men clung to their stereotypes was to see each competent woman as the exception while maintaining that any mistake made by a female was proof of the inferiority of the entire female gender. Through the use of these and a number of other devices, the men managed to be, simultaneously, supportive and resistant.

Young men who are not yet in the labor market show the vestiges of subtle sexism. Anne Machung asked men graduating in 1985 from the University of California at Berkeley whether they intended to be married to a woman who works outside the home. "She can work if she wants," was the typical answer but few of the young men envisioned themselves doing housework. According to one senior in the study, whether he would participate in housework and child care "would depend on how much I liked her and how she asked."[10]

It is, of course, not only men who hold deep-seated sexist notions. Some women do too. Think of Phyllis Schlafly and other women who seem all too willing to scold the independent and ambitious jugglers for "abandoning" the family.[11] Even among feminists, an undercurrent of sexism can unfortunately be detected. I have, for example, heard committed feminists declare with a straight face: "Women are as intelligent as men." It is unquestionably true that there are no gender differences in intelligence; yet we may recoil from a sentence that takes as a given that males are the standard against which to measure female accomplishments. How different is the offending sentence from the more neutral sentence: "Women and men are equally intelligent."

One concrete by-product of sex-role expectations is the assumption—an assumption that is so ingrained that even many radical feminists take it for granted—that women must tend the young. Conservatives would have us all live in families where the adult males go out and provide for the others while the adult females nurture and care for those who are dependent.[12] So, too, would some people, women as well as men, who are liberal in other ways. Many feminists have challenged the division of the world according to which females are relegated to home and excluded from the workplace while males are excluded from the home and relegated to the labor force. Others have claimed (probably correctly) that the only good parent is one who relates well to the needs of the child and also claimed (incorrectly) that females are skilled at relating to others while males are not and perhaps cannot be. This residue of sexist thinking has produced some striking contradictions. Ellen Galinsky, a nationally recognized researcher and child-care advocate, has noted the presence of incongruous attitudes. In one survey, three-quarters of the staff of "an excellent" child-care center thought that "it would be better for young children if their mothers didn't work." In another survey reported by Galinsky, 42 percent of employed mothers of children under the age of twelve endorsed the sentiment that "having a mother who works is bad for children under six."[13] Mothers of tiny infants in yet another study displayed a similar ambivalence. Even though two-thirds of the mothers planned to return to their jobs before the child's first birthday, nearly all of them subscribed to traditional attitudes about exclusive mother care for babies. Nine in ten of the women thought she could meet her child's needs better than any other adult and about half agreed that "only a mother just naturally knows how to comfort her distressed child."[14]

Another and related by-product of sexist thinking is the way that most women think of our employment as the extra job or the second job in the family.[15] Until we think of ourselves as providers—whether or not a partner is present—we cannot help but see our work in the paid labor force as opposed, at some level, to our work within the family. To imagine that the male contributes to the family's welfare through his paid work more than does the female is to perpetuate deep and pervasive sexual inequalities, to stall social change. Until we see women and men as equally responsible for the material well-being of the family, we will be stuck at a bottle-neck of sex-role stereotyping.[16]

The same point was foreshadowed fifteen years ago, in a compelling paper by sociologists Rose Laub Coser and Gerald Rokoff.[17] They proposed that the biggest strain that occurs in the dual-career family is the strain on assumed social status. In America status is intimately linked to one's employment; and so the employed wife presents a potential threat to the very core of the system by which high and low statuses are assigned to various families. What if her occupation surpasses his in prestige? The existence of even a few noticeable examples in which the wife's job carried more prestige than the husband's would challenge the unspoken rule that the status of the family is to be determined by the most senior male in the family. In the American system it is presumed that only when there is no male present should a female function as status bearer. A woman who wishes simultaneously to have a male partner and to take her own nonfamily work so seriously that she might attain status in the occupational world poses a grave contradiction for the entire system.

Coser and Rokoff called attention to the hypocrisies of social scientists. Rather than admit that it is the system that they wish to protect (and their privileged place in it), many social scientists, Coser and Rokoff noted, would pretend that it is the woman whom they seek to shelter. Outwardly they address the strain that a working mother and wife experiences, but it is not her strain that is actually at issue. What is at issue is the strain that she produces for the system.

Individualism and Collective Responsibility

If sexism keeps women tied to home and makes life more difficult for the juggler than it need be, so does our adherence to individualism. We are uncomfortable with the communal approach to life, especially when this approach is facilitated by the workings of the government. Only when it comes to the formal schooling of children do we assume that the state's responsibilities override the privacy rights of parents.[18] In almost all other ways, we are committed to an ideal of individual responsibility.

A commitment to individual responsibility has much to recommend it. The pioneer spirit deserves to be revered, and in many ways, I endorse it. Yet I also think we have invested too much in the cowboy image—the image of some strong, never-complaining person, going it alone—to our great detriment. Of course, people should be responsible for their actions, but the philosophy of taking responsibility for ourselves too often subverts the impulse to take communal responsibility for the welfare of all. And individualism can turn nasty and punitive. In the words of T. Berry Brazelton, whom I quoted before: "If there is an implicit bias in the United States, it is this: Families should be self-sufficient, and if they're not, they deserve to suffer."[19]

The most fragile and most precious parts of our juggling acts are children. But even as we acknowledge responsibility for our own children, we have a need and a right to think of society's responsibility. We must work together as a society to assure the right of every child to a full life, free of hunger, safe from destruction, war, and violence, and as safe as can be from the ravages of physical and mental ill health. We must work together to tend and attend to every growing child.

In opposition to the ideal of social responsibility for the welfare of children is the presumption that the raising of children is to be conducted exclusively within the confines of the isolated nuclear family. The increasingly public nightmare of child abuse has not yet led most Americans to question the validity of a system that leaves children almost entirely under the thumb of their biological parents. Ironically, it may be the public scandals about child-care centers that lead people to see that for women and children, the American family can be a violent institution. Local newspapers are beginning to carry stories about abuse in centers and to include by way of reference statistics about the family. My local paper, the *Daily Hampshire Gazette,* for example, carried a story on the McMartin child-care scandal trial and noted that "children are nearly twice as likely to be molested in their own household as in a day care center."[20]

Child-care policies in our country are lamentable. As well-known researchers, Sandra Scarr, Deborah Phillips, and Kathleen McCartney observe: "Considerations of 'who should provide child care?' are mired in an acrimonious debate involving the schools, community-based child-care programs, and church-housed programs. . . . We are unlikely ever to see child care and leave policies in the United States that resemble European or Canadian policies."[21]

Scarr, Phillips, and McCartney go on to document "a national ambivalence" about child care. In 1988, for example, more than forty bills were introduced into Congress that contained provisions for child care. National policymakers are evidently aware of the pressing need. Yet, direct federal funding for child care has decreased dramatically since 1980. Adjusting the spending for real dollars, the cuts have amounted to 18 percent! Among the industrialized countries, the United States is the only one that does not have have a job-protected maternal leave policy.[22]

Ambivalence about other care may be better than out-and-out opposition. Opposition to governmental responsibility was strong in the early 1970s when special interest groups organized against passage of the comprehensive child-care bill. Richard Nixon vetoed the bill on the grounds that he did not want the federal government to "invade" the privacy of the family. And the judicial branch of government was sometimes as stubborn as the executive. In 1974 the Supreme Court overturned a regulation established by the Equal Employment Opportunities Commission (EEOC) concerning maternity leave. The EEOC had declared that denial of maternity leave constituted sex discrimination; the Court disagreed.[23]

Whatever the future may bring, the current lack of proper parental leave policies and of adequate other care makes it much harder than it need be for women and men to juggle various life demands. The difficulty falls, of course, more on the women than the men. Some national survey data collected from 1968 to 1979 show that absenteeism is greater among employed women with children than among employed men with children or employed women without children.[24] In other national surveys, a noticeable percentage of employed women conceive of the lack of adequate child care as the major restraint on the hours they work.[25]

Of course, in the long run, it is not primarily women and men who bear the greatest burden from our nation's inadequate child-care policies. In the long run, it is the children who suffer the most. Substantiating the reality are some statistics assembled by Helen Blank of the Children's Defense Fund and presented in 1985 at a special pediatric roundtable.[26] Among the chilling figures she presented were these:

✦ In Los Angeles County, 135,000 children under the age of five and 300,000 children aged five to fourteen need child care or after-school care; but there is no licensed and regulated child care for them.

✦ In Maine about 25,000 children aged six to twelve spend an average of four hours a week as latchkey children, and each week 500 children under age five spend some time without any adult supervision or care.

✦ In New Mexico an estimated 50,000 children need other care while 3,700 receive it.

Other unhappy facts, presented by other researchers, confirm the impression that ours is a country where a professed interest in children's welfare is not realized in fact.

✦ Among the middle and upper classes, more than 50 percent of three and four year olds go to nursery school; among lower-income families, only a quarter do, presumably for lack of funds.[27]

✦ Despite the publicity about flextime, only about 12 percent of people working full time can vary the hours that they begin or end work.[28]

✦ Nearly two-thirds of school principals responded to a survey on child care by saying that they thought their own schools ought to provide better care for children before and after school; and less than one-fourth said their school already had an after-school program.[29]

✦ As many as 70 percent of American youngsters under the age of ten regularly care for themselves and a substantial portion of these children also care for a younger sibling.[30]

Some people claim it is a woman's job to care for her children. I agree. I am responsible for my children, but my maternal responsibilities cannot and should not be discharged by my acting in isolation, without asking for or accepting the help of others.

When I go on a trip, it is my responsibility to get myself from Point A to Point B. Because I cannot afford a chauffeur, I drive myself. I do not assume that someone else is responsible for driving me. But when I climb into my car, I do not expect to have to go pave the roads for my journey. The existence of a national network of well-paved highways in no measure invades my privacy and rights as a private citizen. And speed limits do not trammel my rights unnecessarily. In just the same way, the existence of a minimally adequate network of child-care institutions would not invade my rights as a mother, and the creation of child-care policies would not unnecessarily limit my opportunities and obligations as a parent. This point was made some years ago by Letty Pogrebin and holds true today.[31] As Pat Schroeder and others have repeatedly argued, a national family policy that acknowledges "the rich diversity of American families" could help all women and men meet the economic and social demands of family life.[32]

Structural, Not Personal Reasons

The question reverberates: Why is it so hard for so many people to combine productive labor and domestic life? The answer, as we have seen, clearly implicates the system in which we live. The core issue is one of structures, and the great need is for structural change.

Yet many people continue to frame the issues in personal failures. Naomi cries at the Chinese restaurant; Dana grabs my arm at the Yale conference; and Kendall sends a poignant letter to her colleagues. Meanwhile, many of the women whom I interview—similar to women in a number of other studies—confess that while they have a marvelous time combining different life roles, they feel that they might do better if they were more planful, clever, or efficient.[33] In short, even women who are lively, vibrant, and highly successful feel guilty.

Confessions appear in print as well. Georgia Witkin-Lanoil writes in the introduction to her book, *The Female Stress Syndrome:*

> I was a full-time college professor, full-time psychotherapist, full-time mother, full-time author of textbooks, part-time clinical supervisor, part-time consultant, semi-efficient homemaker, and inefficient bookkeeper.
>
> I was full-time stressed and part-time guilt-ridden. Like most working mothers, I was haunted by a long list of *shoulds*.[34]

More sadly, Sylvia Hewlett describes her reaction to the stillbirth of twins:

> Afterward, for quite a long time, life was truly hard to bear. . . . I mourned my children with an intensity that frightened me. In addition to my grief, I was coping with an overwhelming sense of responsibility. . . . For a while I believed that I was living proof of the conservative wisdom that women could not have both careers and babies.[35]

To frame the issues in personal terms means more than accepting personal responsibility for failure. It also means having to look for personal solutions when structural ones might be more useful.[36] "If women lived in a culture that presumed active fatherhood," observed Arlie Hochschild, "they wouldn't need to devise personal strategies to bring it about."[37] But the culture does not presume that fathers should be involved in the day-to-day, nitty-gritty of child rearing; and individual women are left, again and again, to develop individually tailored means of coping.[38]

Even when the father wishes to coparent, the two adults are left to create their own family solutions to the challenges of combining work and home life. Someone usually has to sacrifice his or her involvement in work when two careers and more than two people live within one family. Given sex discrimination and given the tendency of women to marry a man slightly older and more established than themselves, it is usually true that the husband generates a larger income than the wife and also has more potential for career growth. And so it is usually the wife who makes sacrifices for the husband—especially after the arrival of children, when families need money.[39] Not only do many women cut back on the hours when working outside the home; they also switch their jobs to enable the husband to locate or relocate for his work. According to Lisa Silberstein: "It can be expected that moves organized around the husband's career often will have a deleterious impact on the woman's career progress. A positive feedback loop is thus established: Women begin in lower-paying jobs and are likely to remain there."[40] In reinventing individual solutions to the structural and systemic problems that face them, families that include a juggler inadvertently help to perpetuate the problems that make life stressful for the juggler. The reinvention of solutions by each family is troubling for another reason. Much energy is expended and much time is consumed; and yet the time and energy do not really diminish the problems.

When I think of the problems that beset women and men who every week need to arrange the car pools, line up the babysitters, schedule meetings and appointments, get to the store before it closes, and keep the checkbook balanced; when I think of the many recurrent little problems, I think of mosquitos. I hate mosquitos and wish only that the feeling was reciprocated. But, alas, it is not. In the summer I keep a swatter by my desk. If I could just fix the screen door, I would spend a lot less time each summer swatting the insects. The same applies—metaphorically—to the juggling families who are trying, in the words of public policy analysts Sheila Kamerman and Alfred Kahn, to "manage productive roles in the labor force at the same time as they fulfill productive roles with the family—at home."[41] Only when we shift the focus away from the individual woman or the individual family and to the society in which we all live will we bring about lasting improvements in the ways that families can work. In the long run, if we don't want to agonize, we must organize![42]

Changing Conceptions Through Metaphor Analysis

While we are waiting for the screen door of parental leaves and good child care to be constructed, we need to keep the mosquito bites to a minimum. While we are waiting for Congress to create a viable system of national other care or for our employers to institute on-site child care arrangements, we do not have to just sit around and scratch. There is much that we can do as individuals to improve our situation. The need for collective action does not cancel out the necessity of individual action.

What strategies can we use to minimize the stresses of juggling without jeopardizing the benefits? Most strategies involve cognitive reframing—that is, rethinking realities. From cognitive reframing may come behavioral changes.

One strategy is simply to lower aspirations. Given that the diversity of juggling cheers us and that variety adds spice to life, it should theoretically be possible for a woman to feel happy and fulfilled by simply telling herself that it is okay to be "pretty good" in many different roles (rather than great in any one role). In theory, this strategy fits well with what we know about the buffering effects of multiple roles. In theory, having a job, even a mediocre one, ought to help one feel reconciled to having an unclean house while having a house, even a shabby one, ought to help one feel reconciled to an unfulfilling job. When there is no choice, and problems and disappointments are in fact inevitable, then resigning oneself to them is good.

But there are many times when defeat is not inevitable and when it is unhealthy to resign to disappointment. As a psychologist, I am convinced that most adults come to recognize that they possess some talents and lack others. Certainly, we should not try to excel in areas where we lack talent. We should strive for excellence in areas where our talents lie. Trying to convince yourself that a few dustballs do not matter if, in fact, they really do matter to you is a bad strategy. Attempting to resign yourself to a low-paying job when money is a prime motivator for you is another bad strategy. So, too, is the desire to find refuge in many middling accomplishments when you know, inside, that you are capable of more.

When women seek to relieve the stresses of juggling by swallowing their true ambitions to excel in any one domain, they are heading for trouble. If she decides to settle, the contemporary juggler writes herself a ticket to the land of bland emotions and depressions whose previous tenant was the upper-middle-class housewife. We all have to make-do, to settle sometimes. But to permit oneself to be uniformly mediocre is both a mark of and an inducement to depression. The life in which there are no public performances, no moments in which one stands to be challenged and evaluated, is a sorry life indeed. The way to make juggling less stressful is not to give up striving for anything that one truly wants.

Metaphor Analysis

Another, much more therapeutic strategy is to engage in a mental exercise technique that I frequently use in teaching. In this metaphor analysis technique, we make liberal use of imagery—such as the juggling metaphor—to discover which elements of our lives need the most attention and which need less attention now. Clarifying these distinctions can help reduce stress.

To illustrate metaphor analysis, we return to my friend Naomi whose lunch with me was described in chapter 1. Naomi's life roles included mother, friend, daughter, lover, worker, community activist, and ex-wife as well as research assistant. She was an active, high-achieving woman, but one who felt nearly overwhelmed by her many responsibilities.

The first step is for Naomi to imagine herself as a juggler (as she in fact did, and as many women imagine themselves). Each life role is an Indian club. Next she should focus in her mind's eye on each club, asking in turn about each:

1. Is it fragile or sturdy?
2. Is it beautiful? Ugly? A little of each?
3. Is it weighted in a way that makes it easy to catch or difficult to catch?
4. How does it feel when I grasp it? Toss it?
5. Is its flight path predictable and smooth or wobbly and uncertain?
6. Does it exert any gravitational pull on any of the other clubs?
7. How would I feel if it were harmed? Broken or dented?

The more concrete the questions, the better.

By becoming extremely specific in the questions she asks, Naomi should begin to see important distinctions that would otherwise remain conceptually remote. She might realize, for example, that she holds the following opinions about her current life-partner, Jim Day:

1. He is sturdy (e.g., he won't go away if you are a half hour late getting home).
2. He is predictable (e.g., he is sure always to forget your birthday *or* is sure to never forget your birthday).
3. He is beautiful and it would be a great shame if he were harmed or broken (e.g., if he did somehow mind that you were home late once again, if his feelings were somehow hurt, it would bother you).

About her younger child, she would see that he seems extremely beautiful, somewhat wobbly, and—as is appropriate to a person his age—quite fragile. If you are a half an hour late for him, his world falls apart.

What about her angry ex-husband? He would be fragile, hard to catch, and hard to launch, unpredictable, and ugly. She would also see that the angry ex-husband exerts a strong gravitational pull on the wonderful boys.

And so it goes with each Indian club. Once Naomi has fixed a quite detailed image of each separate item in her mind and has used these images to illuminate distinctions, she is ready to conjure up images of the action. She should watch the internal movie of herself juggling all the clubs to see when she feels happy and satisfied and when she feels worried. She could see when and how she attends to the the children, to her job, to her friends. She might notice how much attention she gives to the ex-husband—ironically much more than to steady, dependable Jim.

If Naomi were to give herself over to the process, she would be able to use metaphor analysis to help reduce the stress of juggling without minimizing the pleasures of balancing different life roles.[42] She would gain the composure that comes from knowing she is prepared for an emergency. And she would lose none of the fun of combining roles.

I know that I have benefited from repeated use of metaphor analysis. The conceptual clarity it brings to life has helped me decide which actions to follow and which to avoid. I have observed:

✦ First, some roles are, in and of themselves bothersome. Using the juggling metaphor: Some Indian clubs are ugly and will be a source of displeasure whether they sit on a shelf or are tossed in the air with other clubs.[43] (If you find this, you are similar to most other people for research shows that *stress within* a given role usually exceeds stress *between* roles.)

+ Second, even when I can eliminate the ugly Indian clubs from my juggling act, I sometimes experience stress when juggling. Stress comes from worry. Often we are just as bothered by what might happen as by what is happening. We worry, for example, that a fall will weaken a club, perhaps in ways that will only be detected with the passage of time. When all the clubs are unquestionably sturdy, we do not worry about dropping them. When all the clubs are made of rubber, we can juggle many of them with little stress, for a mistake is inconsequential. But if even one club is made of porcelain, the entire act is infused with tension.

+ Third, the joys of juggling are distinct from the stresses. To keep everything aloft is exhilarating, whether the clubs are made of porcelain or rubber. But keeping everything aloft produces much more stress when the clubs are porcelain than when they are rubber. The exhilaration and the fun do not simply go hand-in-hand with the stress.

Another juggler might also discover, if she is like me, that she sometimes treats sturdy clubs as if they were very delicate. Whenever she does, she is creating unnecessary stress. Certainly, she should notice whether every club is, in fact, as sturdy as it appears. (Just because a husband doesn't cry doesn't mean he has no feelings.) Do not assume that every club will shatter if dropped. Remember, sturdiness and value are distinguishable. Even the most beautiful and valuable club can prove very hardy.

A juggler might also notice, furthermore, that she worries about bungling the act sometimes out of concern for her own image rather than out of concern for the Indian clubs themselves. Sometimes she does not wish to drop even the most ugly and worthless club because she knows or imagines that some audience will disapprove. "She's no good at this; look at how she let a club drop." Again, she may be creating unnecessary stress for herself. If the club is worthless or if it is sturdy, don't worry when it drops. Audience members probably won't mind, even if they are paying attention.

My friend Dot had convinced herself that life was full of dangers because she saw every mistake as irretrievable. She thought that if a club she had launched in the air fell and broke, her act would be ruined for once and all. This attitude made her very anxious when she was offered two jobs—one in Maine and one in Connecticut.

Dot was working herself into a real lather. At the base of her dilemma was the nagging worry: What if it turns out that I made the wrong choice? Just at her moment of greatest doubt, Dot read a newspaper article about male and female styles in making career choices. Men, said the newspaper, tend to think of choices as two-year options while women think of the initial choice as determining the rest of one's life. Dot pulled herself together instantaneously and accepted the job in Connecticut. If it turns out to be a mistake, she thought, I'll leave after eighteen months. If the club cracks when it drops, I'll get a replacement.

Similarly, journalist Betty Rollin has reflected on her capacity for worry and has wondered if women may be more prone than men to what she calls the "I'm-over-my-head-and-this-time-they're-going-to-catch-me" feeling. It was her conviction that men do not feel like crying when they are faced with a big challenge. She tested her conviction by asking a young male producer about his experiences:

"When you're on a story," I asked him, "do you ever think that it is not going to work out?"
"Sure," he said merrily, "All the time!"
"Do you worry about it?"
"Sometimes," he said, not sounding sure.
"When it doesn't work out, do you usually figure it's your fault?"
"No," he said, sounding sure.
"Suppose it is your fault. Does it make you feel terrible?"
"Nah," he said.
"Why not?"
He looked at me. "Aren't I entitled to make a mistake once in a while?"[44]

As a juggler, you may feel that some audiences (your critical relative, your male chauvinist boss, your spiteful neighbor, your own misguided conscience) are watching and waiting for you to make a mistake, to drop a club or cause some midair collision. And this feeling may be correct. But perhaps you do not need to worry about audience reaction as much as you assume. Examining your assumptions and discovering which life roles you should pay more attention to and which you can safely ignore is the aim of the metaphor analysis.

From Concepts to Action

Using metaphor analysis, it may be possible to find ways to reduce some of the unnecessary stress. Yet, even having eliminated the excess, a juggler may find that she is left with more tension and conflict than she would like. She has too many fragile and valued clubs in the act to be able to relax. This is how Naomi felt the day we went for lunch.

What can Naomi do next? The next step is to ask herself if she must catch each falling club with her own hands. How does a woman not worry about the fragile and precious club that is speeding earthward and that she knows she will not be able to catch? She juggles over a safety net. Naomi never once thought about safety nets. Circus jugglers use safety nets when they practice, and tightrope walkers use them as frequently as possible. A great saving in emotional energy comes from knowing that we have backup resources and personnel in case of emergencies.

It is the knowledge that one cannot afford to make a mistake that creates stress. Whether one is an air traffic controller, a neurosurgeon, a student taking an exam, a concert pianist, or the mother of a toddler, it is worry about possible mistakes that results in the state of vigilance most often associated with stress diseases in the body. As jugglers we worry most about our children because children are, indeed, vulnerable creatures.

In our modern society, safety nets are not often part of the permanent scenery. But one can weave them, even in her role as mother of dependent young. What I have advised Naomi to do, and what I would advise everyone to do who is feeling stressed by juggling home and work is to build a network of adults who accept responsibility to help out with the children in the event of an emergency, no matter how minor.

I have tried to follow my own advice. Here is a vivid, if somewhat extreme, example of how we have sewn safety nets to help the Crosby family with its many juggling acts. For the last thirteen years, my husband and I have had a commuter marriage. During the academic term, we typically spend half of the week together in our principal residence. The other half of the week, I stay put while Travis, my husband, lives elsewhere. Eleven years ago we were living in New Haven, Connecticut, with our elder child aged six, and I was pregnant with our second child. The second child was due to be born in March. Travis, Matthew, and I were all at our respective schools, teaching and learning during the month of March. Given my age at the time and the rapidity of my first labor, we felt it necessary to plan for almost any eventuality.

My greatest fear was that I would go into labor at 2:30 P.M., just when I was supposed to be collecting Matthew from first grade on a day when Travis was out of town. My next greatest fear was that I would go into labor in the middle of the night in the middle of the week. Husbands were welcome in the delivery room even in those days, but first-graders were not. My fears, you see, were totally realistic and not the wild imaginings of a neurotic woman.

Starting in late January, we installed extensive safety nets. Because of the possibility of daytime labor, we had a list of friends, primarily other junior faculty members, who agreed to stay by a phone during certain hours of the day and, if needed, to collect Matthew from school and keep him until Travis could make it back to town. And for evenings and nights, we had graduate students come and live with Matthew and me at our apartment whenever Travis was absent. We could not afford to offer any pay for the babysitting work, but the students were kind, and I provided dinner and breakfast for them as well as clean sheets and a pleasant, if somewhat crowded, place to stay.

The weaving of nets was not without costs. So much arranging, cooking, cleaning, and scheduling was naturally a bit wearing. Even more "costly" at first (but only at first) was the breaking down of social barriers. It is unusual for faculty and graduate students to share the intimacies of daily life, and it took me a minute to feel at ease, for example, yelling at Matthew in front of company. To show your own parental short temper in front of an audience is rarely easy; the experience is even more charged when the audience is supposed to admire and revere you and to go to the library for you.

The benefits of the arrangement, both expected and unexpected, far outweighed the costs. In addition to peace of mind, our original goal, we gained a number of amusing stories and, better yet, a number of good friends. There is nothing so cementing as being trench buddies, especially in a war in which no one gets hurt. Best of all, the adult friendships were not forged at Matthew's expense. We shared responsibility for his well-being; we did not abdicate it, a difference appreciable to any child, young or old.

Myths and Realities

Most jugglers today derive a great deal of pleasure from life. And, like most women in contemporary American society, they also feel stressed, stretched, and tired to the point of exhaustion. Metaphor analysis and other techniques can reduce the stress without reducing the pleasure. But no amount of thought and individual planning will make women free of stress. To function with less stress, they would need to live in a society that values women and children more than ours does and in a culture that does not impose the burden of individualism on women, children, and men.

With the advent of jugglers has come an extraordinary amount of attention to the issue of women's distress. As I have argued throughout the book, some of this attention arouses suspicion; even the friendly stories of care-worn jugglers often seem like thinly veiled descriptions of female inadequacy and failure. But some of the attention is helpful. Scholars and others have correctly identified that there is stress, and from the accumulated data it is now also possible to see clearly the sources of the stress—namely, sexism and overly individualistic ideology. Over a decade ago, writer and activist Jessie Bernard wrote: "Changing sex-specialized norms and sex-typed behavior is not a take-it-or-leave-it option. It is a fundamental imperative. The question is not whether to do it, but rather how to do it."[45]

Today we can point to some of the ways that jugglers have been making changes and also see more clearly than before the steps needed to continue the process. We can, for example, see the need for communitywide and even nationwide child-care programs. We can see how urgently we must fashion good and affordable other care and how we must develop parental leave policies.[46]

Ultimately, then, the choice is ours. We can paint unrealistic pictures of the juggler—displaying her now as a problemfree paragon of glamour and now as a modern hag. Or we can see in the juggler a real person who strives to overcome the obstacles that nature and society put in her path and who does so with vigor and determination. Taking the latter course, we can use the situation to illuminate the features of our social structure that create unnecessary obstacles and unneeded heartache, and we can work to change those features. "It is possible," wrote Alan Pifer when he was president of the Carnegie Foundation, to turn away from our laments and worries and "to regard the new phenomenon of women's large-scale entry into the labor force as an unprecedented opportunity for building a better nation."[47] And it is possible, desirable, and perhaps even obligatory, to regard the growing number of women who are simultaneously spouse, parent, and paid worker as affording us all a chance to fashion social environments that promote healthy communities, families, and individuals.

⋆ ENDNOTES ⋆

CHAPTER 1: THE ISSUES AND THE METAPHORS

1. Carl N. Degler (1980), *At Odds: Women and the Family in America from the Revolution to the Present* (New York: Oxford University Press).

2. Cynthia Fuchs Epstein (1987), "Multiple Demands and Multiple Roles: The Conditions of Successful Management," in Faye J. Crosby, ed., *Spouse, Parent, Worker. On Gender and Multiple Roles,* pp. 23–35 (New Haven, Conn.: Yale University Press). For excellent sources on the history of women's involvement in productive and family work, see Naomi Gerstel and Harriet Engel Gross, eds., *Families and Work* (Philadelphia: Temple University Press, 1987). Part 1 of this comprehensive anthology is entitled "Work and Families in Historical Perspective: The Making of Separate Spheres." Also relevant is the piece by Ruth Schwartz Cowan in another section of Gerstel and Gross's book. See also, Ann Oakley (1974), *Woman's Work. The Housewife, Past and Present* (New York: Random House Vintage Books).

3. The calculation is made from figures presented on p. 97 of Andrea A. LaCroix and Suzanne G. Haynes (1987), "Gender Differences in the Health Effects of Workplace Roles," in Rosalind C. Barnett, Lois Biener, and Grace K. Baruch eds., *Gender and Stress,* pp. 96–121 (New York: Free Press). LaCroix and Haynes derive their figures from government statistics. Corroboration for these estimates comes from a survey conducted by Patrick C. McKendry, Kent G. Hamdorf, Connor M. Walter, and Colleen I. Murry (1985), "Family and Job Influences on Role Satisfaction of Employed Rural Mothers," *Psychology of Women Quarterly* 9, 242–57. Half of their sample of 4-H mothers reported that they worked for financial reasons and half said they worked for enjoyment.

4. This was the clear finding of Claire Sokoloff in her dissertation study of career development issues in young MBAs. Sokoloff's dissertation was completed in 1985 at the School of Organization and Management of Yale University. The evidence is also clear in Kathleen Gerson's book, *Hard Choices. How Women Decide about Work, Career, and Motherhood* (Berkeley: University of California Press, 1985). See also (1) Marie Christine Doerfler

and Phyllis Post Kammer (1986), "Workaholism, Sex, and Sex-Role Stereotyping among Female Professionals," *Sex Roles* 14, 551–60; (2) Marsha Katz (1988), "Have Women's Career and Family Values Changed?" in Suzanna Rose and Laurie Larwood, eds., *Women's Careers, Pathways and Pitfalls,* 95–104 (New York: Praeger); (3) Mirra Komarovsky (1985), *Women in College: Shaping New Feminine Identities* (New York: Basic Books); (4) U.S. Bureau of the Census (1983), *Marital Status and Living Arrangements: March 1982* (Washington D.C.: U.S. Government Printing Office, Current Population Reports, Series P–20, No. 380).

5. The phrase was used at a professional meeting in Toronto in 1988. The popular press then applied it when discussing an article in the *Harvard Business Review* written by Felice Schwartz, the president of an organization called Catalyst. Because Catalyst has a reputation as an innovative outfit that helps women in corporations, many were surprised to hear what could be construed as essentially antifemale views from its president. See: Felice N. Schwartz (1989), "Management Women and the New Facts of Life," *Harvard Business Review,* January–February, 65–76. Schwartz's article produced a furor, and Schwartz wrote an op-ed piece on March 22, 1989, entitled "The Mommy-Track Isn't Anti-Woman" to defend her point of view, *New York Times,* March 22, 1989, A27:1. Subsequent letters to the editors, including one from Representative Pat Schroeder, commented—mostly critically—on the idea of separating those women who are serious about their careers from those who are willing to trade promotions and high salaries for flexibility. (See *New York Times,* April 2, 1989, sec. 4, p. 30). Also see *New York Times,* May 21, 1989, sec. 3, p. 2. The *Harvard Business Review* ran additional articles and letters in subsequent issues, especially in the May–June 1989, issue. See also: Ellen Hopkins (1990), " 'Mommy Track' dearest," *Working Woman,* October, 116–18, 120, and 148.

6. For an in-depth look at contemporary role theory and how it applies to gender, see Graham L. Staines (1986), "Men and Women in Role Relationships," in Richard D. Ashmore and Frances K. Del Boca, eds., *The Social Psychology of Female-Male Relations. A Critical Analysis of Central Concepts,* 211–58 (New York: Academic Press).

7. These and similar findings are presented in a dense and informative book by John Fernandez entitled *Child Care and Corporation Productivity Resolving Family/Work Conflicts* (Lexington, Mass.: D. C. Heath, 1986). Fernandez, an executive at AT&T, calls for more corporate child care. He notes that for every twenty preschool and school-age children of employed mothers, there is one spot in a nongovernment child care facility. Fernandez's statistics also show that fathers do not express the degree of conflict voiced by mothers.

8. Lisa R. Silberstein (1987), *The Dual-Career Couple: A System in Transition* (Ph.D. diss., Yale University), 152.

9. Kathleen McCartney and Deborah Phillips (1988). "Motherhood and Child Care," in Beverly Birns and Dale F. Hay, eds., *The Different Faces of*

Motherhood 157–183 (New York: Plenum). The quotation appears on p. 173.

10. Mary Jane S. Van Meter and Samuel Agronow (1982), "The Stress of Multiple Roles: The Case for Role Strain among Married College Women," *Family Relations* 31, 131–38.

11. See, for example, Marjorie Hansen Shaevitz, *The Superwoman Syndrome* (New York: Warner, 1985).

12. A great number of scholars currently look at the link between gender and economics in our country. One pioneering source is Mary Jo Bane. Relevant and readable books by Bane include: *Here to Stay* (New York: Basic Books, 1978); *The Nation's Families, 1960–1990,* with George Masnick (Boston: Auburn House, 1980); and *Household Composition and Poverty: Which Came First?* (Madison: University of Wisconsin, 1985). More recently, Ruth Sidel has written a disturbing account of the feminization of poverty in her book, *Women and Children Last: The Plight of Poor Women in Affluent America* (New York: Penguin Books, 1987). In her frequently cited piece entitled, "The Feminization of Poverty: Women, Work and Welfare," Diana Pearce points out that two out of three persons over age sixteen and living in poverty are women. The plight of black women is even worse than the plight of white women, as Linda Burnham notes in "Has Poverty Been Feminized in Black America?" Both Pearce's and Burnham's chapters appear in R. Lefkowitz and A. Wilthorm, eds., *For Crying Out Loud: Women and Poverty in the United States.* (New York: Pilgrim Press, 1986).

13. The 1984 Bureau of National Affairs Report is cited (p. 138) in Fernandez, *Child Care and Corporate Productivity.* Most sources agree about the value of flextime. See: (1) S. D. Nollen (1979), "Does Flextime Improve Productivity?" *Harvard Business Review,* September–October, 12–22; (2) W. D. Hicks and R. J. Klimoski (1981), "The Impact of Flextime on Employee Attitudes," *Academy of Management Journal* 24, 333–41; (3) Steward Young Blood and Kimberly Chambers-Cook (1984), "Child Care Assistance Can Improve Employee Attitudes and Behavior," *The Personnel Administrator,* February, 45–46 and 93–95; and (4) Julian Barling and Allison Barenburg (1984), "Some Personal Consequences of 'Flextime' Work Schedules," *The Journal of Social Psychology* 123, 137–38.

One study showed that government workers with a flextime system reported fewer scheduling conflicts between home and work than other government workers. H. Bohen and A. Viveras-Long (1981), *Balancing Job and Family Life: Do Flexible Schedules Help?* (Philadelphia: Temple University Press).

Most recently, Seila M. Rothman and Emily Menlo Marks cite strong evidence in favor of flextime. A survey by the American Management Association of 196 corporations discovered that 97 percent of the corporations found flextime to improve worker morale and 48 percent saw flextime schedules as increasing productivity. Rothman and Marks report the data in a chapter called "Adjusting Work and Family Life: Flexible Work Schedules and Family Policy." The chapter appears in the anthology edited by Gerstel and Gross and cited in note 2. However, individual coping was the most powerful predictor of outcomes, while formal flextime was unrelated with the well-being of working parents, according to Marybeth Shim, Nora Wong, Patricia Simko and Blanca Ortiz-Torres (1989), "Promoting the Well-Being of Working Parents Coping, Social Support, and Flexible Job Schedules," *American Journal of Community Psychology* 17, 31–55.

14. Catalyst (1982 Fall), *Resources on Parenting and Child Care* (New York: Catalyst Career and Family Center). Cited in Lucia Albino Gilbert (1985), *Men in Dual Career Families: Current Realities and Future Prospects* (Hillsdale, N.J.: Erlbaum), 43–44. It has been documented that on-site care can make good economic sense. For example, Intermedics, a company in Freeport, Texas, saved thousands of hours of absenteeism and had vastly reduced employee turnover within two years of setting up on-site child care, according to Barbara Adolf and Karol Rose (1985), *Employer's Guide to Child Care* (New York: Praeger).

15. Barbara Butler and Janis Wasserman (1988), "Parental Leave: Attitudes and Practices in Small Businesses," in Edward F. Zigler and Meryl Frank, eds., *The Parental Leave Crisis. Toward a National Policy,* pp. 223–32 (New Haven: Yale University Press).

16. Edward F. Zigler, Meryl Frank, and Barbara Emmel (1988), "Introduction," in Edward F. Zigler and Meryl Frank, eds., *The Parental Leave Crisis,* p. xxxiii. For a fascinating study of Sweden's situation see: Phyllis Moen (1989), *Working Parents: Transformations in Gender Roles and Public Policies* (Madison: University of Wisconsin Press).

17. See Naomi Gerstel and Harriet Gross (1987), "State Policy and Employers' Policy," in Naomi Gerstel and Harriet Gross, eds., *Families and Work,* pp. 457–68. Concerning the policies of Third World nations specifically see Peggy Pizzo (1988), "Uncertain Harvest: Maternity Leave Policies in Developing Nations," in Edward F. Zigler and Meryl Frank, eds., *The Parental Leave Crisis,* pp. 276–90.

18. These statistics come from a special issue of the *Harvard Women's Law Review* 11, Spring 1988, 171–95. The issue is entitled: "Maternity Leave Policies: An International Survey." Also see: Sheila B. Kamerman and Alfred J. Kahn (1981), *Childcare, Family Benefits, and Working Parents: A Study in Comparative Policy* (New York: Columbia University Press).

19. Eunice McCarthy (1988), *Transitions to Equal Opportunity at Work in Ireland: Problems and Possibilities* (Dublin: Employment Equality Agency).

20. Florence Denmark (1990), "Aspects of Family Interaction in Cross-Cultural Perspective" (Round table discussion at the Fourth International Interdisciplinary Congress on Women, New York, New York). Francine du Plessix Gray (1990), *Soviet Women: Walking the Tightrope* (New York: Doubleday). See especially, chapter 16.

21. Judith Viorst (1986), *Necessary Losses: The Loves, Illusions, Dependen-*

cies, and Impossible Expectations That All of Us Have to Give Up in Order to Grow (New York: Fawcett Gold Medal).

22. Evelyn Fox Keller has written widely on the topic of ideology and science. Her book, *Reflections on Gender and Science* (New Haven, Conn.: Yale University Press, 1987) brings together many of her essays. Also relevant are: A. R. Buss (1978), "The Structure of Psychological Revolutions," *Journal of the History of the Behavioral Sciences* 14, 57–64. Kenneth Gergen (1985), "The Social Constructionist Movement in Modern Psychology," *American Psychologist* 40(3), 266–75. Rhoda Unger, Richard D. Draper, and Michael Pendergrass (1986), "Personal Epistemology and Personal Experience," *Journal of Social Issues* 42, no. 2, 67–79. Another very insightful observer is Edward E. Sampson. In *Justice and the Critique of Pure Psychology* (New York: Plenum Press, 1983), Sampson analyzes how psychologists' points of view and unstated assumptions penetrate their scientific investigations.

23. Both quotations come from page 23 of T. Berry Brazelton (1986), "Issues for Working Parents," *American Journal of Orthopsychiatry* 56, 14–25. See also T. Berry Brazelton (1985), *Working and Caring* (Reading, Mass.: Addison-Wesley).

24. T. Berry Brazelton (1989), "Working Parents," *Newsweek*, February 13, 66.

25. Adrienne Rich may be the best known of the separatists. In 1977 she published in *Signs* a stinging critique of mainstream feminist psychology in an essay entitled "Compulsory Heterosexuality and Lesbian Existence." The essay was reprinted as a pamphlet by the Antelope Press of Denver, Colorado. One of Rich's most thought-provoking points in the essay was that psychology has been asking the wrong questions about females and sexual orientation. Given that all females start out life loving a woman, the puzzle is not lesbianism but rather heterosexuality. Emotionally, as well as erotically, males may be much more dispensable to females, Rich suggests, than most psychologists seem to assume.

A less extreme view is popular. The idea that females nurture females and that males are "just desserts" has been embraced by quite a few feminists who are more part of the mainstream than is Rich. Lillian Rubin's *Intimate Strangers* (New York: Harper and Row, 1985) argues that women look to women, not men, for emotional support because women are oriented toward the family and are interpersonally skilled while men are oriented toward work and have little talent for interpersonal understanding. More optimistic is Barbara Ehrenreich's view. This cofounder of *Ms.* ends her book, *The Hearts of Men: American Dreams and the Flight from Commitment* (Garden City, N.Y.: Anchor Books, 1983) saying "I would like to think that a reconciliation between the sexes is still possible" (p. 181).

26. Wilkinson produces this and many other catchy phrases in an elegantly written brief book, *The Pursuit of American Character* (New York: Harper and Row, 1988). Wilkinson points out that Americans seem caught

in a dilemma: We simultaneously strain toward community and maintain our addiction to individualism. Also relevant is Edward E. Sampson (1988), "The Debate on Individualism: Indigenous Psychologies of the Individual and Their Role in Personal and Societal Functioning," *American Psychologist* 43, 15–22.

27. William Kahn and Faye J. Crosby (1985), "Change and Status: Discriminating between Attitudes and Discriminatory Behavior," in Laurie Larwood, Barbara A. Gutek, and Anne H. Stromberg, eds., *Women and Work, an Annual Review*, vol. 1, 215–38 (Beverly Hills, Calif.: Sage).

28. Barbara Gutek and Veronica Nieva (1982), *Women and Work. A Psychological Perspective* (New York: Praeger).

29. Laurie Chassin, Antonette Zeiss, Kristina Cooper, and Judith Reaven (1985), "Role Perception, Self-Role Congruence and Marital Satisfaction in Dual-Worker Couples with Pre-School Children," *Social Psychology Quarterly* 118, 301–11.

CHAPTER 2: COSTS

1. Lisa Silberstein (1987), *The Dual-Career Marriage: A System in Transition* (Ph.D. diss., Yale University). The first quotation is from p. 183, the second from p. 193, and the third from p. 181.

2. David L. Chambers (1989), "Accommodation and Satisfaction: Women and Men Lawyers and the Balance of Work and Family," *Law and Social Inquiry* 14, 251–87. The first three quotations appear on p. 266, the last on p. 281. Other researchers have found that women scientists who have families mind the lack of time, too. See Jonathan Cole and Harriet Zuckerman (1987), "Marriage, Motherhood, and Research Performance in Science," *Scientific American* 256, no. 2, 119–25.

3. D. G. Fournier and J. D. Engelbrecht (1982), "Assessing Conflicts between Family Life and Employment" (Paper presented at Work and Family Conference, Oklahoma State University). The research is cited on p. 102 of Rena Repetti (1987), "Linkages between Work and Family Roles," *Applied Social Psychology Annual* 7, 98–127. Similar findings with a different sample are discussed by Phyllis Moen and Donna Dempster-McClain (1987), "Employed Parents: Role Strain, Work Time, and Preferences for Working Less," *Journal of Marriage and the Family* 49, 579–90.

4. Janet Reis and Roger Burton (1984), "Maternal Employment and Child Socialization Practices. Intracultural Tests of Cross-Cultural Theory," *Journal of Comparative Family Studies* 15, 1–16.

5. Ruth Anderson-Kulman and Michelle A. Paludi (1986), "Working Mothers and the Family Context. Predicting Positive Coping," *Journal of Vocational Behavior* 28, 241–53. Similarly, Joseph H. Pleck and Michael Rustad found that working mothers manage by reducing their sleep and eliminating free time. Joseph H. Pleck and Michael Rustad (1980), *Husbands' and Wives' Time in Family Work and Paid Work in the 1975–1976 Study*

of Time Use (Wellesley, Mass.: Wellesley College Center for Research on Women).

6. Sara Yogev (1981), "Do Professional Women Have Egalitarian Marital Relationships?" *Journal of Marriage and the Family* 43, 865–71.

7. Arlie Hochschild with Anne Machung (1989), *The Second Shift: Working Parents and the Revolution at Home* (New York: Viking Press). Hochschild's book was very favorably reviewed in the *New York Times* on Sunday, June 25, 1989 (p. 3). Accompanying the review was an interview, entitled "Mothers with Dark Circles." Wrote the interviewer: "Ms. Hochschild said that she would drive to work in the morning after doing interviews with exhausted working mothers and worry about the naive young women in the classes she teaches at the University of California, Berkeley. 'These kids have no idea what is coming.' "

8. "Time Poor Women. Housekeeping Goes First," *Psychology Today,* June 1989, 12–13.

9. *New York Times.* August 21, 1989, p. A14.

10. See Karen D. Fox and Sharon Y. Nickols (1983), "The Time Crunch: Wife's Employment and Family Work," *Journal of Family Issues* 4, 61–82.

11. In *The Biological Clock: Reconciling Careers and Motherhood in the 1980s,* Molly McKaughan gives her impressions of how contemporary career women are coping with their desires for children. Her conclusions are based on interviews with more than 100 women and on the answers that 1,000 readers of *Working Woman* magazine provided to a questionnaire that appeared in the May 1985 issue of the magazine. Doubleday published McKaughan's book in 1987. Also of interest is Kathleen Gerson's *Hard Choices: How Women Decide about Work, Career, and Motherhood* (Los Angeles: University of California Press, 1985). Gerson presents many fascinating quotations from her interviews with two groups of women living around San Francisco. The first sample included female graduates of a local college and the second included women who were attending a local community college. Other researchers also report that women who are students in medical schools have little investment in the motherhood role, while women who teach in medical schools are much more invested. For the latter, the biological clock has rung. (Sylvia Fava and Rosalie Genovese [1983], "Family Work and Individual Development in Dual-Career Marriages: Issues for Research," *Interweave of Social Roles* 3, 163–83.)

12. Carole A. Wilk (1986), *Career Women and Childbearing: A Psychological Analysis of the Decision Process* (New York: Van Nostrand), 261. In addition to counseling couples, Wilks conducted a study of twenty-four white, middle-class, childless women in dual-career marriages, interviewing them in-depth about their decisions regarding children and about their marriages. Wilk notes that while some young career women are frightened of the demands that children place on an insecure career, some older, more established women are frightened of the demands that children place on people with too many job responsibilities.

13. Ann C. Crouter (1984), "Spillover from Family to Work: The Neglected Side of the Work-Family Interface," *Human Relations* 37, 425–42.

14. A survey of working parents in one midwestern city showed that time shortages are more severe for women than for men. The presence of school-age children and preschoolers in the home had a statistically reliable and noticeable effect on time shortages. See: Patricia Voydanoff and Robert K. Kelly (1984), "Determinants of Work-Related Family Problems among Employed Parents," *Journal of Marriage and the Family* 46, 881–92. Children's ability to soak up all the available time is no doubt one reason why at least one researcher has found that housewives have no more leisure time than employed women. See: Rosemary Deem (1986), *All Work and No Play? The Sociology of Women and Leisure* (Milton Keynes, England: The Open University). Quite informative is Susan Maizel Chambre's review of Deem's book in the June 1990 issue of *Gender and Society*.

15. Emily Abel (1988), "Who Really Cares?" *The Women's Review of Books* 5, no. 8, 12. Also: Tish Sommers and Laurie Shields with the Older Women's League Task Force on Caregivers, and Judy MacLean (1987), *Women Take Care: The Consequences of Caregiving in Today's Society* (Gainesville, Fla.: Triad Publishing). For a moving personal account, see Jo Ann Miller (1987), "The Sandwich Generation," *Working Mother Magazine*, 46–52.

16. Anita Shreve (1987), *Remaking Motherhood. How Working Mothers Are Shaping Our Children's Future* (New York: Viking), 118.

17. There are a number of relevant articles. They include: (1) Lisa Berkman (1980) "Physical Health and Social Environment: A Social Epidemiological Perspective," in Leon Eisenberg and Arthur Kleinman, eds., *The Relevance of Social Science for Medicine*, 51–75 (Boston: D. Reidel); (2) Lisa Berkman and Leonard Syme (1979), "Social Networks, Host Resistance, and Mortality: A Nine-Year Follow-Up Study of Alameda County Residents," *American Journal of Epidemiology* 109, 186–204; (3) S. Maes, A Vingerhoets, and G. Van Heck (1987), "The Study of Stress and Disease: Some Developments and Requirements," *Social Science and Medicine* 25, 567–78; (4) Lori Schmied and Kathleen Lawler (1986), "Hardiness, Type A Behavior, and the Stress-Illness Relation in Working Women," *Journal of Personality and Social Psychology* 51, 1218–23; (5) Abigail Stewart and Patricia Salt (1981), "Life Stress, Life-Styles, Depression, and Illness in Adult Women," *Journal of Personality and Social Psychology* 40, 1063–69; (6) Mary Van Sell, Arthur P. Brief, Randall S. Schuler (1981), "Role Conflict and Role Ambiguity," *Human Relations* 34, 43–71. Also very intriguing is the work of a researcher at Columbia University named Karasek, who proposes that work stress exists when the resources are inadequate to the demands of the job. Karasek's work is discussed by Rosalind Barnett and the late Grace Baruch in a book they and Lois Biener edited entitled *Gender and Stress* (New York: Free Press, 1987).

18. The passage appears in A. M. Washton (1989), *Cocaine Addiction* (New York: W. W. Norton), 193. It is quoted by Lois Biener in 1990 article,

"Substance Abuse in Women: A Consequence of Emancipation or the Lack of It," in *Psychology of Women Newsletter* 17, no. 2, 8–9. Biener also comments: "the available data provides no support for the popular belief that working women suffer from multiple role strain and as a consequence resort to alcohol, illicit drugs, or cigarettes" (p. 8). Many data support Biener's view. See: R. W. Wilsnack, S. C. Wilsnack, and A. D. Klassen (1984), "Women's Drinking and Drinking Problems: Patterns From a 1981 National Survey," *American Journal of Public Health* 74, 1231–38. R. W. Wilsnack and R. Cheloha (1987), "Women's Roles and Problem Drinking Across the Lifespan," *Society for the Study of Social Problems* 34, 231–48. Ingrid Waldron and D. Lye (1989), "Employment, Unemployment, Occupation and Smoking," *American Journal of Preventative Medicine* 5, 142–49.

19. Garry B. Trudeau. Commencement speech at Smith College, Northampton, Massachusetts, on May 17, 1987. The speech appears in the *Smith Alumnae Quarterly* 78, no. 4 (Summer 1987), 4–8. The passage quoted appears on p. 7.

20. Lois M. Verbrugge and Deborah L. Wingard (1987), "Sex Differentials in Health and Mortality," *Women and Health* 12, 103–46. See also Allan Johnson (1977), "Recent Trends in Sex Mortality Differential in the United States," *Journal of Human Stress* 3, 22–32.

21. Lois M. Verbrugge (1986), "Role Burdens and Physical Health of Women and Men," *Women and Health* 11, 47–77. Black women still have lower overall mortality rates than both black and white men, according to the *Statistical Abstract of the United States: 1990,* by the U.S. Bureau of the Census, 1990.

22. Bonnie Strickland (1988), "Sex-Related Differences in Health and Illness," *Psychology of Women Quarterly* 12, 381–99.

23. Verbrugge and Wingard, "Sex Differentials," 104.

24. Strickland, "Sex-Related Differences," 383.

25. The actual number of men who die from coronary heart disease is greater than the number of women who die of coronary heart disease, but coronary heart disease is the leading cause of death for both. See: Centers for Disease Control (1989), "Trends in Lung Cancer Incidence—United States, 1973–1986," *Morbidity and Mortality Weekly Report* 38, 505–6, 511–13.

26. Charles Dickens (1978), "Sex Roles, Smoking, and Smoking Cessation," *Journal of Health and Social Behavior* 19, 324–34. However, several studies show no differences in the prevalence of cigarette smoking between employed and nonemployed women. See: (1) Suzanne Haynes and Manning Feinleib (1980), "Women, Work, and Coronary Heart Disease: Prospective Findings from the Framingham Heart Study," *American Journal of Public Health* 70, 133–41. (2) H. P. Hazuda, S. M. Haffner, M. P. Stern, J. A. Knapp, C. W. Eifler, and M. Rosenthal (1986), "Employment Status and Women's Protection against Coronary Heart Disease," *American Journal of Epidemiology* 123, 623–40. (3) Ingrid Waldron (1988), "Gender and Health-

Related Behavior," in D. S. Gochman, ed., *Health Behavior: Emerging Research Perspectives,* 193–208 (New York: Plenum).

27. Glorian Sorenson, Phyllis Pirie, Aaron Folsom, Russell Luepker, David Jacobs, and Richard Gillum (1985), "Sex Differences in the Relationship between Work and Health: The Minnesota Heart Study," *Journal of Health and Social Behavior* 26, 379–94.

28. Strickland, "Sex-Related Differences." Other studies have confirmed that—no surprise—younger women are healthier than older women (Judith H. Hibbard and Clyde R. Pope [1987], "Women's Roles, Interest in Health and Health Behavior," *Women and Health* 12, 67–84). Also relevant is the fact that elderly women are one and a half times more likely than elderly men to be poor. One in five elderly women lives in poverty (Lois Grau [1988], "Illness-Engendered Poverty among the Elderly," *Women and Health* 13, 103–18).

29. In fact, in the United States in 1980, the age-adjusted mortality rate for each of the twelve leading causes of death was higher for men than for women. See: D. L. Wingard (1984), "The Sex Differential in Morbidity, Mortality, and Lifestyle," *Annual Review of Public Health* 5, 433–58. Various explanations have been developed to account for women's advantage in mortality. For biological explanation, see: (1) E. R. Ramey (1982), "The Natural Capacity for Health in Women," in P. W. Berman and E. R. Ramey, eds., *Women: A Developmental Perspective*, NIH Publication No. 82-2298, pp. 3–12 (Washington, D.C.: U.S. Department of Health and Human Services); (2) Cheryl B. Travis (1988), *Women and Health Psychology: Biomedical Issues* (Hillsdale, N.J.: Erlbaum). For hormonal explanation, see: (1) J. A. Hamilton, B. L. Parry and S. J. Blumenthal (1988), "The Menstrual Cycle in Context: I. Affective Syndromes Associated with Reproductive Hormonal Changes, *Journal of Clinical Psychology* 49, 474–79; (2) J. A. Hamilton, B. L. Parry, and S. J. Blumenthal (1988), "The Menstrual Cycle in Context: II. Human Gonadal Steroid Hormone Variability," *Journal of Clinical Psychology* 49, 480–84. For a proposed interaction model of biological and behavioral characteristics, see: Karen Matthews (1989), "Interactive Effects of Behavior and Reproductive Hormones on Sex Differences in Risk for Coronary Heart Disease," *Health Psychology* 8, 373–87.

30. Phyllis Moen, Donna Dempster-McClain, and Robin M. Williams, Jr. (1989), "Social Integration and Longevity: An Event History Analysis of Women's Roles and Resilience," *American Sociological Review* 54, 635–47.

31. Researcher Lois Verbrugge proposed that women are more frequently ill than men but suffer from problems that are serious but not life threatening. The result is symptoms, disability, and medical care but not death. Men are sick less often than women but their illnesses and injuries are more severe, and men have higher rates of chronic diseases that are the leading causes of death. See: Lois M. Verbrugge (1989), "The Twain Meet: Empirical Explanations of Sex Differences in Health and Mortality," *Journal of Health and Social Behavior* 30, 282–304.

32. Suzanne Haynes and Manning Feinleib (1980), "Women, Work, and Coronary Heart Disease: Prospective Findings from the Framingham Heart Study," *American Journal of Public Health* 70, 133–41. Also see Andrea Z. LaCroix and Suzanne G. Haynes (1987), "Gender Differences in Health Effects of Workplace," in Rosalind C. Barnett, Lois Biener, and Grace K. Baruch, eds., *Gender and Stress*, 96–121.

33. A substantial number of studies show a strong relationship between wealth and health: the richer one is, the healthier one is likely to be. Women are economically poorer, and poverty creates health problems. See: (1) Deborah Belle (1990), "Poverty and Women's Mental Health," *American Psychologist* 45, 385–89; (2) Donald Binsacca, Judith Ellis, Deborah Martin, and Diana Petitti (1987), "Factors Associated with Low Birth Weight in an Inner-City Population: The Role of Financial Problems," *American Journal of Public Health* 77, 505–6; (3) Ralph Catalano and David Dooley (1983), "Health Effects of Economic Instability: A Test of Economic Stress Hypothesis," *Journal of Health and Social Behavior* 24, 46–60; (4) Valentino Dardanoni and Adam Wagstaff (1987), "Uncertainty, Inequalities in Health and the Demand for Health," *Journal of Health Economics* 6, 283–90; (5) Harriet O. Duleep (1986), "Measuring the Effect of Income on Adult Mortality Using Longitudinal Administrative Record Data," *Journal of Human Resources* 21, 238–51. On the connection between poverty and mental health, see Peggy A. Thoits (1982), "Life Stress, Social Support and Psychological Vulnerability: Epidemiological Considerations," *Journal of Community Psychology* 10, 341–62. Another reason to conclude that employment is not the cause of poor health in women is that women's health has long been poorer than men's—even when most women were not in the paid labor force. For trends over time, see Philip Cole (1974), "Morbidity in the United States," in E. Gartley Jaco, ed., *Patients, Physicians, and Illness*, 30–52 (Glencoe, Ill.: Free Press). Finally, it may be important to note how changing social mores influence the patterns of findings. Lois Verbrugge reports that two major studies no longer reveal health disadvantages to mothers who are employed as clerical workers. (See Lois Verbrugge [1984], "Physical Health of Clerical Workers in the U.S., Framingham and Detroit," *Women and Health* 9, 17–41.) And one recent study even shows an advantage among employed women. (Helen P. Hazuda, Steven M. Haffner, Michael P. Stern, J. Ava Knapp, Clayton W. Eifler, and Marc Rosenthal [1986], "Employment Status and Women's Protection against Coronary Heart Disease," *American Journal of Epidemiology* 123, 623–40.) For a complete review of the most current research on women's health and employment, and especially of longitudinal studies, see: Rena L. Repetti, Karen A. Matthews, and Ingrid Waldron (1989), "Employment and Women's Health: Effects of Paid Employment on Women's Mental and Physical Health," *American Psychologist* 44, 1394–1401.

34. Lois M. Verbrugge (1987), "Role Responsibilities, Role Burdens, and Physical Health," in Faye J. Crosby, ed., *Spouse, Parent, Worker*, 154–66.

35. Susan Faludi (1989), "Diary of a Mad Supermom," *Mother Jones,* June, 39–41.

36. Two studies report less stress among jugglers than others. They are: (1) Elaine Cumming, Charles Lazer, and Lynne Chisholm (1975), "Suicide as an Index of Role Strain among Employed and Not Employed Married Women in British Columbia," *Canadian Review of Sociology and Anthropology* 12, 462–70; (2) Raymond Rochrane and Mary Stopes-Roe (1981), "Women, Marriage, Employment, and Mental Health," *British Journal of Psychiatry* 139, 373–81. Three studies report more stress among jugglers than others. They are: (1) Judith M. Gerson (1985), "Women Returning to School: The Consequences of Multiple Roles," *Sex Roles* 13, 77–91; (2) Rosalind C. Barnett and Grace K. Baruch (1985), "Women's Involvement in Multiple Roles and Psychological Distress," *Journal of Personality and Social Psychology* 49, 135–45; (3) Suzan N. Lewis and Cary L. Cooper (1987), "Stress in Two-Earner Couples and Stage in the Life-Cycle," *Journal of Occupational Psychology* 60, 289–303. The majority of studies show no difference in stress or role conflict when jugglers and others are compared. Among those finding no differences are: (1) Susan Welch and Alan Booth (1977), "Employment and Health among Married Women with Children," *Sex Roles* 3, 385–97; (2) Walter R. Gove and Michael R. Geerken (1977), "The Effect of Children and Employment on the Mental Health of Married Men and Women," *Social Forces* 56, 66–76; (3) Lilly J. Schubert Walker and James L. Walker (1980), "Trait Anxiety in Mothers," *Psychological Reports* 47, 295–99; (4) Constance L. Shehan (1984), "Wives' Work and Psychological Well-Being: An Extension of Gove's Social Role Theory of Depression," *Sex Roles* 11, 881–99; (5) Nancy Fugate Woods (1985), "Employment, Family Roles and Mental Ill Health in Young Married Women," *Nursing Research* 34, 4–10; (6) Joseph Stokes and Judith Peyton (1986), "Attitudinal Differences between Full-Time Homemakers and Women who Work Outside of the Home," *Sex Roles* 15, 299–310; (7) Nicholas Beutell and Marianne O'Hare (1987), "Work-Nonwork Conflict among MBAs: Sex Differences in Role Stressors and Life Satisfaction," *Work and Stress* 1, 35–41; (8) Dona Alpert and Amy Culbertson (1987), "Daily Hassles and Coping Strategies of Dual-Earner and Nondual-Earner Women," *Psychology of Women Quarterly* 11, 359–66. For an interesting integrative review of the early work, see: Sara Yogev (1982), "Happiness in Dual-Career Couples: Changing Research, Changing Values," *Sex Roles* 8, 593–605.

37. Nicholas J. Beutell and Jeffrey H. Greenhaus (1983), "Integration of Home and Nonhome Roles: Women's Conflict and Coping Behavior," *Journal of Applied Psychology* 68, 43–48. Despite the data showing low inter-role conflict, the researchers concluded: "It seems clear that married women who participate in multiple roles run the risk of experiencing conflict among those roles" (p. 46).

38. Joseph H. Pleck and Graham L. Staines (1982), "Work Schedules and Work-Family Conflict in Two-Earner Couples," in Joan Aldous, ed., *Two*

Paychecks: Life in Dual-Earner Families, 68–87 (Beverly Hills, Calif.: Sage). Meanwhile, 31 percent of the men in the study felt their home lives and work lives interfered with each other. More recently, Ellen Galinsky and her associates at the Families and Work Institute of New York used Pleck and Staines's measure and found that between 31 and 49 percent of workers at various employment sites reported at least some interference between work and home. The amount of interference was greater where the employer expected workers to work long hours and where job autonomy was low.

39. Carol-Ann Emmons, Monica Biernat, Linda Beth Tiedje, Eric L. Lang, and Camille B. Wortman (1990), "Stress, Support, and Coping among Women Professionals with Preschool Children," in John Eckenrode and Susan Gore, eds., *Stress between Work and Family,* 61–93 (New York: Plenum Press).

40. Janet Dreyfus Gray (1983), "The Married Professional Woman: An Examination of Her Role Conflicts and Coping Strategies," *Psychology of Women Quarterly* 7, 235–43.

41. Robert A. Cooke and Denise M. Rousseau (1984), "Stress and Strain from Family Roles and Work-Role Expectations," *Journal of Applied Psychology* 69, 252–60. Similarly, other researchers questioned 185 professional women in major cities around the country. The women filled out a 7-point stress scale and 7-point coping scale. The average stress score was 4.2, but the average coping score was 5.01. (Margaret R. Elman and Lucia A. Gilbert [1984], "Coping Strategies for Role Conflict in Married Professional Women with Children," *Family Relations* 33, 317–27. Low levels of inter-role stress have also been documented among psychologists. See: Barbara A. Gutek, Lilian Klepa, and Sabrina Searle-Porter (1989), "Understanding the Failure to Perceive Work-Family Conflict" (Paper presented at the Academy of Management Conference, Washington, D.C.).

42. Emmons et al., "Stress, Support and Coping." Joseph H. Pleck (1979), "Men's Family Work: Three Perspectives and Some New Data," *Family Coordinator* 28, 481–88. On the distinction between stress and coping see: Linda Beth Tiedje, Camille B. Wortman, Geraldine Downey, Carol Emmons, Monica Biernat, and Eric Lang (1990), "Women with Multiple Roles: Role-Compatibility, Perceptions, Satisfaction, and Mental Health," *Journal of Marriage and the Family* 52, 63–72.

43. The evidence on this point is not crystal clear. Fathers have more personal time in their day than do mothers (especially employed mothers). But employed fathers and mothers may feel equally pressed for time because subjective reality does not always match objective reality. A few studies look at inter-role conflict among men and women in dual-career families, and they give no evidence of sex differences. See: (1) Carole K. Holahan and Lucia A. Gilbert (1979), "Conflict between Major Life Roles: Women and Men in Dual-Career Couples," *Human Relations* 32, 451–67; (2) Nicholas J. Beutell and Marianne O'Hare (1987), "Work-Nonwork Conflict among MBAs: Sex Differences in Role Stressors and Life Satisfaction," *Work and Stress* 1, 35–

41; (3) Suzan Lewis and Cary Cooper (1987), "Stress in Two-Earner Couples and Stage in the Life-Cycle," *Journal of Occupational Psychology* 60, 289–303. C. Aneshensel, R. Frerichs, and V. Clark found that sex differences were minimal among the employed with few family roles but generally increased as the roles became more divergent. Thus, parenthood is a greater stressor for women than for men. See: C. Aneshensel, R. Frerichs, and V. Clark (1981), "Family Roles and Sex Differences in Depression," *Journal of Health and Social Behavior* 22, 379–93.

44. For a beautiful depiction of the subtle ways in which these gender dynamics are maintained, see Robert S. Weiss (1987), "Men and Their Wives' Work," in Faye J. Crosby, ed., *Spouse, Parent, Worker,* 109–21.

45. In fact, one fairly old study of women and men in the Chicago area asked people about their time demands with questions such as "Does it seem as if others are always making demands on you?" and "Do you often feel that it is impossible to finish anything?" and "When you try to do something at home, are you almost always interrupted?" The study also asked people about their desire to be alone and their feelings of loneliness, among other things. In families with one or two children, housewives experienced more time demands and more loneliness and had a greater desire to be alone than employed wives. See Walter R. Gove and Michael R. Geerken, "The Effect of Children and Employment on the Mental Health of Married Men and Women."

46. Barbara A. Gutek, Rena L. Repetti, and Deborah L. Silver (1988), "Nonwork Roles and Stress at Work," in Cary L. Cooper and Roy Payne, eds., *Causes, Coping, and Consequences of Stress at Work,* 141–74 (London: Wiley). J. S. House and E. M. Cottington (1986), "Health and the Workplace," in L. H. Aiken and D. Mechanic, eds., *Applications of Social Science to Clinical Medicine and Health Policy,* 392–416 (New Brunswick, N.J.: Rutgers University Press).

47. See Cynthia Epstein (1988), *Deceptive Distinctions: Sex, Gender, and the Social Order* (New Haven, Conn.: Yale University Press). Also: Veronica Nieva and Barbara A. Gutek (1981), *Women and Work: Psychological Perspectives* (New York: Praeger).

48. Many studies demonstrate that worker attitudes that appear to differ according to sex actually differ as a function of a person's status, position, or job in an organization. See: (1) Denise Del Vento Bielby and William T. Bielby (1984), "Work Commitment, Sex-Role Attitudes, and Women's Employment," *American Sociological Review* 49, 234–47; (2) Jeanne Brett Herman and Karen Kuczynski Gyllstrom (1977), "Working Men and Women: Inter- and Intra-Role Conflict," *Psychology of Women Quarterly* 1, 319–33; (3) Nancy C. Jurik and Gregory J. Halemba (1984), "Gender, Working Conditions and Job Satisfaction," *The Sociological Quarterly* 25, 551–66; (4) William B. Lacy, Janet L. Bokemeier, and Jon M. Shepard (1983), "Job Attribute Preferences and Work Commitment of Men and Women in the United States," *Personnel Psychology* 36, 315–29; (5) Jon Lorence (1987), "A

Test of 'Gender' and 'Job' Models of Sex Differences in Job Involvement," *Social Forces* 66, 121–42; (6) Clifford Mottaz (1986), "Gender Differences in Work Satisfaction, Work-Related Rewards, and the Determinants of Work Satisfaction," *Human Relations* 39, 359–78. Another factor that also matters more than gender is a person's status as breadwinner. Analyses of national data show that a person's feelings about working depended on whether or not the individual provides the primary financial support for the family and did not depend on whether the individual was male or female. See: Jack K. Martin and Sandra L. Hanson (1985), "Sex, Family Wage-Earning Status, and Satisfaction with Work," *Work and Occupations* 12, 91–109.

49. Faye J. Crosby, Jacqueline Golding, and Andrea Resnick (1983), "Discontent among Male Lawyers, Female Lawyers, and Female Legal Secretaries," *Journal of Applied Social Psychology* 13, 183–90.

50. In a study by Uma Sekaran, men and women were found to be similar in cognitively associating their career salience, self-esteem derived from job, and confidence in their own competence on the job. Also, both husbands and wives were found to attribute their effectiveness to the same factors—some related to family dynamics and others to satisfactions from the workplace. However, women do not perceive themselves to be as job involved, which might be reflective of their heavy family responsibilities which may prevent them from getting job involved. See: Uma Sekaran (1983), "How Husbands and Wives in Dual-Career Families Perceive their Family and Work Worlds," *Journal of Vocational Behavior* 22, 288–302.

51. Strong evidence of persistent sex discrimination appears in Barbara R. Bergmann (1986), *The Economic Emergence of Women* (New York: Basic Books). Even conservative economists present data that show large gaps between male and female salaries. See, for example, the article by Peter Kuhn (1987), "Sex Discrimination in Labor Markets: The Role of Statistical Evidence," *American Economic Review* 77, 567–83.

52. On the nonintentional nature of discrimination, see selected chapters in Fletcher A. Blanchard and Faye J. Crosby, eds., *Affirmative Action in Perspective,* published in 1989 by Springer-Verlag in New York. See also Faye J. Crosby, Ann Pufall, Rebecca Claire Snyder, Marion O'Connell, and Peg Whalen (1989), "The Denial of Personal Disadvantage among You, Me and all the Other Ostriches," in Mary Crawford and Margaret Gentry, eds., *Gender and Thought,* 79–99 (New York: Springer-Verlag).

53. Donald J. Trieman and Patricia A. Roos (1983), "Sex and Earnings for Industrial Society: A Nine-Nation Comparison," *American Journal of Sociology* 89, 612–50.

54. The money to purchase services has been found significant in reducing the conflict between the demands at home and work. See: Deborah Belle (1982), *Social Support, Lives in Stress: Women in Depression* (Beverly Hills, Calif.: Sage).

55. Several different reviews show this. (1) Jeanne J. Fleming (1988), "Public Opinion on Change in Women's Rights and Roles," in Sanford M.

Dornbusch and Myra H. Strobes, eds., *Feminism, Children, and the New Families,* 47–66 (New York: Guilford Press). William Kahn and Faye J. Crosby (1985), "Change and Stasis: Discriminating between Attitudes and Discriminatory Behavior," in Laurie Larwood, Barbara A. Gutek, and Ann H. Stromberg, eds., *Women and Work: An Annual Review,* vol. 1, 215–38 (Beverly Hills, Calif.: Sage); (2) Karen Oppenheim Mason and Yu-Hsia Yu (1988), "Women's Familial Roles: Changes in the United States, 1977–1985," *Gender and Society* 2, 39–57.

56. The figure of 59 percent is the percent of a man's earnings that a woman typically has earned. See Barbara Bergmann.

57. Christopher Ruhm has shown that women and men do not find new jobs of comparable levels, even when they occupied comparable jobs before being laid off. His analysis appears in *Affirmative Action in Perspective.* If employed women face discrimination, housewives do, too. See: Andrea Tyree and Rebecca Hicks (1988), "Sex and the Second Moment of Prestige Distributions," *Social Forces* 66, 1028–37.

58. Faye J. Crosby (1982), *Relative Deprivation and Working Women* (New York: Oxford University Press). See also Faye J. Crosby (1984), "Relative Deprivation in Organizational Settings," in Barry Staw and L. L. Cummings, eds., *Research in Organizational Behavior,* vol. 6, 51–93 (Greenwich, Conn.: JAI Press).

59. As Voydanoff and Kelly show, the less adequate an employed mother's income, the more time strain she feels.

60. Barbara A. Gutek (1985), *Sex and the Workplace* (San Francisco: Jossey-Bass).

61. Rena L. Repetti (1987), "Individual and Common Components of the Social Environment at Work and Psychological Well-Being," *Journal of Personality and Social Psychology* 52, 710–20.

62. The quotation appears on pp. 167–68 of Alan Guttmacher's widely used book *Pregnancy and Birth: A Book for Expectant Mothers* (New York: Viking). Current evidence, incidentally, challenges the old medical advice. Physicians no longer think that young women automatically bear the healthiest babies or that older women automatically run greater risks. See Phyllis Kernoff Mansfield (1988), "Midlife Childbearing. Strategies for Informed Decisionmaking," *Psychology of Women Quarterly* 12, 445–60.

63. The first edition of Benjamin Spock's book appeared in 1946. For an interesting discussion of Spock and how he came to recognize his sexism, see pp. 120–21 in Gloria Norris and Jo Ann Miller (1984), *The Working Mother's Complete Handbook* (New York: New American Library).

64. Rosalind C. Barnett and Grace K. Baruch (1987), "Mothers' Participation in Childcare," in Faye J. Crosby, ed., *Spouse, Parent, Worker,* 91.

65. The demanding nature of motherhood has now been shown to call for assertiveness, independence, and leadership—all stereotypically masculine traits. No doubt that is why new mothers show the best psychological adjustment if they possess masculine traits and why feminine traits do not

enhance adjustment, according to researchers at the University of Colorado. See: Evelyn Sillen Bassoff (1984), "Relationship of Sex-Role Characteristics and Psychological Adjustment in New Mothers," *Journal of Marriage and the Family* 46, 449–54.

66. Among the systematic studies are these: (1) Rosalind C. Barnett and Grace K. Baruch (1985), "Women's Involvement in Multiple Roles and Psychological Distress." Paul D. Cleary and David Mechanic (1983), "Sex Differences in Psychological Distress among Married People," *Journal of Health and Social Behavior* 24, 111–21; (2) Claude S. Fischer and Stacey J. Oliker (1983), "A Research Note on Friendship, Gender, and the Life Cycle," *Social Forces* 62, 124–33; (3) Susan Gore and Thomas W. Mangione (1983), "Social Roles, Sex Roles, and Psychological Distress," *Journal of Health and Social Behavior* 24, 300–12; (4) Walter R. Gove and Michael Hughes (1979), "Possible Causes of the Apparent Sex Differences in Physical Health: An Empirical Investigation," *American Sociological Review* 44, 126–46; (5) Karen A. Polonko, John Scanzoni, and Jayne Teachman (1982), "Childbearing and Marital Satisfaction," *Journal of Family Issues* 3, 545–73; (6) Thomas G. Power and Ross D. Parke (1984), "Social Network Factors and the Transition to Parenthood," *Sex Roles* 10, 949–72; (7) Leonard I. Pearlin (1975), "Sex Roles and Depression," in Nancy Datan and L. Ginsberg, eds., *Lifespan Developmental Psychology: Normative Life Crises,* 191–207 (New York: Academic Press); (8) Joseph Veroff, Elizabeth Douvan, and Ronald Kulka (1981), *The Inner American* (New York: Basic Books).

67. Fischer and Oliker, "A Research Note on Friendship."

68. Jeannette R. Ickovics (1987), *Striking a Balance after the Birth of a Child?* (Master's thesis, George Washington University).

69. It did not matter if there were also other children in the family. As the youngest child got older, the women in the study became less depressed.

70. Pearlin, "Sex Roles and Depression," p. 199.

71. Some of the literature on American individualism is summarized in Rupert Wilkinson's *The Pursuit of American Character* (New York: Random House, 1988). On the question of how psychologists view individualism, Edward Sampson has written a number of very provocative essays, including his classic 1977 article entitled "Psychology and the American Ideal" that appeared in the *Journal of Personality and Social Psychology* 35, 767–82.

72. The psychological literature on stress has burgeoned in the last decade. The exact definition of stress is much debated, but its ill effects are not to be questioned. Chief among the stress theorists is Richard Lazarus of the University of California at Berkeley. Among his numerous books and articles, perhaps the standard text on stress is Richard S. Lazarus and Susan Folkmann (1984), *Stress, Appraisal and Coping* (New York: Springer).

That vigilance produces poor health in women is clear. Analyses of the National Health Surveys of 1975–77 show that mothers of disabled children experience more health problems than other mothers. Spouse's health status was also an important predictor of wife's own health. Charlotte Muller

(1986), "Health and Health Care of Employed Women and Homemakers: Family Factors," *Women and Health* 11, 7–25.

73. Mary Jo Bane (1980), *Here to Stay* (New York: Basic Books).

74. Edward Z. Tronick, Gilda A. Morelli, and Steve Winn (1987), "Multiple Caretaking of Efe (Pygmy) Infants," *American Anthropologist* 89, 96–106.

75. Thomas S. Weisner and Ronald Gallimore surveyed 186 nonindustrialized societies. In three-fifths of the societies, the infant was considered the exclusive responsibility of the mother, while in two-fifths of the societies the care of the infant was to be shared. In only one-fifth of the societies was child care, after infancy, treated as the exclusive responsibility of the family into which the child was born. Weisner and Gallimore (1977), "Child and Sibling Caretaking," *Current Anthropologist* 18, 169–90.

76. Urie Bronfenbrenner (1972), *Two Worlds of Childhood* (New York: Simon & Schuster).

77. Suzanne Buchanan (1987), "Evolution of Parental Rights in Education," *Journal of Law and Education* 16, 339–49.

78. Working mothers speak of their guilt. See: Barbara Berg (1986), *The Crisis of the Working Mother, Resolving the Conflict between Family and Work.* (New York: Summit). Caroline Bird (1979), *The Two Paycheck Marriage* (New York: Rawson, Wade Publishers). John P. Fernandez (1986), *Child Care and Corporate Productivity. Resolving Family/Work Conflicts* (Lexington, Mass.: Lexington Books, D. C. Heath). Judith Gerson, "Women Returning to School." Guilt even seems to show up in women's dreams (Monique Lortie-Lussier, Christine Schwab, and Joseph DeKoninck [1985], "Working Mothers versus Homemakers: Do Dreams Reflect the Changing Roles of Women?" *Sex Roles* 12, 1009–21).

79. Kathryn T. Young and Edward Zigler (1986), "Infant and Toddler Day Care: Regulations and Policy Implications," *American Journal of Orthopsychiatry* 56, 43–55.

80. The government study is cited in Deborah Phillips (1986), "The Federal Model Child Care Standards of 1985: Step in the Right Direction or Hollow Gesture?" *American Journal of Orthopsychiatry* 56, 56–64.

81. One study found a constraint on social support from all sources except the spouse and hypothesized that this finding may be due to the social norms about the appropriateness of requesting or receiving support for the task of combining work and parenting. See Marybeth Shinn, Nora Wong, Patricia Simko, and Blanca Ortiz-Torres (1989), "Promoting the Well-Being of Working Parents: Coping, Social Support, and Flexible Job Schedules," *American Journal of Community Psychology* 17, 31–55.

82. Carol B. Stack (1974) *All Our Kin. Strategies for Survival in a Black Community* (New York: Harper and Row Torchbooks, 1974), 44. The benefits of shared responsibility for children has also been shown among Hispanics and Caucasians. See Elsa Hernandez Holtzman and Lucia Gilbert (1987), "Social Support Networks for Parenting and Psychological Well-

Being among Dual-Earner Mexican-American Families," *Journal of Community Psychology* 15, 176–86. Also S. McLanahan (1981), "Network Structure, Social Support, and Psychological Well-Being in the Single Parent Family," *Journal of Marriage and the Family* 43, 601–12.

83. Stack, *All Our Kin*, 89.

CHAPTER 3: AND BENEFITS

1. In our town one of the elementary schools publishes a directory of parents. I extracted from the list the names of all women whom I knew to be married and to work full-time outside the home. I telephoned all the names. Every woman who was in town agreed to a brief interview. This sampling procedure yielded seventeen women. To round out the numbers, I interviewed three more acquaintances.

2. Cynthia Fuchs Epstein (1981), *Women in Law* (New York: Basic Books).

3. Cynthia Fuchs Epstein (1987), "Multiple Demands and Multiple Roles: The Conditions of Successful Mangement," in Faye J. Crosby, ed., *Spouse, Parent, Worker. On Gender and Multiple Roles*, 23–35 (New Haven, Conn.: Yale University Press). The quotation appears on p. 26.

4. Epstein (1987), "Multiple Demands," 27–28.

5. Lisa Silberstein (1987), *The Dual-Career Marriage: A System in Transition* (Ph.D. diss., Yale University).

6. Myra Marx Ferree (1976), "Working Class Jobs: Housework and Paid Work as Sources of Satisfaction," *Social Problems* 23, 431–41. The problem for working-class women is not their own attitudes but the attitudes of their husbands or partners, who can feel threatened (especially if the woman holds a nontraditional job). Also Ferree has continued to write on the theme in more recent years. See Jean Reith Schroedel (1990), "Blue-Collar Women: Paying the Price at Home on the Job," in Hildreth Grossman and Nia Lane Chester, eds., *The Experience and Meaning of Work in Women's Lives*, 241–60 (Hillsdale, N.J.: Erlbaum).

7. Rena Repetti (1985), *The Social Environment at Work and Psychological Well-Being* (Ph.D. diss., Yale University). See also the article that summarizes the research: Rena Repetti (1987), "Individual and Common Components of the Social Environment at Work and Psychological Well-Being," *Journal of Personality and Social Psychology* 52, 710–20.

8. It is interesting to note the (possibly coincidental) link between rates of depression and the advent of the cult of domesticity.

9. Martin Seligman (1973), "Fall into Helplessness," *Psychology Today* 7 (June), 43–48.

10. Nan Lin and Walter M. Ensel (1984), "The Depression Mobility and Its Social Etiology: The Role of Life Events and Social Support," *Journal of Health and Social Behavior* 25, 176–88. Paul D. Cleary (1987), "Gender Differences in Stress-Related Disorders," in Rosalind C. Barnett, Lois Biener,

and Grace K. Baruch, eds., *Gender and Stress,* 39–72 (New York: Free Press). Lyn Abramson, Lauren Alloy, and Gerald Metalsky (1988), "The Cognitive Diathesis-Stress Theories of Depression: Toward an Adequate Evaluation of the Theories' Validities," in Lauren B. Alloy, ed., *Cognitive Processes in Depression,* 3–30 (New York: Guilford Press).

11. Gerald C. Davison and John M. Neale (1982), *Abnormal Psychology. An Experimental Clinical Approach,* 3d ed. (New York: John Wiley & Sons).

12. Leonore Radloff (1977), "The CES-D Scale: A Self-Report Depression Scale for Research in the General Population," *Journal of Applied Psychological Measurement* 1, 385–401. Further confirmation of the scale's reliability has come from other researchers as well. See: (1) Myrna M. Weissman, Diane Sholomskas, Margaret Pottenger, Brigitte A. Prusoff, and Ben Z. Locke (1977), "Assessing Depressive Symptoms in Five Psychiatric Populations: A Validation Study," *American Journal of Epidemiology* 106, 203–14; (2) J. Craig and Pearl A. Van Natta (1979), "Influence of Demographic Characteristics on Two Measures of Depressive Symptoms, *Archives of General Psychiatry* 36, 149–54; (3) Catherine E. Ross and John Mirowsky (1984), "Components of Depressed Mood in Unmarried Men and Women," *American Journal of Epidemiology* 119, 997–1004.

13. Cleary, "Gender Differences in Stress-Related Disorders." The female-male ratio is estimated to hold true among depressed people who do not seek treatment, according to John W. Fix (1980), "Gove's Specific Sex-Role Theory of Mental Illness: A Research Note," *Journal of Health and Social Behavior* 24, 260–67.

14. Among the best scholarly books on gender and depression are (1) Myrna M. Weissman and Eugene S. Paykel (1974), *The Depressed Woman* (Chicago: University of Chicago Press); (2) Helen Block Lewis (1976), *Psychic War in Men and Women* (New York: New York University Press); (3) Susan Nolan-Hoeksema (1990), *Sex Differences in Depression* (Stanford, Calif.: Stanford University Press). Two excellent books for the general reader on the topic of gender and mental health are: Phyllis Chesler (1972), *Women and Madness* (Garden City, N.Y.: Doubleday) and Maggie Scarf (1980), *Unfinished Business* (Garden City, N.Y.: Doubleday). The number of scholarly articles examining why females suffer depressions is large. Among the most comprehensive review articles are (1) Carol S. Aneshensel, Ralph R. Frerichs, and Virginia A. Clark (1981), "Family Roles and Sex Differences in Depression," *Journal of Health and Social Behavior* 22, 379–93; (2) Constance Hammen (1982), "Gender and Depression," in Ihsan Al-Issa, ed., *Gender and Psychopathology,* 133–52 (New York: Academic Press); (3) Susan Nolen-Hoeksema (1987), "Sex Differences in Unipolar Depression: Evidence and Theory," *Psychological Bulletin* 101, 259–82; (4) Catherine E. Ross, John Mirowsky, and Joan Huber (1983), Dividing Work, Sharing Work, and In-Between: Marriage Patterns and Depression," *American Sociological Review* 48, 809–23; (5) Peter Warr and Glenys Parry (1982), "Paid Employment and Women's Psychological Well-Being," *Psychological Bulletin* 91, 498–516;

(6) Myrna Weissman and Gerald Klerman (1977), "Sex Differences and the Epidemiology of Depression," *Archives of General Psychiatry* 41, 949–58.

15. Nancy Felipe Russo (1990), "Overview: Forging Priorities for Women's Mental Health," *American Psychologist* 45, 368–73. The final report of the task force, edited by Ellen McGrath, Gwendolyn Puryear Keita, Bonnie R. Strickland, and Nancy Felipe Russo, can be obtained from the American Psychological Association in Washington, D.C. It is entitled *Women and Depression: Risk Factors and Treatment Issues.*

16. Myrna Weissman and Gerald Klerman (1987), "Gender and Depression," in Ruth Formanek and Anita Gurian, eds., *Women and Depression. A Lifespan Perspective,* 3–15 (New York: Springer Publishing). See also: Elizabeth McNeal and Peter Cimbolic (1986), "Antidepressants and Biochemical Theories of Depression," *Psychological Bulletin* 99, 361–74.

17. The classic source on the question is B. Dohrenwend and B. S. Dohrenwend (1969), *Social Status and Psychological Disorder* (New York: John Wiley). The most authoritative new book, containing many relevant articles by leading experts was edited by Rosalind Barnett, Lois Biener, and Grace Baruch and entitled *Gender and Stress.*

18. William W. Dressler (1985), "Extended Family Relationships, Social Support, and Mental Health in a Southern Black Community," *Journal of Health and Social Behavior* 26, 39–48. Barbara Reskin and Shelly Coverman (1985), "Sex and Race in the Determinants of Psychophysical Distress: A Reappraisal of the Sex-Role Hypothesis," *Social Forces* 63, 1038–59. Deborah Belle (1990), "Poverty and Women's Mental Health," *American Psychologist* 45, 385–89.

19. Joy P. Newman (1986), "Gender, Life Strains, and Depression," *Journal of Health and Social Behavior* 27, 161–78. Leonard I. Pearlin (1975), "Sex Roles and Depression," in Nancy Datan and L. Ginsberg, eds., *Lifespan Developmental Psychology: Normative Life Crises,* 191–207 (New York: Academic Press).

20. First to point out the differences in depressions between single-earner and dual-earner families were two sociologists; see Ronald Kessler and J. M. McRae (1981), "Trends on the Relationship between Sex and Psychological Distress, 1957–1976," *American Sociological Review* 46, 443–52. Also relevant are (1) Fred B. Bryant and Joseph Veroff (1984), "Dimensions of Subjective Mental Health in American Men and Women," *Journal of Health and Social Behavior* 25, 116–35; (2) Myra Marx Ferree (1984), "Class, Housework, and Happiness: Women's Work and Life Satisfaction," *Sex Roles* 11, 1057–74; (3) Jacqueline M. Golding (1989), "Role Occupancy and Role-Specific Stress and Social Support as Predictors of Depression," *Basic and Applied Social Psychology* 10, 173–95; (4) Constance L. Shehan (1984), "Wives' Work and Psychological Well-Being: An Extension of Gove's Social Role Theory of Depression," *Sex Roles* 11, 881–94.

21. About half of the empirical studies show that housewives are more depressed than employed women; but half show no difference between

housewives and working women. One reason for the inconsistency is that different researchers use different samples. Some, for example, take parental status into account but others do not. Some limit the sample to a given age bracket and others do not. Some include only educated women, (who face relatively little adversity) but others include women with varying degrees of education. Consistently, however, the data show that employed women react to life stresses differently than do housewives. On this point, see: (1) Evelyn Mostow and P. Newberry (1975), "Work Role and Depression in Women: A Comparison of Workers and Housewives in Treatment," *American Journal of Orthopsychiatry* 45, 538–48; (2) Glenys Parry (1986), "Paid Employment, Life Events, Social Support, and Mental Health in Working-Class Mothers," *Journal of Health and Social Behavior* 27, 193–208; (3) Abigail J. Stewart and Patricia P. Salt (1981), "Life Stress, Life-Styles, Depression and Illness in Adult Women," *Journal of Personality and Social Psychology* 40, 1063–69.

22. Grace K. Baruch and Rosalind C. Barnett (1987), "Role Quality and Psychological Well-Being," in Faye J. Crosby, ed., *Spouse, Parent, Worker,* 63–73. See also Grace Baruch and Rosalind Barnett (1986), "Role Quality, Multiple Role Involvement, and Psychological Well-Being in Midlife Women," *Journal of Personality and Social Psychology* 51, 578–85.

23. Denise B. Kandel, Mark Davis, and Victoria H. Raveis (1985), "The Stressfulness of Daily Social Roles for Women: Marital, Occupational, and Household Roles," *Journal of Health and Social Behavior* 26, 64–78.

24. Golding, "Role Occupancy and Role-Specific Stress."

25. Lerita Coleman, Toni C. Antonucci, and Pamela K. Adelmann (1987), "Role Involvement, Gender, and Well-Being," in Faye J. Crosby, ed., *Spouse, Parent, Worker,* 138–53.

26. Walter R. Gove and Carol Zeiss (1987), "Multiple Roles and Happiness," in Faye J. Crosby, ed., *Spouse, Parent, Worker,* 125–37.

27. See the review of studies in Mary Holland Benin and Barbara Cable Nienstedt (1985), "Happiness in Single- and Dual-Earner Families: The Effects of Marital Happiness, Job Satisfaction, and Life Cycle," *Journal of Marriage and the Family* 47, 975–84.

28. See the review of studies in Sara Yogev (1982), "Happiness in Dual-Career Couples: Changing Research, Changing Values," *Sex Roles* 8, 593–605.

29. Faye J. Crosby (1982), *Relative Deprivation and Working Women* (New York: Oxford University Press).

30. David Bersoff and Faye J. Crosby (1984), "Job Satisfaction and Family Status," *Personality and Social Psychology Bulletin* 10, 79–83.

31. One study followed a random sample of forty-nine new mothers from the time they gave birth to the era of kindergarten. The study found some evidence of self-selection into the work force. Mothers who ranked high on career orientation tended to return to work more often and earlier than others. Mothers who saw themselves as disorganized and susceptible to stress returned less (and later). Karen Christman Morgan and Ellen Hock (1984),

"A Longitudinal Study of Psychosocial Variables Affecting the Career Patterns of Women with Young Children," *Journal of Marriage and the Family* 46, 383–90.

32. Women show higher rates of restricted activity due to minor illness than do men. See: Walter Gove and M. Hughes (1979), "Possible Causes of the Apparent Sex Differences in Physical Health: An Empirical Investigation," *American Sociological Review* 44, 126–46. Ingrid Waldron (1976), "Why Do Women Live Longer than Men—Part 1," *Journal of Human Stress,* March, 2–13.

33. Ronald C. Kessler and James A. McRae Jr. (1982), "The Effects of Wives' Employment on the Mental Health of Married Men and Women," *American Sociological Review* 47, 216–27.

34. Concerning physical symptoms, Ingrid Waldron (1980) found the same. See: "Employment and Women's Health: An Analysis of Causal Relationships," *International Journal of Health Services* 10, 435–54.

35. David L. Chambers (1989), "Accommodation and Satisfaction: Women and Men Lawyers and the Balance of Work and Family," *Law and Social Inquiry* 14, 251–87. See especially, pp. 277–78.

36. Deborah Belle, ed. (1982), *Lives in Stress: Women and Depression* (Beverly Hills, Calif.: Sage).

37. Joseph Veroff, Elizabeth Douvan, and Richard Kulka (1981), *The Inner American* (New York: Basic Books).

38. Good working conditions, good social support, and feelings of closeness all matter when one considers how life roles affect well-being. Prominent among recent studies that show this are (1) Walter Gove and Carol Zeiss, "Multiple Roles"; (2) Judith Hibbard and Clyde Pope (1985), "Employment Status, Employment Characteristics, and Women's Health," *Women and Health* 10, 59–77; (3) Mary Clare Lennon (1987), "Sex Differences in Distress: The Impact of Gender and Work Roles," *Journal of Health and Social Behavior* 28, 290–305; (4) Joseph Pleck (1985), *Working Wives/Working Husbands* (Beverly Hills, Calif.: Sage) especially relevant information given on p. 110; (5) Rena Repetti (1987), "Linkages between Work and Family Roles," in Stuart Oskamp, ed., *Applied Social Psychology Annual,* vol. 7. *Family Processes and Problems,* 98–127 (Beverly Hills, Calif.: Sage).

39. More precisely, Baruch and Barnett found the following correlations:

| | *Psychological Well-Being* | | |
	Self-Esteem	*Pleasure*	*Depression*
Number of roles	.16	.23	− .14
Wife role (among married)	.35	.70	− .45
Mother role (among mothers)	.34	.34	− .42
Worker role (among employed)	.36	.49	− .35

All the correlations are reliable, but the correlations between role quality and the measures of well-being are much stronger than those between role quantity and well-being.

Some readers may be wondering what a correlation is. In a technical sense, when two items are correlated, they tend to change in ways that are related to each other. If my mood, as measured with your Mood Scale, is correlated with my sibling's successes, as measured with your Sibling Success Scale, then change in success means change in mood. Let's assume that the correlation is positive. In this case, when one measure goes up, so does the other. When my sister is awarded the prize as the best petunia grower in Franklin County, my mood elevates and when, days later, she wins the Nobel Peace Price, I am ecstatic. Now let's assume the correlation is negative. In this case, my sister's horticultural success dampens my mood a little, and her winning of the Nobel Prize sends me into a deep depression. A perfect positive correlation is written $+1.0$. A perfect negative correlation is -1.0. A zero means that there is no correlation between two factors. A correlation of $+.30$ between two measures indicates that they are fairly closely related, positively; while a correlation of $-.30$ means that they are fairly closely related, but in a negative or inverse way. Similarly, a correlation of $+.70$ shows a robust positive association between two variables, and a correlation of $-.70$ shows a robust negative association.

It is not only for suburban women that the quality of marriage proves influential. Among woman who live and work on farms, there is also a strong connection between the supportiveness of a woman's husband and the amount of role strain she experiences. The greater the support, the less the strain. See: Alan D. Berkowitz and H. Wesley Perkins (1984), "Stress among Farm Women: Work and Family as Interacting Systems," *Journal of Marriage and the Family,* 46, 161–66.

40. Nancy Pistrang (1984), "Women's Work Involvement and the Experience of New Motherhood," *Journal of Marriage and the Family* 46, 433–47.

41. Rena Repetti (1988), "Family and Occupational Roles and Women's Mental Health," in Rosalind M. Schwartz, ed., *Women at Work* (Los Angeles: UCLA Institute of Industrial Relations, 1988). In the same study, greater job involvement was associated with ratings of more social support and satisfaction at work and with more conflict at home.

CHAPTER 4: EXPLAINING THE LINK

1. Walter Gove (1972), "Sex, Marital Status, and Mental Illness," *Social Forces* 51, 34–55. The quotations appear on p. 34. Gove has continued to champion his thesis about the psychological benefits of dual roles and has published a long list of articles on the topic. For a recent statement, see Walter R. Gove and Carol Zeiss (1987), "Multiple Roles and Happiness," in Faye J. Crosby, ed., *Spouse, Parent, Worker,* 125–37 (New Haven, Conn.: Yale University Press).

2. See William J. Goode (1960), "A Theory of Role Strain," *American Sociological Review* 25, 483–96, for the view that was dominant until very

recently. At the time that Gove first proposed his views, some others also expressed doubt about the inevitability of role conflict for women. Especially eloquent were Rose L. Coser and Gerald Rokoff (1971), "Women in the Occupational World: Social Disruption and Conflict," *Social Problems* 18, 535–54. For a positive view of multiple roles also see: (1) S. Marks (1977), "Multiple Roles and Role Strain: Some Notes on Human Energy, Time, and Commitment," *American Sociological Review* 42, 921–36; (2) Sam D. Sieber (1974), "Toward a Theory of Role Accumulation," *American Sociological Review* 39, 567–78; (3) Peggy A. Thoits (1983), "Multiple Identities and Psychological Well-Being: A Reformulation and Test of the Social Isolation Hypothesis," *American Sociological Review* 48, 174–87; (4) Peggy A Thoits (1987), "Negotiating Roles," in Faye J. Crosby, ed., *Spouse, Parent, Worker,* 11–22.

3. For an elaboration on these concepts, see F. S. Hall and D. T. Hall (1979), *The Career Couple* (Reading, Mass.: Addison-Wesley).

4. Pamela Roby and Lynet Uttal (1988), "Trade Union Stewards: Coping with Union, Work, and Family Responsibilities," in Barbara A. Gutek, Laurie Larwood, and Anne H. Stromberg, eds., *Women and Work. An Annual Review,* vol. 3, 215–48 (Newbury Park, Calif.: Sage). Jean Reith Schroedel (1990), "Blue-Collar Women: Paying the Price at Home on the Job," in Hildreth Grossman and Nia Lane Chester, ed., *The Experience and Meaning of Work in Women's Lives,* 241–60. (Hillsdale, N.J.: Erlbaum). Essentially the same finding emerged in three other studies. See: (1) Barbara Gutek and Denise A. Stevens (1979), "Effects of Sex of Subject, Sex of Stimulus Due, and Androgyny Level on Evaluations in Work Situations Which Evoke Sex Role Stereotypes," *Journal of Vocational Behavior* 14, 23–32; (2) Helen Lopata, Debra Barnewolt, and Kathleen Norr (1980), "Spouses' Contributions to Each Others' Roles," in Fran Pepitone-Rockwell, ed., *Dual-Career Couples,* 111–41 (Beverly Hills, Calif.: Sage); (3) Beth Vanfossen (1981), "Sex Differences in the Mental Health Effects of Spouse Support and Equity," *Journal of Health and Social Behavior* 22, 130–43. However, Marybeth Shinn, Nora Wong, Patricia Simko, and Blanca Ortiz-Torres (1989) found no differences in spouse support. See: "Promoting the Well-Being of Working Parents: Coping, Social Support, and Flexible Job Schedules," *American Journal of Community Psychology* 17, 31–55.

5. Jonathan R. Cole and Harriet Zuckerman (1987), "Marriage, Motherhood, and Research Performance in Science," *Scientific American* 256, no. 2, 119–25. For similar findings a decade earlier, see: Thomas W. Martin, Kenneth J. Berry, and R. Brooke Jacobsen (1975), "The Impact of Dual-Career Marriages on Female Professional Careers," *Journal of Marriage and the Family* 37, 734–42. More important then the fact of marital status is marital history. See: Sharon K. Houseknecht, Suzanne Vaughan, and Anne Slatham (1987), "The Impact of Singlehood on the Career Patterns of Professional Women," *Journal of Marriage and the Family* 49, 353–56. A fascinating personal account of marriage and career is given by Janet T. Spence

(1988), "Autobiographical Sketch," in Agnes N. O'Connell and Nancy Felipe Russo, eds., *Models of Achievement. Reflections of Eminent Women in Psychology,* 189–203 (Hillsdale, N.J.: Erlbaum).

6. For an early statement, see Cynthia F. Epstein (1971), "Law Partners and Marital Partners: Strains and Solutions in the Dual Career Family Enterprise," *Human Relations* 24, 549–64. For a much more complete account, see Cynthia Epstein's *Women in Law* published by Basic Books in 1981.

7. Rosanna Hertz (1986), *More Equal than Others: Women and Men in Dual Career Marriages* (Berkeley: University of California Press). The quotation appears on pp. 78–79.

8. Lisa Silberstein (1987), *The Dual-Career Marriage: A System in Transition* (Ph.D. diss., Yale University), 98.

9. Concerning the division of labor in the family, see chapter 2, pp. 48–51.

10. In a recent survey of approximately 150 professional married mothers of preschool children, more than half of the respondents acknowledged that marriage had proved more beneficial than harmful to their jobs. See: Carol-Ann Emmons, Monica Biernet, Linda Beth Tiedje, Eric L. Lang, and Camille B. Wortman (1990), "Stress, Support, and Coping among Women Professionals with Preschool Children," in John Eckenrode and Susan Gore, eds., *Stress between Work and Family,* 61–93 (New York: Plenum Press).

11. Pat Schroeder, with Andrea Camp and Robyn Lipner (1989), *Champion of the Great American Family* (New York: Random House).

12. Paula Slomin Derry (1990), *Motherhood and Professional Life of Female Psychotherapists* (Bristol, Indiana: Wyndham Hall Press). The quotations appear on pp. 68–73.

13. Entitled "Balancing Acts," the article appeared in *The Women's Review of Books* V, no. 10–11 (July 1988), 29.

14. Alice Walker (1983), "A Writer Because of, Not in Spite of, Her Children," in *In Search of Our Mothers' Gardens,* 66–70 (New York: Harcourt, Brace, Jovanovich). The review originally appeared in 1976.

15. Walker, *In Search of Our Mothers' Gardens.*

16. The differentiation between material and psychological should not be overdrawn. People's emotional well-being depends on their own material well-being and of the material conditions of those around them. This point is powerfully demonstrated in Deborah Belle's book *Lives in Stress* (Beverly Hills, Calif.: Sage, 1982). Also see: Geraldine Downey and Phyllis Moen (1987), "Personal Efficacy, Income, and Family Transitions. A Longitudinal Study of Woman-Headed Households," *Journal of Health and Social Behavior* 28, 320–33.

17. David Chambers (1989), "Accommodation and Satisfaction: Women and Men Lawyers and the Balance of Work and Family," *Law and Social Inquiry* 14, 251–87. The quotation appears on p. 266.

18. Silberstein, *Dual-Career Marriage,* 209.

19. David Bakan (1966), *The Duality of Human Existence* (Boston: Bea-

con Press.) The quotation comes from p. 15. Bakan's distinction has been applied by psychologists at the University of Texas to personality types. The person who is agentic is one who usually accomplishes things. The one who is communal seeks good companionship. A person can be both agentic and communal. Typically little boys are socialized to be agentic and little girls to be communal, say Spence and Helmreich. See Janet T. Spence and Robert L. Helmreich (1978), *Masculinity and Femininity: Their Psychological Dimensions, Correlates, and Antecedents,* 4–16 (Austin: University of Texas Press). See also Janet T. Spence (1984), "Masculinity, Femininity, and Gender-Related Traits: A Conceptual Analysis and Critique of Current Research," *Progress in Experimental Personality Research* 13, 1–97.

20. Abigail J. Stewart and Janet E. Malley (1987), "Role Combination in Women: Mitigating Agency and Communion," in Faye J. Crosby, ed., *Spouse, Parent, Worker,* 44–62. The quotation appears on p. 47.

21. Abigail J. Stewart and Patricia Salt (1981), "Life Stress, Life-Styles, Depression, and Illness in Adult Women," *Journal of Personality and Social Psychology* 40, 1063–69.

22. It is possible that some background variable or personality factor caused some women both to choose to be jugglers and, later, to be resilient. Rena Repetti brought this observation to my attention.

23. Stewart and Malley, "Role Combination."

24. Some psychologists propose that it is the daily hassles that lead to depression as much as the major life events. For a proponent of the daily hassles view, see: Allen D. Kramner, James C. Coyne, Catherine Schaefer, and Richard S. Lazarus. (1981), "Comparison of Two Modes of Stress Measurement: Daily Hassles and Uplift versus Major Life Events," *Journal of Behavioral Medicine* 4, 1–39. For a recent integrative survey, see: Shelley Taylor (1990), "Health Psychology: The Science and the Field," *American Psychologist* 45, 40–50.

25. Robert J. Lifton (1969), *Thought Reform and the Psychology of Totalism: A Study of Brainwashing in China* (New York: W. W. Norton). Edgar Schein, Inge Schneier, and Curtis H. Baker (1961), *A Socio-Psychological Analysis of "Brainwashing" of American Civilian Prisoners by the Chinese Communists* (New York: W. W. Norton).

26. D. Brewer and E. B. Doughtie (1980), "Induction of Mood and Mood Shifts," *Journal of Clinical Psychology* 36, 215–26.

27. Susie Orbach and Luise Eichenbaum (1988), *Between Women: Love, Envy, and Competition in Women's Friendships* (New York: Viking). Jane Ciabattari (1989), "Will the '90s Be the Age of Envy?" *Psychology Today,* December, 46–50.

28. Daniel Kahneman and Dale Miller (1986), "Norm Theory: Comparing Reality to Its Alternatives," *Psychological Review* 93, 136–53.

29. Many researchers have found that the relationship between stress in one life role and mental health problems is attenuated among people who are involved in other life roles. Among the research reports demonstrating the

presence of buffering are: (1) Rosalind Barnett and Grace Baruch (1985), "Women's Involvement in Multiple Roles and Psychological Distress," *Journal of Personality and Social Psychology* 49, 135–45; (2) Mary Holland Benin and Barbara Cable Nienstedt (1985), "Happiness in Single- and Dual-Earner Families: The Effects of Marital Happiness, Job Satisfaction, and Life Cycle," *Journal of Marriage and the Family* 47, 975–84; (3) Denise B. Kandel, Mark Davies, and Victoria H. Raveis (1985), "The Stressfulness of Daily Social Roles for Women: Marital, Occupational and Household Roles," *Journal of Health and Social Behavior* 26, 64–78; (4) Pat M. Keith and Robert B. Schafer (1985), *Family Relations* 34, 227–33; (5) Neal Krause (1984), "Employment Outside the Home and Women's Psychological Well-Being," *Social Psychiatry* 19, 41–48; (6) James M. LaRocco, James S. House, and John P. French, Jr. (1980), "Social Support, Occupation Stress, and Health," *Journal of Health and Social Behavior* 21, 202–18; (7) Glenys Parry (1986), "Paid Employment, Life Events, Social Support, and Mental Health in Working-Class Mothers," *Journal of Health and Social Behavior* 27, 193–208; (8) Leonard I. Pearlin and Joyce S. Johnson (1977), "Marital Status, Life Stress, and Depression," *American Sociological Review* 42, 704–15; (9) Peggy A. Thoits (1982), "Conceptual, Methodological, and Theoretical Problems in Studying Social Support as a Buffer Against Life Stress," *Journal of Health and Social Behavior* 23, 145–59; (10) Sheldon Cohen and Thomas Wills (1985), "Stress, Social Support and the Buffering Hypothesis," *Psychological Bulletin* 98, 310–57. For a review of some of the studies, see also: Peter Warr and Glenys Parry (1982), "Paid Employment and Women's Psychological Well-Being," *Psychological Bulletin* 91, 498–516. For a distinction between buffering and counterbalancing, see Peggy A. Thoits (1984), "Explaining Distributions of Psychological Vulnerability," *Social Forces* 63, 453–80.

30. Rena L. Repetti and Faye J. Crosby (1984), "Gender and Depression: Exploring the Adult-Role Explanation," *Journal of Social and Clinical Psychology* 2, 57–70.

31. Rosalind C. Barnett and Grace K. Baruch (1987), "Social Roles, Gender, and Psychological Distress," in Rosalind C. Barnett, Lois Biener, and Grace K. Baruch, eds., *Gender and Stress,* 122–43 (New York: Free Press).

32. Silberstein, *Dual-Career Marriage,* p. 171.

33. Faye J. Crosby (1990), "Divorce and Work Life among Women Managers," in Hildreth Grossman and Nia Lane Chester, eds., *The Experience and Meaning of Work in Women's Lives,* 121–42.

34. Ronnie Janoff-Bulman and Irene Hanson Frieze (1987), "The Role of Gender in Reactions to Criminal Victimization," in Barnett, Biener, and Baruch, eds., *Gender and Stress* 159–84.

35. Sylvia A. Hewlett (1986), *A Lesser Life. The Myth of Women's Liberation in America* (New York: William Morrow). The quotation appears on p. 43.

36. Patricia Linville (1987), "Self-complexity as a Cognitive Buffer

against Stress-Related Illness and Depression," *Journal of Personality and Social Psychology* 52, 663–76.

37. Barton J. Hirsch (1980), "Natural Support Systems and Coping with Major Life Changes," *American Journal of Community Psychology* 8, 159–72.

38. Joseph Veroff, Elizabeth Douvan, and Richard Kulka (1981), *The Inner American* (New York: Basic Books).

39. Grace K. Baruch and Rosalind C. Barnett (1987), "Role Quality and Psychological Well-Being," in Faye J. Crosby, ed., *Spouse, Parent, Worker*, 63–73.

40. Cynthia Fuchs Epstein (1987), "Multiple Demands and Multiple Roles: The Conditions of Successful Management," in Faye J. Crosby, ed., *Spouse, Parent, Worker*, 23–35. The quotation comes from p. 23.

CHAPTER 5: WHAT ABOUT THE CHILDREN?

1. Ellen Hock, Karen Christman Morgan, and Michael D. Hock (1985), "Employment Decisions Made by Mothers of Infants," *Psychology of Women Quarterly* 9, 383–402.

2. Several studies report that research on the impact of a mother's work has singled out the mother's belief that she should be employed as a critical variable in relation to positive outcomes for children. See: M. R. Yarrow, P. Scott, L. DeLeeuw, and C. Meining (1962), "Childrearing in Families of Working and Non-Working Mothers," *Sociometry* 25, 122–40. Similarly, T. Mason and R. Espinoza found that family stress is more likely if family members have different expectations, particularly in relation to whether or not the mother should be employed. T. Mason and R. Espinoza (1983), *Executive Summary of the Final Report: Working Parents Project* (Washington, D.C.: National Institute of Education).

3. The caption is cited in Lucia Albino Gilbert (1985), *Men in Dual-Career Families. Current Realities and Future Prospects* (Hillsdale, N.J.: Erlbaum), p. 74.

4. Anna Freud and Dorothy Burlingham ran a shelter for children and infants. They summarized their views in *Infants Without Families: The Case for and Against Residential Nurseries* (New York: International University Press, 1944). In 1951, John Bowlby published a monograph entitled *Maternal Care and Mental Health* (Geneva: World Health Organization) and later he developed the theme in his extremely influential *Attachment and Loss* (New York: Basic Books, 1969). Bowlby, like Anna Freud, thought that the mother-infant tie was crucial for later emotional development. While the views of Freud and Bowlby are not as widely accepted now as they used to be, some contemporary scholars still champion their point of view. Especially influential is *Beyond the Best Interests of the Child* in which legal scholars Joseph Goldstein and Albert Solnit join forces with Anna Freud and use separation anxiety as the major argument against joint or split custody of children in divorce (New York: Free Press, 1973).

5. Benjamin Spock (1957), *Baby and Child Care* (New York: Meredith Press).

6. Betty Freidan (1973), *The Feminine Mystique* (New York: Dell). See also B. Welter (1966), "The Cult of True Womanhood, 1820–1860," *American Quarterly,* Summer, pt. 1, 151–74.

7. Lois Wladis Hoffman and F. Ivan Nye (1974), "Preface," in Lois W. Hoffman and F. Ivan Nye, eds., *Working Mothers. An Evaluative Review of the Consequences for Wife, Husband, and Child* (San Francisco: Jossey-Bass, 1974), ix. The earlier book, *The Employed Mother in America,* edited by F. Ivan Nye and Lois Wladis Hoffman was published in 1963 by Rand McNally in Chicago.

8. Lois Wladis Hoffman (1974), "Effects on Child," in Lois Hoffman and F. I. Nye, eds., *Working Mothers,* 165.

9. Ibid., 166. In 1985 Hoffman updated her review with an article in volume 7 of *Child Development Research.* The updated chapter bears the wonderful title: "The Effects on Children of Maternal and Paternal Employment."

10. Sandra Scarr (1984), *Mother Care/Other Care* (New York: Basic Books).

11. Scarr, *Mother Care/Other Care,* 4.

12. Ibid., 5.

13. Ibid., 31.

14. Ibid., 176.

15. On effective instruction, see B. F. Skinner (1953), *Science and Human Nature* (New York: Macmillan) and *Beyond Freedom and Dignity* (New York: Knopf, 1971). Skinner was the famous psychologist who has demonstrated that learning occurs most rapidly when correct responses are rewarded and incorrect ones ignored. Even those psychologists who dislike Skinner's philosophy have to agree with him on this point.

16. K. Alison Clarke-Stewart (1989), "Infant Day Care: Maligned or Malignant?" *American Psychologist* 44, 266–73.

17. See, especially, the excellent review article by Kathleen McCartney and Anatasia Galanopoulos (1988), "Child Care and Attachment: A New Frontier the Second Time Around," *American Journal of Orthopsychiatry* 58, no. 1, 16–24. McCartney and Galanopoulos review the methodological problems inherent in conducting research on child care.

18. See Kathleen McCartney (1984), "Effect of Quality of Day Care Environment on Children's Language Development," *Developmental Psychology* 20, 244–60. Also see: (1) Lois Wladis Hoffman (1989), "Effects of Maternal Employment in the Two Parent Family," *American Psychologist* 44, 283–92; (2) Martin Woodhead (1988), "When Psychology Informs Public Policy. The Case of Early Childhood Intervention," *American Psychologist* 43, 443–54.

19. Elizabeth Jaeger and Marsha Weinraub (1990), "Early Nonmaternal Care and Infant Attachment: In Search of Process" in Kathleen McCartney

(ed.), *Child Care and Maternal Employment: A Social Ecology Approach* (San Francisco: Jossey-Bass, 1990), 71–90.

20. The one method to show some differences is the Ainsworth Stranger Anxiety Test where the child is left for a brief while in the presence of a stranger. Observers then code what occurs when the mother returns to the room. If the child continues playing and does not acknowledge the mother's return, the child can be coded as being emotional upset. For a review of the Ainsworth Stranger Anxiety Situation and other methods of studying attachment, see Sandra Scarr, Deborah Phillips, and Kathleen McCartney (1990), "Facts, Fantasies and the Future of Child Care in the United States," *Psychological Science* 1, 26–35.

Also see some of the work of Jay Belsky, one of the most outspoken critics of child care. Among his numerous publications are (1) Jay Belsky and L. D. Steinberg (1978), "The Effects of Day Care: A Critical Review," *Child Development* 49, 929–49; (2) Jay Belsky (1985), "The Science and Politics of Day Care," in K. L. Shotland and M. Maks, eds., *Social Science and Social Policy* (Beverly Hills: Sage); (3) Jay Belsky (1986), *Infant Day Care: A Cause for Concern? Zero to Three*. Bulletin of the National Center for Clinical Infant Programs (Washington, D.C.: Superintendent of Documents); (4) Jay Belsky and Michael J. Rovine (1988), "Nonmaternal Care in the First Year of Life and the Security of Infant-Parent Attachment," *Child Development* 59, 157–67. Belsky continues to see in the accumulated evidence a strong possibility that the child-care experience disrupts the social development of the infant. He has most recently reiterated his views in a chapter entitled "A Reassessment of Infant Day Care," that appears in a thoughtful and comprehensive book, *The Parental Leave Crisis. Toward a National Policy,* edited by Edward F. Zigler and Meryl Frank (New Haven, Conn.: Yale University Press, 1988).

Other studies of child care show mixed findings concerning the attachment of infants to their mother or parents. See Jan Basom Schubert, Sharon Bradley-Johnson, and James Nuttal (1980), "Mother-Infant Communication and Maternal Employment," *Child Development* 51, 246–49. Brian E. Vaughn, Frederick L. Gove, and Byron Egeland (1980), "The Relationship between Out-of-Home Care and the Quality of Infant-Mother Attachment in an Economically Disadvantaged Population," *Child Development* 51, 1203–14. Thomas J. Gamble and Edward Zigler (1986), "Effects of Infant Day Care: Another look at the Evidence," *American Journal of Orthopsychiatry* 56, 26–42. Peter Barglow, Brian E. Vaughn, and Nancy Molitor (1987), "Effects of Maternal Absence Due to Employment on the Quality of Infant-Mother Attachment in Low-Risk Sample," *Child Development* 58, 945–54. P. Lindsay Chase-Lansdale and Margaret Tresch Owen (1987), "Maternal Employment in a Family Context: Effects on Infant-Mother and Infant-Father Attachments," *Child Development* 58, 1505–12.

A big issue is whether or not early child care arrangements have long lasting effects. The best source on the topic is a book edited by Adele Eskeles

Gottfried and Allen W. Gottfried (1988), *Maternal Employment and Children's Development and Longitudinal Research* (New York: Plenum Press). The book contains nine chapters by sixteen experts reporting on four different longitudinal studies.

21. Edward Zigler and R. Cascione (1980), "On Being a Parent," in the National Institute of Education, *Parenthood in Changing Society* (Urbana: ERIC Clearinghouse of Elementary and Early Childhood Education, University of Illinois), 83. Cited in S. Scarr, *Mother Care/Other Care*), 201. For empirical confirmation of the claim that children arrive somewhat preprogrammed, see E. Waters, Brian E. Vaughn, and Byron Egeland (1980), "Individual Differences in Infant-Mother Attachment Relationships at Age One: Antecedents in Neonatal Behavior in an Urban Economically Disadvantaged Sample," *Child Development* 51, 208–16. Also: Susan B. Crockenberg (1981), "Infant Irritability, Mother Responsiveness, and Social Support Influences on the Security of Infant-Mother Attachment," *Child Development* 52, 857–65. Finally: Jay Belsky and Michael Rovine (1987), "Temperament and Attachment Security in the Stranger Situation: An Empirical Reapproachment," *Child Development* 58, 787–95.

22. *APA Monitor* 17, no. 2 (December 1986), 1. The same link between mothers' work and children's unsupervised time appears in other publications, but some psychologists see latchkey children as a community issue. See: Bryan E. Robinson, Bobbie H. Rowland, Mick Coleman (1986), *Latchkey Kids: Unlocking Doors for Children and Their Families* (Lexington, Mass.: D.C. Heath).

23. Francine Prose (1990), "Confident at 11, Confused at 16." *New York Times Magazine,* January 7, pp. 22, 23, 25, 37, 39, 40, 45 and 46.

24. Carol Gilligan (1982), *In a Different Voice* (Cambridge, Mass.: Harvard University Press), 8.

25. Gilligan, *In a Different Voice,* 8, italics added.

26. Ibid., 17.

27. Ibid., 100.

28. Helen Block Lewis (1976), *Psychic War in Men and Women* (New York: Universities Press). Lewis discusses female affectionateness on p. 233 and male lack of it on p. 263.

29. Nancy J. Chodorow (1978), *The Reproduction of Mothering: Psychoanalysis and the Sociology of Gender* (Berkeley: University of California Press), 169. Chodorow has further developed in her thinking. See: Nancy J. Chodorow (1990), *Feminism and Psychoanalytic Theory* (New Haven, Conn.: Yale University Press).

30. Lillian Rubin (1983), *Intimate Strangers* (New York: Harper and Row), 191.

31. Ibid., 198.

32. Rachel T. Hare-Mustin and Jeanne Maracek (1988), "The Meaning of Difference. Gender Theory, Postmodernism, and Psychology," *American Psychologist* 43, 455–64. The passage occurs on p. 462.

33. Rachel T. Hare-Mustin and Jeanne Maracek (1990), "Beyond Difference." in Rachel T. Hare-Mustin and Jeanne Maracek, eds., *Making a Difference: Psychology and Construction of Gender,* 184–201 (New Haven, Conn.: Yale University Press).

34. Elizabeth V. Spelman (1988), *Inessential Woman. Problems of Exclusion in Feminist Thought* (Boston: Beacon Press), 6.

35. See the very interesting *Women Volunteering. The Pleasure, Pain, and Politics of Unpaid Work from 1830 to the Present* by Wendy Kaminer (Garden City, N.Y.: Anchor Press, 1984). Kaminer is sympathetic to the dilemmas faced by those who volunteer especially if they are feminists. Also aware of the ambiguities of volunteers is Arlene K. Daniels (1985), *Invisible Careers: Women Civic Leaders from the Volunteer World* (Chicago: University of Chicago Press). One very interesting finding of a survey conducted in the Boston area is that middle-class employed mothers volunteered as much as middle-class housewives in organizations that centered about services to children. See Lydia O'Donnell and Ann Stueve (1983), "Mothers as Social Agents. Structuring the Community Activities of School-Aged Children," in Helen Z. Lopata and Joseph Pleck, eds., *Interweave of Social Roles: Jobs and Families,* vol. 3, pp. 113–29 (Greenwich, Conn.: JAI Press).

36. Alice Sterling Honig (1984), "Child Care Options and Decisions: Facts and Figurings for Families," in Kathryn M. Borman, Daisy Quarm, and Sarah Gideonse eds., *Women in the Workplace: Effects on Family,* 89–111 (Norwood, N.J.: Ablex Publishing). The study reported by Honig was conducted by R. Goldberg and reported in 1981 at the Annual Meeting of the American Psychological Association. Nobody has documented that children of housewives have higher self-concepts than the children of employed women. Researchers have shown, on the other hand, that some mothers (employed or not) seem to build self-esteem in children while other mothers (employed or not) seem incapable of building self-esteem in their children. (Nicholas Colangelo, David Rosenthal, and David Daltman [1984], "Maternal Employment and Job Satisfaction and Their Relationship to Children's Perceptions and Behaviors," *Sex Roles* 10, 693–702.)

37. For an integrative review see: Joseph H. Pleck (1985), *Working Wives/Working Husbands* (Beverly Hills, Calif.: Sage), 122–23. The study that contained the data on how men thought "a person might make a contribution" was published in 1966 and conducted by R. Adamek and W. Goudy.

38. Cynthia Fuchs Epstein (1988), *Deceptive Distinctions. Sex, Gender, and the Social Order* (New Haven, Conn.: Yale University Press), 237.

39. One classic study showed that therapists tend to think of healthy men and healthy adults in the same ways but think of healthy women as different from healthy men (and, more importantly, from healthy adults). See I. Broverman, D. Broverman, F. Clarkson, R. Rosenkrantz, and S. Vogel (1979), "Sex Role Stereotypes and Clinical Judgments of Mental Health," *Journal of Consulting and Clinical Psychology* 34, 1–7. More recently E. Car-

men, N. Russo, and J. Miller (1981) have shown the tranquilizers and stimulants are both prescribed to women far more often than to men. ("Inequality and Women's Mental Health: An Overview," *American Journal of Psychiatry* 138, 1319–35). For a general treatment, see Carol Becker (1987), *The Invisible Drama. Women and the Anxiety of Change* (New York: Macmillan). Becker outlines some of the antifemale attitudes in psychology and especially in therapy but points to ways that psychology, especially therapy, can benefit women. For a more scholarly analysis, see M. Annette Brodsky (1980), "A Decade of Feminist Influence on Psychotherapy," *Psychology of Women Quarterly* 4, 331–44.

40. This is a point made in an article arguing for the need for men's studies. The author of the article, Henry Brod, says on page 264: "The new men's studies is not simply a repetition of traditionally male-biased scholarship . . . Women's studies explores and corrects the effects on women and on our understanding of them—of their exclusion from traditional learning caused by the androcentric elevation of 'man' as generic human. Men's studies similarly looks into the, as yet, largely unrecognized effects of this tally on men and our understanding of them." (Henry Brod [1987], "A Case for Men's Studies," in Michael S. Kimmel, ed., *Changing Men. New Directions for Research in Men and Masculinity*, 263–78 (Newbury Park, Calif.: Sage).

41. Gilligan. *In a Different Voice*, 2.

42. Ibid., 28.

43. Ibid.

44. Ibid.

45. I repeated the experiment with the next year's class and obtained virtually identical results.

46. John P. Robinson has conducted meticulous studies of how Americans spend their time. The average hours per day he reports for time spent all alone (including time asleep) for employed men, employed women, and housewives are 14.0 (Mon.–Fri.), 12.5 (Sat.), 13.5 (Sun.); 14.0 (Mon.–Fri.), 13.5 (Sat.), 15.1 (Sun.); 14.6 (Mon–Fri) 14.6 (Sat.) and 13.6 (Sun.), respectively. Thus, according to Robinson, men are alone less time than either employed women or housewives. See John R. Robinson (1977), *How Americans Use Their Time. A Social-Psychological Analysis of Everyday Behavior* (New York: Praeger), 139.

47. Eleanor E. Maccoby and Carol N. Jackllin (1974), *The Psychology of Sex Differences* (Stanford, Calif.: Stanford University Press). See chapter 7.

48. Ibid., 206–9.

49. Maccoby and Jacklin are, indeed, somewhat outdated. But there are two reasons to believe their conclusions hold still. First, a great number of studies have been conducted since the publication of their book—spurred in part by their book—on the topic of gender differences. These studies rarely find sex differences and rarely find women acting in stereotypically feminine ways. Exemplary is a recent book by Sue Freeman detailing a study of women

in the corporation. Freeman discovered "these women defy stereotypic notions of what is important and motivating to females. They are instrumental rather than socioemotional in their orientation" (p. 31). See: Sue J. M. Freeman (1990), *Managing Lives: Corporate Women and Social Change* (Amherst: University of Massachusetts Press).

Second, a new technology has been developed to assess the stability of gender differences across studies. The new technology, called meta-analysis, represents a considerable advance over the list-them-and-count-them method used by Maccoby and Jacklin and other early reviewers. The logic behind meta-analysis is elegant and easy to comprehend. To understand its advantage, imagine that someone, in the manner of Maccoby and Jacklin, shows you a list of five studies in which researchers looked for sex differences in, say, sensitivity to criticism. Now imagine that studies A, B, C, and D all show males to be more sensitive to criticism and study E shows females to be more sensitive. You might conclude from this that males are more sensitive to criticism than are females. But wait! Imagine that I also tell you that studies A, B, C, and D all included only 10 people each while study E had 1,000 people. Or imagine that I say that the first two studies had slightly unstable measures while C and D had better measures and E had excellent, reliable measures. Meta-analysis allows the scholar to adjust for the inevitable variations between studies in sample sizes and reliability of measures before coming to any conclusions. The meta-analytic studies of gender differences in social behavior show no differences in sociability. Foremost among the studies is Alice Eagly's (1987), *Sex Differences in Social Behavior: A Social-Role Interpretation* (Hillsdale, N.J.: Erlbaum).

50. For the controversial nature of the findings, see: Alice H. Eagly (1989), "Gender and Social Behavior: Adventures in the Study of Sex Differences" (Invited Address presented at the annual meeting of the Association for Women in Psychology, Newport, Rhode Island). Also, contrast the position taken by Alice Eagly in 1978, when she wrote "Sex Differences in Influenceability," *Psychological Bulletin* 85, 86–116, with the position she took about a decade later. Alice H. Eagly and Blair T. Johnson (1990), "Gender and Leadership Style: A Male-Analysis," *Psychological Bulletin* 108, 233–56.)

51. Nancy Eisenberg and Randy Lennon (1983), "Sex Differences in Empathy and Related Capacities," *Psychological Bulletin* 94, 100–131.

52. Nancy Eisenberg, Randy Lennon, and Ruth Karlsson (1983), "Pro-Social Development: A Longitudinal Study," *Developmental Psychology* 19, 846–55.

53. Eagly, *Sex Differences,* 67.

54. Concerning the data on nurturance: see Gail F. Melson and Alan Fogel (1988), "Learning to Care," *Psychology Today* 22, 39, 42, 44 and 45. Concerning the African studies, see: Beatrice B. Whiting and John W. Whiting (1975), *Children of Six Cultures: A Psycho-Cultural Analysis* (Cambridge: Harvard University Press).

55. Edward Hall (1973), *The Silent Langugae* (Garden City, N.Y.: Doubleday).

56. Ladd Wheeler, Harry Reis, and John Nezlek (1983), "Loneliness, Social Interaction, and Sex Roles," *Journal of Personality and Social Psychology* 45, 943–53. Harry T. Reis, Marilyn Senchak, and Beth Solomon (1985), "Sex Differences in the Intimacy of Social Interactions: Further Examination of Potential Explanation," *Journal of Personality and Social Psychology* 48, 1204–17. Harry T. Reis (1986), "Gender Effects in Social Participation: Intimacy, Loneliness, and the Conduct of Social Interaction," in R. Gilmore and Steven Duck, eds., *The Emerging Field of Personal Relationships*, 91–105 (Hillsdale, N.J.: Erlbaum). For the recent follow-up study, see: Harry Reis (1990), *The Impact of Social Interaction on Health during the Transition to Adult Life*. Final Report to the National Science Foundation, Grant Number BNS—8416988.

57. Concerning trust and self disclosure, see: Valerian J. Derlaga and J. Grzelak (1979), "Appropriateness of Self-Disclosure in Social Relationships," in G. J. Chelune, ed., *Self-Disclosure*, 151–76 (San Francisco: Jossey-Bass). Also: Nancy Eisenberg and Jane Stayer (1987), "Introduction: Critical Issues in the Study of Empathy," in Nancy Eisenberg and Jane Stayer, eds., *Empathy and Its Development*, 3–13 (New York: Cambridge University Press). There is, however, some new evidence that self-disclosure, especially reciprocal self-disclosure, is more central to women's friendships than to men's friendships in college. (See: Elizabeth Mazur [1989], "Predicting Gender Differences in Same-Sex Friendships from Affiliation, Motive and Value," *Psychology of Women Quarterly* 13 277–91.) Concerning trust and gender, see: Ken J. Rotenburg (1984), "Sex Differences in Children's Trust in Peers," *Sex Roles* 11, 953–57. Also see Scott Swain (1989), "Covert Intimacy: Closeness in Men's Friendships," in Barbara J. Risman and Pepper Schwartz, eds., *Gender in Intimate Relationships. A Microstructural Approach*, 71–86 (Belmont, Calif.: Wadsworth Publishing).

58. On male bonding, see Lionel Tiger (1984), *Men in Groups,* 2d ed. (New York: Marion Boyars). Tiger became famous for the view that men form intimate bonds among themselves in ways that are unlike the connections between men and women or between women. The research does not bear out his claims. (See: Paul H. Wright [1982], "Men's Friendships, Women's Friendships, and the Alleged Inferiority of the Latter," *Sex Roles* 8, 1–20.) Nor, of course, do the empirical data support Gilligan's parallel claim that intimacy belongs to females. For a well-reasoned review of Gilligan, see Anne Colby and William Damon (1983), "Listening to a Different Voice," *Merrill-Palmer Quarterly* 29, 473–81. Many other reviewers agree with Colby and Damon that the ideas are exciting but that few studies really support them.

59. Francesca M. Cancian (1986), "The Feminization of Love," *Signs: Journal of Women in Culture and Society* 11, 692. She makes a similar point in her book, *Love in America: Gender and Self-Development* (New York: Cambridge University Press, 1987).

60. Carol Tavris (1982), *Anger: The Misunderstood Emotion* (New York: Simon and Schuster).

61. Maccoby and Jacklin, *The Psychology of Sex Differences,* 230–31.

62. Janet Hyde (1984), "How Large Are Gender Differences in Aggression? A Developmental Meta-analysis," *Developmental Psychology* 20, 722–36. Also see Alice Eagly, *Sex Differences in Social Behavior,* chapter 3.

63. Judith Lewis Herman with Lisa Hirschman (1981), *Father-Daughter Incest.* (Cambridge, Mass.: Harvarfd University Press).

64. Barbara A. Gutek (1985), *Sex and the Workplace. The Impact of Sexual Behavior and Harassment on Women and Organizations* (San Francisco: Jossey-Bass).

65. Daisy Quarm (1984), "Sexual Inequality: The High Cost of Leaving Parenting to Women," in Kathryn M. Borman, Daisy Quarm, and Sarah Gideonse, eds., *Women in the Workplace,* 187–208. The reference to the low incidence of rape among some other societies occurs on p. 196. Cross-cultural anthropological studies show a relationship between the frequency of rape and male political and economic dominance. See: Peggy Reeves Sanday (1981), *Female Power and Male Dominance: On the Origins of Sexual Inequality* (New York: Cambridge University Press). Statistics within the United States also support the proposal that violent cultures tolerate and even promote rape. See Diana E. H. Russell (1984), *Sexual Exploitation. Rape, Child Sexual Abuse, and Workplace Harassment* (Beverly Hills, Calif.: Sage). Especially revealing are the figures on p. 144.

66. Lillian Messinger (1984), *Remarriage: A Family Affair* (New York: Plenum Press), 108.

67. Bill Cosby (1986), *Fatherhood* (Garden City, N.Y.: Doubleday).

68. Joseph H. Pleck (1987), "American Fathering in Historical Perspective," in Michael S. Kimmel, ed., *Changing Men,* 83–97. The quotation appears on page 94.

69. Ann C. Couter, Maureen Perry-Jenkins, Ted L. Huston, and Susan M. Mattalel (1987), "Processes Underlying Father Involvement in Dual-Earner and Single-Earner Families," *Developmental Psychology* 23, 341–440. M. Ann Easterbrooks and Wendy A. Goldberg (1988) also found that the husbands of employed women devoted more time to child care than did the husbands of housewives. Their findings appear in an article, "Effects of Early Maternal Employment on Toddlers, Mothers, and Fathers," *Developmental Psychology* 21, 774–83.

70. Barbara J. Risman (1989), "Can Men 'Mother'? Life as a Single Father," in Barbara Risman and Pepper Schwartz, *Gender in Intimate Relations,* 155–64. The quotation appears on p. 163. See also: Shirley M. H. Hanson (1986), "Parent-Child Relationships in Single-Father Families," in Robert A. Lewis and Robert E. Salt, eds., *Men in Families,* 181–95 (Beverly Hills, Calif.: Sage).

71. Wade C. Mackey (1985), *Fathering Behaviors: The Dynamics of the Man-Child Bond* (New York: Plenum Press).

72. Researchers who have studied the kind of work children do within the home found that 40 percent of the families studied regularly required their children to do chores around the house when the children were under five years old and that nine out of ten families expected household work by children five and over. On average the younger children spent about two hours a week on chores and the older children five. See: Lynn K. White and David B. Brinkerhoff (1987), "Children's Work in the Family: Its Significance and Meaning," in Naomi Gerstel and Harriet Gross, eds., *Work and Family,* 204–18. Also: Jacqueline J. Goodnow (1988), "Children's Household Work: Its Nature and Functions," *Psychological Bulletin* 103, 5–26.

73. M. Ann Easterbrooks and Wendy A. Goldberg, "Effects of Early Maternal Employment."

74. Lea Ybarra (1982), "When Wives Work: The Impact on the Chicano Family," *Journal of Marriage and the Family* 44, 169–78.

75. Lisa Silberstein, (1987), *The Dual-Career Marriage: A System in Transition* (Ph.D. diss., Yale University). Another recently published study of eighty male engineers working for a company in New Jersey confirmed Silberstein's conclusion that men do not take children to the office. See: Robert Zussman (1987), "Work and Family in the New Middle Class," in Naomi Gerstel and Harriet Gross, eds., *Families and Work,* 338–46.

76. The study was conducted by Patricia Kain Kumb and cited by Anita Shreve (1987), *Remaking Motherhood: How Working Mothers Are Shaping Our Children's Future* (New York: Viking). The study is described on p. 101.

77. The evidence is reviewed in Michael E. Lamb (1982), "Maternal Employment and Child Development: A Review," in Michael E. Lamb ed., *Nontraditional Families: Parenting and Child Development,* 45–70 (Hillsdale, N.J.: Erlbaum). On pp. 59 and 60, Lamb cites nineteen separate studies published between 1960 and 1972. More recently Cookie W. Stephan and Judy Corder (1985) have found that adolescents from dual-earner families are less stereotypic than adolescents from single-earner families. ("The Effects of Dual-Career Families on Adolescents' Sex-Role Attitudes, Work and Family Plans, and Choices of Important Others," *Journal of Marriage and the Family* 47, 321–29.) Also, female college students whose mothers have worked since they were young were less stereotypically feminine, by their own account, than others. (See: Andrey E. Tolman, Kristina A. Diekmann, and Kathleen McCartney [1989], "Social Connectedness and Mothering: Effects of Maternal Employment and Maternal Absence," *Journal of Personality and Social Psychology* 56, 942–49.) Of course, times change and maternal employment is more acceptable today than in the past and sex-role stereotyping is becoming less rigid than in the past. On the later point see: Nancy L. Galambos, Anne C. Petersen, and Kathleen Lenerz (1988), "Maternal Employment and Sex Typing in Early Adolescence: Contemporaneous and Longitudinal Relations," in Adele Gottfried and Allen Gottfried, eds., *Maternal Employment,* 155–89. Finally, for evidence that children in dual-career families are less stereotyped in their behavior (specifically, in the household

tasks they perform), see: Susan M. McHale, W. Todd Bartko, Ann C. Coater, and Maureen Petty-Jenkins (n.d.), "Children's Household Work and Psychological Functioning, *Child Development* forthcoming.

78. See: (1) Bonnie E. Carson (1984), "The Father's Contribution to Child Care: Effects on Children's Perceptions of Parental Roles," *American Journal of Orthopsychiatry* 54, 123–36; (2) Norma Radin (1982), "Primary Caregiving and Role-Sharing Fathers," in M. E. Lamb, ed., *Nontraditional Families and Child Development,* 173–204; (3) Norma Rading and Graeme Russell (1983), "Increased Father Participation and Child Development Outcomes," in Michael E. Lamb and Abraham Sagi, eds., *Fatherhood and Family Policy,* 191–218 (Hillsdale, N.J.: Erlbaum).

79. Norman Bell and Ezra Vogel, eds. (1968), *A Modern Introduction to the Family,* rev. ed. (New York: Free Press). The passage appears on p. 586.

80. David McClelland (1961), *The Achieving Society* (New York: Free Press).

81. Ann C. Crouter, Shelley M. MacDermed, Susan M. McHale, and Maureen Perry-Jenkins (n.d.), "Parental Monitoring and Perceptions of Children's School Performance and Conduct in Dual- and Single-Earner Families," *Developmental Psychology,* forthcoming.

82. Janet Reis and Roger Burton (1984), "Maternal Employment and Child Socialization Practices: An Intercultural Test of Cross-Cultural Theory," *Journal of Comparative Family Studies* 15, 1–16.

83. Howard Hayghe (1978), "Marital and Family Characteristics of Workers," *Monthly Labor Review* 3, March 1977, 51–54.

84. U.S. Department of Labor (1980), *Perspectives on Working Woman. A Databook.* Bulletin 2080 (Washington, D.C.: Bureau of Labor Statistics).

85. Howard Hayghe (1982), "Dual-Career Families. Their Economics and Demographic Characteristics," in Joan Aldous, ed., *Two Paychecks. Life in Dual-Earner Families,* 27–40 (Beverly Hills, Calif.: Sage).

86. Leonard Silk (1989), "Rich and Poor: The Gap Widens," *New York Times,* May 12, p. D2.

87. Helen Axel (1988), "Playing Catch-Up," *Across the Board* 25, 30–31. Also see table 1 in Kristin Moore, Daphne Spain, and Suzanne Bianchi (1984), "Working Wives and Mothers," *Marriage and Family Reviews* 7, 77–98.

88. Census Bureau, U.S. Department of Commerce (1980), *American Families and Living Arrangements* (Washington, D.C.: Goverment Printing Office). Letha Scanzoni and John Scanzoni (1976), *Men, Women and Change: A Sociology of Marriage and Family* (New York: McGraw-Hill). See also Caroline Bird (1979), *The Two-Paycheck Marriage. How Women at Work Are Changing Life in America* (New York: Rawson, Wade Publishers). See especially pages 229–30.

89. Srully Blotnick (1985), *Otherwise Engaged. The Private Lives of Successful Career Women* (New York: Facts on File). In a recent survey of female graduates of a midwestern university, young women were more likely than

older women to say that they would not have children. Most women seemed interested in careers, and the young women did not seem to wish to allow children to interfere with careers. (See Marsha Katz [1988], "Have Women's Career and Family Values Changed?" in Suzanna Rose and Laurie Larwood, eds., *Women's Careers. Pathways and Pitfalls*, 95–104 (New York: Praeger).

90. Martha Minow, quoted in Elizabeth Spelman, *Inessential Woman*, 57.

CHAPTER 6: AH, MEN

1. Carol Orsborn (1986), *Enough Is Enough. Exploding the Myth of Having It All* (New York: Putnam's), 30.

2. Beth Vanfossen (1981) found that instrumental support from husbands reduced the impact that role overload had on depression. In a sample of employed women, those who felt overwhelmed suffered less if they believed that they could count on their husbands for help with family problems. Overloaded women unsure of husband's support had higher rates of depression. See: "Sex Differences in the Mental Health Effects of Spouse Support and Equity," *Journal of Health and Social Behavior* 22, 130–43.

3. Rena Repetti (1987) reported that women bank workers' ratings of strong familly cohesion, an indicator of support, were associated with perceptions of a more positive social climate at work. See: "Linkages between Work and Family Roles," in Stuart Oskamp, ed., *Applied Social Psychology Annual 7, Family Processes and Problems*, 98–127 (Beverly Hills, Calif.: Sage).

4. Janet G. Hunt and Larry L. Hunt (1987), "Male Resistance in Dual-Earner Households. Three Alternative Explanation," in Naomi Gerstel and Harriet Engel Gross, eds., *Families and Work*, 192–203 (Philadelphia: Temple University Press). On page 192, they note: "The news about men in dual-earner households, which has been out for some time, has inspired little intellectual curiosity. . . . Male resistance, in short, has been treated as basically not interesting and not legitimate."

5. In two engrossing documentary films entitled *Love Stories: Women, Men* and *Romance and Men* a number of men speak their minds freely. They believe that women's liberation has stripped them of their rights and made life very difficult. (Both films are directed by Richard Broadman and produced by Richard Broadman, John Grady, Judith Smith, and Kersti Yllo. See also Barbara Ehrenreich (1983), *The Hearts of Men. American Dreams and the Flight from Commitment* (Garden City, N.Y.: Doubleday).

6. For a scholarly and well-reasoned presentation of the view that men have been impediments to progress, see Peggy Thoits (1987), "Negotiating Roles," in Faye J. Crosby, ed., *Spouse, Parent, Worker: On Gender and Multiple Roles*, 11–22 (New Haven, Conn.: Yale University Press).

7. Dylan Thomas (1965), *Under Milk Wood. A Play for Voices* (New York: New Directions), 52, the fourth woman declares "Men are brutes on the quiet."

8. Here again we come to the issue of whether or not women and men are

quintessentially different. Many reasonable feminists argue compellingly that women and men differ little from each other in basic personality styles. Women behave "like men" when they are placed in stereotypically male situations and men behave "like women" when they find themselves in stereotypically female situations. A good collection of essays on the topic occurs in the book, *Making a Difference, Psychology and the Construction of Gender*, edited by Rachel T. Hare-Mustin and Jeanne Maracek and published in 1990 by Yale University Press.

9. Catherine E. Ross, John Mirowsky, and Joan Huber (1983), "Dividing Work, Sharing Work, and In-Between: Marriage Patterns and Depression," *American Sociological Review* 48, 809–23. Also see: Patricia M. Ulbrich (1988), "The Determinants of Depression in Two-Income Marriages," *Journal of Marriage and the Family* 50, 121–31.

10. Rena L. Repetti (1987), "Family Process and Problems: Social Psychological Aspects," *Applied Social Psychology Annual* 7, 98–127.

11. Joan Huber and Glenna Spitze (1983), *Sex Stratification, Children, Housework, and Jobs* (New York: Academic Press), 221.

12. Teresa L. Jump and Linda Haas (1987), "Fathers in Transition: Dual-Career Fathers Participating in Child Care," in Michael S. Kimmel, ed., *Changing Men: New Directions in Research on Men and Masculinity*, 98–114 (Newbury Park, Calif.: Sage).

13. Shelly Coverman and Joseph F. Sheley (1986), "Change in Men's Housework and Child-Care Time, 1965–1975," *Journal of Marriage and the Family* 48, 413–22. For further confirmation of the lack of change in men's participation in family labor, see: (1) Catherine W. Berheide (1984), "Women's Work in the Home: Seems Like Old Times," *Marriage and Family Review* 7, 37–55; (2) Sharon Y. Nickols and Edward J. Metzen (1982), "Impact of Wife's Employment upon Husband's Housework," *Journal of Family Issues* 3, 199–216; (3) Glenna Sitze (1986), "The Division of Task Responsibility in U.S. Households: Longitudinal Adjustments to Change." *Social Forces* 64, 689–701. In a national probability sample interviewed in 1974, furthermore, husbands in dual-earner families contributed nine minutes more per day to housework than did husbands in single-earner families but saved nine minutes per day in total work time (housework plus paid work). Meanwhile, wives in dual-earner families spent three hours more per day in total work time than did wives in single-earner families. See: Michael Geerken and Walter R. Gove (1983), *At Home and at Work. The Family's Allocation of Labor* (Beverly Hills, Calif.: Sage).

14. Elizabeth Maret and Barbara Finlay (1984), "The Distribution of Household Labor among Women in Dual-Earner Families," *Journal of Marriage and the Family* 46, 357–64. For a review of several additional studies, see: Chaya S. Piotrokowski and Rena L. Repetti (1984), "Dual-Earner Families," *Marriage and Family Review* 7, 99–124. More recent studies include: Joni Hersch (1985), "Effects of Housework on Earnings of Husbands and Wives: Evidence from Full-Time Piece Rate Workers," *Social Science Quar-*

terly 66, 210–17. Karen Seccombe (1986), "The Effects of Occupational Conditions upon the Division of Household Labor: An Application of Kohn's Theory," *Journal of Marriage and the Family* 48, 839–48.

15. Sarah Fenstermaker Berk (1985), *The Gender Factory. The Apportionment of Work in American Households* (New York: Plenum).

16. Joseph H. Pleck (1985), *Working Wives/Working Husbands* (Beverly Hills, Calif.: Sage). Harriet Presser found that the major factor leading fathers to be primary child care providers during wives' working hours is not paternal unemployment, but husbands and wives working different shifts. See Harriet B. Presser (1988), "Shift Work and Child Care among Dual-Earner American Parents," *Journal of Marriage and the Family* 50, 3–14.

17. J. Beckett and A. Smith (1981), "Work and Family Roles: Egalitarian Marriage in Black and White Families," *Social Service Review* 55, 314–26. Cited in Bonnie E. Carlson (1984), "The Father's Contribution to Child Care," *American Journal of Orthopsychiatry* 54, 123–36.

18. Maureen Mahoney (1987), "Supports for New Mothers" (Paper presented at the International Council of Psychologists, New York, New York, August).

19. Berk, *The Gender Factory*.

20. Pleck, *Working Wives/Working Husbands*.

21. Jay Belsky and Brenda L. Volling (1987), "Mothering, Fathering, and Marital Interaction in the Family Triad during Infancy," in Phyllis W. Berman and Frank A. Pedersen, eds., *Men's Transitions to Parenthood: Longitudinal Studies of Early Family Experience*, 37–63 (Hillsdale, N.J.: Erlbaum).

22. Linda Nyquist, Karla Slivken, Janet T. Spence, and Robert L. Helmreich (1985), "Household Responsibilities in Middle-Class Couples: The Contribution of Demographic and Personality Variables," *Sex Roles 12,* 15–34.

23. Keith M. Kilty and Virginia Richardson (1985), "The Impact of Gender on Productive and Social Activities," *Journal of Sociology and Social Welfare* 12, 162–85. Also relevant is the finding that a man's job involvement and his identification with the employer (organization) is less among men married to working women than among men married to housewives. (See: Sam Gould and James D. Werbel [1983], "Work Involvement: A Comparison of Dual Wage Earner and Single Wage Earner Families," *Journal of Applied Psychology* 68, 313–19.)

24. Grace K. Baruch and Rosalind C. Barnett (1981), "Fathers' Participation in the Care of Their Preschool Children," *Sex Roles* 7, 1043–55. Bonnie Carlson (1984), "The Father's Contribution to Child Care." B. Shelton found that increase in domestic work was relatively greater among younger husbands and those with egalitarian sex role attitudes. See: B. A. Shelton (1989), " 'Real' change or Pseudo Change? Sources of Change in Men's and Women's Domestic Labor Time, 1975–1981," (State University of New York at Buffalo). Cited in: Joseph Pleck (August 1990), "Family-Supportive Employer Policies: Are They Relevant to Men?" (Proceedings of

the 98th Annual Convention of the American Psychological Association). Perceptions can be as important as reality. Sara Yogev and Jeanne Brett found that husbands and wives were more likely to be satisfied with their marriage if they perceive their spouse as doing more than his or her share of child care or housework, even if the actual time spent in such tasks varies from minutes to hours. See Sara Yogev and Jeanne Brett (1983), "Patterns of Work and Family Involvement among Single- and Dual-Earner Couples: Two Competing Analytical Approaches." (Washington, D.C.: Office of Naval Research). Cited in Ellen Gralinsky (1986), "Family Life and Corporate Policies," in Michael W. Yogman and T. Berry Brazelton, eds., *In Support of Families*, 109–45 (Cambridge, Mass.: Harvard University Press).

25. Carol-Ann Emmons, Monica Biernet, Linde Beth Tiedje, Eric L. Lang, and Camille B. Wortman (1990), "Stress, Support, and Coping among Women Professionals with Preschool Children," in John Eckenrode and Susan Gore, eds., *Stress between Work and Family*, 61–93 (New York: Plenum).

26. *New York Times*. August 21, 1989. p. A14.

27. Mexican wives, for example, do more housework than Americans: Catherine A. Ross, John Mirowski, and Patricia Ulbrich (1983), "Distress and the Traditional Female Role: A Comparison of Mexicans and Anglos," *American Journal of Sociology* 89, 670–82.

28. Carol C. Nadelson and Theodore Nadelson (1980), "Dual-Career Marriages: Benefits and Costs," in Fran Pepitone-Rockwell, ed., *Dual-Career Couples*, 91–109 (Beverly Hills, Calif.: Sage).

29. Berk, *The Gender Factory*, 209.

30. Camille Wortman and Darrin R. Lehman (1985) found that ineptly provided support may exacerbate rather than alleviate the recipient's feelings of distress. See: "Reactions to Victims of Life Crises: Support Attempts that Fail," in Irvin G. Sarason and Barbara R. Sarason, eds., *Social Support: Theory, Research, and Applications*, 463–89 (Dordrecht, the Netherlands: Martinus Nijhoff).

31. Lucia Albino Gilbert (1985), *Men in Dual-Career Families: Current Realities and Future Prospects* (Hillsdale, N.J.: Erlbaum), 52.

32. The seminal article was written by E. E. LeMasters (1957), "Parenthood as Crisis," *Marriage and Family Living* 19, 352–55. Recent studies are much more sophisticated, but they show the same results. Here is a list of some of the recent studies: (1) Darla Rhyne (1981), "Bases of Marital Satisfaction among Men and Women," *Journal of Marriage and the Family 43*, 941–55; (2) Holly Waldron and Donald K. Routh (1981), "The Effect of the First Child on the Marital Relationship," *Journal of Marriage and the Family* 43, 785–88; (3) Norvald D. Glenn and Sara McLanahan (1982), "Children and Marital Happiness: A Further Specification of the Relationship," *Journal of Marriage and the Family* 44, 63–72; (4) Karen A. Polonko, John Scanzoni, and Jay D. Teachman (1982), "Childlessness and Marital Satisfaction: A Further Assessment," *Journal of Family Issues* 3, 545–73; (5) Jay Belsky, Graham B. Spanier, and Michael Rovine (1983), "Stability and

Change in Marriage across the Transition to Parenthood," *Journal of Marriage and the Family* 45, 567–77; (6) Jay Belsky, Mary Lang, and Michael Rovine (1985), "Stability and Change in Marriage across the Transition to Parenthood: A Second Study," *Journal of Marriage and the Family* 47, 855–65.

It is important to keep in mind that marital satisfaction is not synonymous with life satisfaction or happiness. The birth of a child causes most people to feel more dissatisfied with marriage than before, but the birth of a child also brings happiness and life satisfaction to most people. See Steven L. Nock (1981), "Family Life-Cycle Transitions: Longitudinal Effects on Family Members," *Journal of Marriage and the Family* 43, 703–14.

33. Gloria Norris and Jo Ann Miller (1984), *The Working Mother's Complete Handbook* (New York: New American Library). The quotation is from p. 247.

34. Other researchers have noted the same patterns. See, for example: Erica Wimbush (1987), "Transitions: Changing Work, Leisure and Health Experiences among Mothers with Young Children," in Patricia Allatt, Teresa Keil, Alan Bryman, and Bill Bytheway, eds., *Women and the Life Cycle: Transitions and Turning-Points,* 149–63 (New York: St. Martin's Press).

35. Michael R. Frone and Robert W. Rice (1987), "Work-Family Conflict: The Effect of Job and Family Involvement," *Journal of Occupational Behavior* 8, 45–53.

36. Dafna Izraeli and Naomi Silman (1990), "Wives Who Earn Less, Equal, and More Than Their Husbands" (Paper presented at the Fourth International Interdisciplinary Conference on Women, New York, New York, June).

37. Henriette Faraggi is quoted on p. 168 of Sylvia F. Fava and Rosalie G. Genovese (1983), "Family, Work, and Individual Development in Dual-Career Marriages: Issues for Research," *Research in the Interweave of Social Roles* 3, 163–85. Ridley found that the ease with which family and work roles were integrated by members of dual-career families influenced the extent of their perceived career salience and career commitment. Carl A. Ridley (1973), "Exploring the Impact of Work Satisfaction and Involvement on Marital Interaction When Both Partners Are Employed," *Journal of Marriage and the Family* 35, no. 2, 229–44.

38. An insightful and poignant account of the discrepancy between rhetoric and reality appears in *The Second Shift: Working Parents and the Revolution at Home* (New York: Viking). Written by Arlie Hochschild with the help of Anne Machung, the book chronicles how we have adopted a rhetoric of role redefinition when, in fact, all that has happened in most families is a kind of role-expansion. Domestic tasks are only one issue to produce family frictions. See: Carol Rubin and Jeff Rubin (1989), *When Families Fight: How to Handle Conflict with Those You Love* (New York: Morrow). For a quick overview of their work on family conflicts, see their article in the December 1988 issue of *Psychology Today.*

39. Robert Kuttner (1989), "She Minds the Child, He Minds the Dog," *New York Times Book Review,* June 25, p. 3 and p. 26.

40. Of course, every wife sees reality differently, and the realities we see depend on our expectations. A study by Suzanne Allen and Richard Kalish found that women who are married when they are between 25 and 29 years old had significantly greater expectations for an egalitarian marriage than the women who married younger. See: Suzanne M. Allen and Richard A. Kalish (1984), "Professional Women and Marriage," *Journal of Marriage and the Family* 46, 375–82.

41. Nancy Newhouse, ed. (1985), *Hers: Through Women's Eyes* (New York: Billard Books).

42. Anna Quindlen, "Off on an Adventure: Living Life, Unexamined," *New York Times,* December 1, 1988, p. C1.

43. Several studies have found that women and men differ in their estimates of how much time they and their spouses spend in domestic labor, with each side underestimating the efforts of the other. See: (1) John G. Condran and Jerry G. Bode (1982), "Rashomon, Working Wives, and Family Division of Labor: Middletown, 1980," *Journal of Marriage and the Family* 44, 421–27; (2) Michael Geerken and Walter R. Gove (1983), *At Home and at Work,* especially p. 95; (3) Patrick C. McKenry, Sharon J. Price, Philip B. Gordon, and Nancy M. Rudd (1986), "Characteristics of Husbands' Family Work and Wives' Labor Force Involvement," in Robert A. Lewis and Robert E. Salt, eds., *Men in Families,* 73–83 (Beverly Hills, Calif.: Sage); (4) New York Times Poll. *New York Times,* August 21, 1989, p. A14. And at least one investigator has documented how men remain blind to the work of their wives: Aafke Komter (1989), "Hidden Power in Marriage," *Gender and Society* 3, 187–216.

44. Graham L. Staines with Pam L. Libby (1986), "Men and Women in Role Relationships," in Richard D. Ashmore and Frances K. DelBoca, eds., *The Social Psychology of Female-Male Relations,* 211–58 (New York: Academic Press). See especially, p. 226.

45. Laurie Chassin, Antonette Zeiss, Kristina Cooper, Judith Reaven (1985), "Role Perception, Self-Role Congruence and Marital Satisfaction in Dual-Worker Couples with Preschool Children," *Social Psychology Quarterly* 48, 301–11.

46. Robert S. Weiss (1987), "Men and Their Wives Work," in Faye J. Crosby, ed., *Spouse, Parent, Worker,* 109–21. The quotation appears on p. 115.

47. Ibid, 120.

48. Komter, "Hidden power."

49. For a discussion of the genetic argument, see Eleanor Maccoby (1990), "Gender and Relationships: A Developmental Account," *American Psychologist* 45, 513–20.

50. May Sarton (1980), "Entry for Tuesday, February 20, 1979," *Recovering: A Journal* (New York: W. W. Norton), 60.

51. Marjorie L. deVault (1987), "Doing Housework: Feeding and Family Life," in Naomi Gerstel and Harriet Engel Gross, eds., *Families and Work*, 178–91.

52. *New York Times*, June 14, 1989, p. D25.

53. *New York Times*, March 27, 1990, p. C4.

54. The lack of an available wife may even cut a man's productivity. Men with Ph.D.s publish fewer articles and hold fewer professional offices if they are married to women with Ph.D.s than if they are married to less educated women, possibly because the Ph.D. wives have careers of their own. See: Marianne Ferber and Joan Huber (1979), "Husbands, Wives, and Careers," *Journal of Marriage and the Family* 41, 315–25.

55. Martha R. Fowlkes (1987), "The Myth of Merit and Male Professional Careers: The Roles of Wives," in Naomi Gerstel and Harriet Engel Gross, eds., *Families and Work*, 347–60.

56. Martha Fowlkes (1980), *Behind Every Successful Man* (New York: Columbia University Press), 173.

57. Ibid., 174

58. Ibid.

59. Lisa R. Silberstein (1986), *Dual-Career Couples: A System in Transition*. (Ph.D. diss., Yale University).

60. Sandra C. Stanley, Janet G. Hunt, and Larry L. Hunt (1986), "The Relative Deprivation of Husbands in Dual-Earner Households," *Journal of Family Issues* 7, 3–20.

61. Roald Dahl (1970), *Fantastic Mr. Fox* (New York: Bantam Skylark), 16–17.

62. For the original thought piece, see: Jessie Bernard (1981), "The Good-Provider Role: Its Rise and Fall," *American Psychologist* 36, 1–12. For an historical overview and a contemporary analysis of the provider role, also see: (1) Jane C. Hood (1986), "The Provider Role: Its Meaning and Measurement," *Journal of Marriage and the Family* 48, 349–59; (2) Clyde W. Franklin II (1984), *The Changing Definition of Masculinity* (New York: Plenum). Recent studies show that men who are attached to the provider role are less happy than other men about performing household labor. See Maureen Perry-Jenkins and Ann C. Crouter (n.d.), "Implications of Men's Provider Role Attitudes for Household Work and Marital Satisfaction," *Journal of Family Issues*. In press.

63. Barbara A. Gutek, Rena L. Repetti, and Deborah L. Silber (1988), "Nonwork Roles and Stress at Work," in Cary L. Cooper and Roy Payne, eds., *Causes, Coping, and Consequences of Stress at Work* 141–74 (New York: John Wiley & Sons).

64. Noel A. Cazenave and George H. Leon (1987), "Men's Work and Family Roles and Characteristics: Race, Gender, and Class Perceptions of College Students," in Michael S. Kimmel, ed., *Changing Men*, 244–62. Interestingly, more black college men than white college men report that they would feel threatened by having a wife earn more than they themselves did.

65. Caroline New and Miriam David (1985), *For the Children's Sake* (London: Penguin Books). The study is cited on p. 217.

66. For an account of the methods, see: Faye J. Crosby (1990), "Divorce and Work Life among Women Managers," in Nia L. Chester and Hildy Grossman, eds., *The Experience and Meaning of Work in Women's Lives,* 121–42 (Hillsdale, N.J.: Erlbaum). In a similar vein, Joseph H. Pleck and Linda Lang (1978) find that men's psychological involvement in their families promotes their own mental health. ("Men's Family Role: Its Nature and Consequences," *Working Paper 10,* Wellesley Center for Research on Women.) A beautiful analysis of men's family roles, and how they relate to work life outside the family, is done by Joseph H. Pleck (1983), "Husbands' Work and Family Roles: Current Research Issues," *Research on the Interweave of Social Roles* 3, 251–333.

67. Graham L. Staines, Kathleen J. Pottick, and Deborah A. Fudge (1986), "Wives' Employment and Husbands' Attitudes toward Work and Life," *Journal of Applied Psychology* 71, 118–28.

68. Kathleen M. Barker (1990), "Work and Home" (Paper presented at the Fourth International Interdisciplinary Conference on Women, New York, New York, June).

69. Robert E. Gould (1974), "Measuring Masculinity by the Size of a Paycheck," in Joseph H. Pleck and Jack Sawyer, eds., *Men and Masculinity,* 96–100 (Englewood Cliffs, N.J.: Prentice-Hall Spectrum). The quoted section appears on p. 98.

70. Virginia Woolf (1938/1984). *Three Guineas* (London: Hogarth Press).

71. Huber and Spitze, *Sex Stratification.* The wives did not report a difference.

72. Janice M. Steil and Beth A. Turetsky (1987), "Marital Influence Levels and Symptomology among Wives," in Faye J. Crosby, ed., *Spouse, Parent, Worker,* 74–90. Another measure of power—freedom from domestic tasks—showed the same pattern. Among couples that considered the wife's career to be of equal or greater importance than the husbands' career, Steil and Turetsky did not find that men increased their household labor. See also: Janice M. Steil and Karen Weltman (1991), "Marital Inequality: The Importance of Resources, Personal Attributes, and Social Norms on Career Valuing and the Allocation of Domestic Responsibilities," *Sex Roles, 24,* 161–79.

73. Pat M. Keith and Robert B. Schafer (1985), "Role Behavior, Relative Deprivation, and Depression among Women in One- and Two-Job Families," *Family Relations* 34, 227–33.

74. David C. Bell, Janet Saltzman Chafetz, and Lori Heggem Horn (1982), "Marital Conflict Resolution. A Study of Strategies and Outcomes," *Journal of Family Issues* 3, 111–32.

75. See Sue J. M. Freeman (1990), *Managing Lives: Corporate Women and Social Change* (Amherst: University of Massachusetts Press). The quotation appears on p. 149.

76. B. F. Skinner (1971), *Beyond Freedom and Dignity* (New York: Knopf).

77. Jesse Geller (1990), " 'That's Interesting'—Reflections on the Sleepy Therapist" (Invited Address at the Eastern Psychological Association, Philadelphia, April).

78. In fact, forcing a verbal disclosure is opposite to creating a feeling of synchrony. As to whether expressive or instrumental support is more typical of some husbands or others, see: Harry Brod (1990), "A Better Class of Men," *Gender and Society* 4, 251–53. Also: J. Jill Suitor (1990), "The Importance of Emotional Support in the Face of Stressful Status Transitions: A Response to Brod," *Gender and Society* 4, 254–57.

79. Nadelson and Nadelson, "Dual-career marriages."

80. Silberstein, *Dual-Career Couples,* 52.

81. Ibid., 226.

82. Ibid.

83. Robert S. Weiss (1990), *Staying the Course: The Emotional and Social Lives of Men Who Do Well at Work* (New York: Free Press). The quotation appears on p. 135.

84. I was able to locate nearly a dozen studies published in the 1980s in which the husbands of working women were compared with the husbands of housewives on some measure of mental health. One of the studies divided its sample into childless couples and others and another limited their sample to couples with children. Neither of these studies found differences between the two groups of husbands. More specifically, Keith and Schafer found no group differences in self-esteem or depression and House found no group differences in well-being. See: (1) Pat M. Keith and Robert B. Schafer (1984), "Role Behavior and Psychological Well-Being: A Comparison of Men in One-Job and Two-Job Families," *American Journal of Orthopsychiatry* 54, 137–45; (2) Elizabeth A. House (1986), "Sex Role Orientation and Marital Satisfaction in Dual- and One-Provider Couples," *Sex Roles* 14, 245–59. Five other studies showed no effects. More specifically, reviewing and reanalyzing a set of earlier studies, Fendrich found no group differences for well-being, self-esteem, and depression. (See Michael Fendrich [1984], "Wives' Employment and Husbands' Distress: A Meta-analysis and a Replication," *Journal of Marriage and the Family* 46, 871–79.) Ross, Mirowski, and Huber found no differences in depression. (See Catherine E. Ross, John Mirowsky, and Joan Huber [1983], "Dividing Work, Sharing Work, and In-between"). Benin and Niedstedt looked at national data for 1978, 1980, 1982, and 1983 and found happiness the same among husbands of housewives and husbands of working wives. (See: Mary Holland Benin and Barbara Cable Nienstedt [1985], "Happiness in Single- and Dual-Earner Families: The Effects of Marital Happiness, Job Satisfaction, and Life Cycle," *Journal of Marriage and the Family* 47, 975–84). Billings and Moos contacted about 500 families and found no differences in the levels of psychological distress reported by husbands

of working wives and husbands of at-home wives. (See: Andrew G. Billings and Rudolf H. Moos [1982], "Work Stress and Stress-Buffering Roles of Work and Family Resources," *Journal of Occupational Behavior* 3, 215–32.) Finally, Locksley found no differences in marital adjustment. (See: Anne Locksley [1980], "On the Effects of Wives' Employment on Marital Adjustment and Companionship," *Journal of Marriage and the Family* 42, 337–46.) On the other hand, four studies—some of them with old samples—did find a difference on various measures, always in favor of the husbands of housewives. See: (1) Sarah Rosenfield (1980), "Sex Differences in Depression: Do Women Always Have Higher Rates?" *Journal of Health and Social Behavior* 21, 33–42; (2) Graham L. Staines, Kathleen J. Pottick, and Deborah A. Fudge (1986), "Wives' Employment and Husbands' Attitudes toward Work and Life, *Journal of Applied Psychology* 71, 118–28. (Some of the findings in Staines, Pottick, and Fudge are also presented in "The Effects of Wives' Employment on Husbands' Job and Life Satisfaction," *Psychology of Women Quarterly* 9 (1985), 419–24. Yet another report on the same data appears in Sandra C. Stanley, Janet G. Hunt, and Larry L. Hunt [1986], "The Relative Deprivation of Husbands.") (3) Catherine A. Ross, John Mirowski, and Patricia Ulbrich (1983), "Distress and the Traditional Female Role"; (4) Ronald C. Kessler and James A. McRae, Jr. (1982), "The Effect of Wives' Employment on the Mental Health of Married Men and Women," *American Sociological Review* 47, 216–27. Finally, one study looked at marital satisfaction among husbands of mothers and husbands of nonmothers and found the former to be better off. (See: Karen A. Polonko, John Scanzoni, and Jay D. Teachman [1982], "Childlessness and marital satisfaction.")

Older studies did seem more aware of the importance of children. For a beautiful review, see: Joseph H. Pleck (1983), "Husbands' work and family roles."

85. Rosalind C. Barnett and Grace K. Baruch (1987). "Mothers' Participation in Childcare: Patterns and Consequences," in Faye J. Crosby, ed., *Spouse, Parent, Worker*, 91–108.

86. Silberstein, *Dual-Career Couples*, 68. On the issue of how younger and older men react to changes in the rules, see the provocative analyses of Joseph H. Pleck, Michael E. Lamb, and James A. Levine (1986), "Epilog: Facilitating Future Change in Men's Family Roles," in Robert A. Lewis and Marvin B. Sussman, eds., *Men's Changing Roles in the Family*, 11–16 (New York: Haworth).

87. Lisa Wenner (1988), "Breast-Feeding and Coparenting," (Northampton, Mass.: Smith College).

88. The study by Thomas, Abrecht, and White was presented in 1982 at the American Psychological Association annual meeting. It is cited by Lucia Albino Gilbert (1985), *Men in Dual-Career Families*.

89. Gilbert, *Men in Dual-Career Families*, 50.

90. Few studies, for example, simultaneously take into account the wife's

employment status and the presence or absence of dependent children in the home. See footnote 75.

91. On this point, see the insightful observations of Rosalind C. Barnett and Grace K. Baruch (1987), "Mothers' Participation in Childcare."

92. Peter Willmott and Michael Young (1974), *The Symmetrical Family* (New York: Pantheon Books). In contrast, see: Talcott Parsons (1951), *The Social System*. (Glencoe, Ill: Free Press).

93. And imbalances in material resources make the resentments deeper. See: Aafke Komter (1989), "Hidden Power in Marriage."

94. Sara Yogev (1981), "Do Professional Women Have Egalitarian Relationships?" *Journal of Marriage and the Family* 43, 865–71. The quotation appears on p. 867.

95. Rosanna Hertz (1986), *More Equal than Others: Women and Men in Dual-Career Marriages* (Berkeley: University of California Press), 80–81.

96. Ibid., 80.

97. Cynthia Fuchs Epstein (1987), "Multiple Demands and Multiple Roles," in Faye J. Crosby, ed., *Spouse, Parent, Worker*, 23–35. And Cynthia Fuchs Epstein (1981), *Women in Law* (New York: Basic Books).

98. Gilbert, *Men in Dual-Career Families*. Lisa Silberstein and Rosanna Hertz also document how some men feel liberated from having to play the provider role.

99. Samuel Osherson and Diana Dill (1983), "Varying Work and Family Choices: Their Impact on Men's Work Satisfaction," *Journal of Marriage and the Family* 45, 339–46.

100. Ross Parke (1981), *Fathers*. (Cambridge, Mass.: Harvard University Press). Also see Michael E. Lamb, ed. (1982), *Nontraditional Families: Parenting and Child Development* (Hillsdale, N.J.: Erlbaum). Especially relevant in the book are the chapters by Lamb, Frodi, Hwang, and Frodi; by Russel; by Radin; and by Sagi. Other insights into the new husband and father occur in: Theodore F. Cohen (1987), "Remaking Men: Men's Experiences Becoming and Being Husbands and Fathers and Their Implications for Reconceptualizing Men's Lives," *Journal of Family Issues* 8, 57–77.

101. Silberstein, *Dual-Career Couples*, 8.

102. Jump and Haas, "Fathers in transition."

103. Gilbert, *Men in Dual-Career Families*, 78.

104. Diane Ehrensaft (1987), *Parenting Together. Men and Women Sharing the Care of Their Children* (New York: Free Press). The quotations appear on pp. 119–20.

105. Ehrenreich, *The Hearts of Men*, 181–82.

CHAPTER 7: THE METAPHORS DECONSTRUCTED

1. Values are changing rapidly. The housewife role used to be revered, albeit with ambivalence. The occupation "housewife" is no longer given much respect. See: Claire Etaugh and Barbara Petroski (1985), "Perceptions

of Women: Effects of Employment Status and Marital Status," *Sex Roles* 12, 329–39. Also see: Arlene Kaplan Daniels (1985), *Invisible Careers: Women Civic Leaders from the Volunteer World* (Chicago: University of Chicago Press); and Myra Marx Ferree (1987), "Family and Job for Working-Class Women: Gender and Class Systems Seen from Below," in Naomi Gerstel and Harriet Gross, eds., *Families and Work,* 289–301 (Philadelphia: Temple University Press).

2. Carole K. Holahan and Lucia A. Gilbert (1979), "Interrole Conflict of Working Women: Careers versus Jobs," *Journal of Applied Psychology* 64, 86–90.

3. Rosalind C. Barnett and Grace K. Baruch (1987), "Social Roles, Gender, and Psychological Distress," in Rosalind C. Barnett, Lois Biener, and Grace K. Baruch eds., *Gender and Stress,* 122–43 (New York: Free Press). The passage appears on p. 133.

4. For a discussion of the changing views and opinions of most Americans, see chapter 2, pp. 20–58.

5. Jennifer Kaylin (1988), "Girls Just Wanna Have . . ." *The New Haven Advocate,* July 11, p. 6.

6. See chapter 6, pp. 146–82.

7. Joanne Martin (1990), "Deconstructing Organizational Taboos: The Suppression of Gender Conflict in Organizations," *Organization Science,* 1(4), 339–59.

8. It is interesting to note, parenthetically, that pregnancy disabilities may not cause nearly as many problems for American commerce and industry as heart attacks. In our country, 135 million staff days are lost per year to heart attacks and 27 million work days are lost due to cardiovascular problems. At every age, males exceed females in frequency and severity of heart problems.

9. Marian Swerdlow (1989), "Men's Accommodations to Women Entering a Nontraditional Occupation: A Case of Rapid Transit Operatives," *Gender and Society* 3, 383–87. The passage appears on p. 374.

10. Anne Machung's study is cited on page 266 of Arlie Hochschild with Anne Machung (1989), *The Second Shift: Working Parents and the Revolution at Home* (New York: Viking).

11. Patricia Yancey Martin, Sandra Seymour, Myrna Courage, Karolun Godbey, and Richard Tate (1988), "Work-Family Policies: Corporate, Union, Feminist, and Pro-Family Leaders' Views," *Gender and Society* 2, 385–400.

12. For a fascinating critique of the conservative point of view, see: Michael E. Lamb (1982), "Maternal employment and child development: A review," in Michael E. Lamb ed., *Nontraditional Families: Parenting and Child Development,* 47–69 (Hillsdale, N.J.: Erlbaum).

13. Ellen Galinsky (1986), "Contemporary Patterns of Child Care," in Nina Gunzenhauser and Bettye M. Caldwell, eds., *Group Care for Young Children,* 13–24 (New York: Johnson and Johnson Baby Products). The quotations are on p. 21.

14. Ellen Hock, M. Therese Gnezda, and Susan McBride (1984), "Mothers of Infants: Attitudes Toward Employment and Motherhood Following Birth of the First Child," *Journal of Marriage and the Family* 46, 425–31.

15. Julia Brannen (1987), "The Resumption of Employment after Childbirth: A Turning-Point within a Life-Course Perspective," in Patricia Allatt, Teresa Keil, Alan Bryman, and Bill Bytheway, eds., *Women and the Life Cycle,* 164–77 (New York: St. Martin's Press).

16. The bottleneck concept comes from Rhona Rapoport and Robert N. Rapoport (1982), "The Next Generation in Dual-Career Family Research," in Joan Aldons ed., *Two Paychecks. Life in Dual-Earner Families,* 229–43 (Beverly Hills, Calif.: Sage). See also: Joseph H. Pleck (1983), "Husband's Paid Work and Family Roles: Current Research Issues," in Helen Lopata and Joseph H. Pleck, eds., *Research in the Interweave of Social Roles: Families and Jobs,* vol. 3, 251–333 (Greenwich, Conn.: JAI Press).

17. Rose L. Coser and Gerald Rokoff (1971), "Women in the Occupational World: Social Disruption and Conflict," *Social Problems* 18, 535–54.

18. Josef Wendel, William Konnert, and Charles Foreman (1986), "Home Schooling and Compulsory School Attendance," *School Law Bulletin* 17, 1–8.

19. T. Berry Brazelton (1990), "Why Is America Failing Its Children?" *The New York Times Magazine,* November 9, pp. 40–43, 50, 90. The passage appears on p. 50.

20. *Daily Hampshire Gazette,* January 19, 1990, p. 1 and p. 8. For current statistics on family violence, see: Mary P. Koss (1990), "The Women's Mental Health Research Agenda," *American Psychologist* 45, 374–80.

21. Sandra Scarr, Deborah Phillips, and Kathleen McCartney (1990), "Facts, Fantasies, and the Future of Child Care in America," *Psychological Science* 1, 26–35. The passage appears on p. 32.

22. Kamerman, S. (n.d.). "Child Care, Women, Work, and the Family: An International Overview of Child Care Services and Related Policies," in J. Lande, S. Scarr, and N. Gunzenhauser, eds., *The Future of Child Care in the United States* (Hillsdale, N.J.: Erlbaum, forthcoming).

23. Nancy Folbre (1987), "The Pauperization of Motherhood: Patriarchy and Public Policy in the United States," in Naomi Gerstel and Harriet Gross, eds., *Families and Work,* 491–511.

24. Paul Leigh (1986), "Correlates of Absence from Work Due to Illness," *Human Relations* 39, 81–100.

25. National Commission of Working Women (1979), *National Survey of Working Women: Perceptions, Problems, and Prospects* (Washington, D.C.: Center for Women and Work, National Manpower Institute). And Harriet B. Presser (1986), "Shift Work among American Women and Child Care," *Journal of Marriage and the Family* 48, 551–63.

26. Helen Blank (1986), "The Special Needs of Single-Parent and Low-Income Families," in Nina Gunzenhauser and Bettye M. Caldwell, eds., *Group Care for Young Children,* 25–35 (New York: Johnson and Johnson Baby

Products). These figures and other similarly alarming ones appear on p. 32.

27. Sheila B. Kamerman (1983), "Child Care Service: A National Picture," *Monthly Labor Review* 106, no. 112, 35–39.

28. Earl F. Mellor (1986), "Shift Work and Flexitime: How Prevalent Are They?" *Monthly Labor Review* 109, no. 11, 14–21.

29. *Raising Kids,* September 1988 issue, p. 2.

30. Wellesley College Center for Research on Women (1990), *Research Report* 9, no. 2, 1.

31. Letty Cottin Pogrebin (1983), *Family Politics: Love and Power on an Intimate Frontier* (New York: McGraw-Hill). See especially pp. 135–36.

32. Pat Schroeder with Andrea Camp and Robyn Lipner (1989), *Champion of the Great American Family* (New York: Random House), 174.

33. Many surveys show some guilt and feelings of inadequacy. Among them: (1) Caroline Bird (1979), *The Two Paycheck Marriage* (New York: Pocket Books); (2) Julia Brannen (1987), "The Resumption of Employment after Childbirth." (3) Myra Marx Ferree (1987), "Family and Job for Working-Class Women." (4) Judith Gerson (1985), "Women Returning to School: The Consequences of Multiple Roles," *Sex Roles* 13, 77–91. (5) Ellen Hock, Karen Christman Morgan, and Michael D. Hock (1985), "Employment Decisions Made by Mothers of Infants," *Psychology of Women Quarterly* 9, 383–402.

34. Georgia Witkin-Lanoil (1984), *The Female Stress Syndrome: How to Recognize It and Live with It* (New York: Newmarket Press). The quotation is from p. 2.

35. Sylvia Ann Hewlett (1986), *A Lesser Life. The Myth of Women's Liberation in America* (New York: William Morrow). The quotation is from p. 27.

36. Patricia Gerald Bourne and Norma Juliet Wikler (1982), "Commitment and the Cultural Mandate: Women in Medicine," in Rachel Kahn-Hut, Arlene Kaplan Daniels, and Richard Colvard, eds., *Women and Work: Problems and Perspectives* (New York: Oxford University Press). Especially interesting is the shape of the argument around page 117.

37. Hochschild with Machung, *The Second Shift,* 194.

38. Margaret R. Elman and Lucia A. Gilbert (1984), "Coping Strategies for Role Conflict in Married Professional Women with Children," *Family Relations* 33, 317–27.

39. See: Diane Ehrensaft (1987), *Parenting Together: Men and Women Sharing the Care of Their Children* (New York: Free Press). Karen D. Fox and Sharon Y. Nickols (1983), "The Time Crunch: Wife's Employment and Family Work," *Journal of Family Issues* 4, 61–82.

40. Lisa Silberstein (1987), *The Dual-Career Marriage. A System in Transition.* (Ph.D., diss., Yale University). The passage is from p. 107.

41. Sheila B. Kamerman and Alfred J. Kahn (1981), *Child Care, Family Benefits, and Working Parents. A Study in Comparative Policy* (New York: Columbia University Press). The quotation is from p. 2.

42. The motto "don't agonize, organize" is attributed to Joe Hill. See: Emily Abel (1988), "Who Really Cares?" *The Women's Review of Books* 5, no. 8, p. 4.

43. That it makes sense to distinguish between the plusses and the minuses of role combination is clear from an insightful analysis of survey data, showing that role combination brings both enhancement and conflict. See: Linda Beth Tiedge, Camille B. Wortman, Geraldine Downey, Carol Emmons, Monica Bierad, and Eric Lang (1990), "Women with Multiple Roles: Role-Compatibility Perceptions, Satisfaction, and Mental Health," *Journal of Marriage and the Family* 52, 63–72.

44. Betty Rollin (1985), "Essay," in Nancy R. Newhouse, ed., *Hers: Through Women's Eyes,* 233–35 (New York: Villard Books). The passage occurs on p. 235.

45. Jessie Bernard (1976), "Change and Stability in Sex-Role Norms and Behaviors," *Journal of Social Issues* 32, no. 2, 207–23. The passage occurs on p. 222.

46. Indeed, as author Anita Shreve (1987) observes: "To continue to ignore the urgent need for reasonably priced, good-quality childcare will not make the American family resume its former shape. It will simply create a strain that may damage those families, may teach the children in those families confusing lessons about their own futures and may ultimately hurt the children in serious ways." *Remaking Motherhood: How Working Mothers Are Shaping Our Children's Future* (New York: Viking). The passage occurs on p. 209.

47. Alan Pifer (1979), "Women Working: Toward a New Society," in Karen Wolk Feinstein, ed., *Working Women and Families,* 1–33 (Beverly Hills, Calif.: Sage). The passage occurs on p. 33.

FURTHER
✦ READING ✦

From the many references cited in the chapter endnotes, I have culled
a few sources that may prove helpful for those who would like to read
further.

<small>JUGGLING</small>

General Books
BIRD, CAROLINE (1979). *The Two Paycheck Marriage*. New York: Rawson, Wade
    Publishers.
HOCHSCHILD, ARLIE with ANNE MACHUNG (1989). *The Second Shift: Working
    Parents and the Revolution at Home*. New York: Viking.
SHREVE, ANITA (1987). *Remaking Motherhood: How Working Mothers Are Shaping
    Our Children's Future*. New York: Viking.

Collections
ALDOUS, JOAN, ed. (1982). *Two Paychecks: Life in Dual-Earner Families*. Beverly
    Hills, Calif.: Sage.
CROSBY, FAYE J., ED. (1987). *Spouse, Parent, Worker. On Gender and Multiple Roles*.
    New Haven, Conn.: Yale University Press.
GERSTEL, NAOMI, AND HARRIET GROSS, eds. (1987). *Families and Work*. Philadel-
    phia: Temple University Press.
GROSSMAN, HILDRETH, AND NIA LANE CHESTER, eds. (1990). *The Experience and
    Meaning of Work in Women's Lives*. Hillsdale, N.J.: Erlbaum.

Research-Oriented Books
FERNANDEZ, JOHN P. (1986). *Child Care and Corporate Productivity. Resolving
    Family/Work Conflicts*. Lexington, Mass.: Lexington Books, D.C. Heath.
GERSON, KATHLEEN (1985). *Hard Choices: How Women Decide about Work, Career,
    and Motherhood*. Berkeley: University of California Press.
GILBERT, LUCIA ALBINO (1985). *Men in Dual-Career Families. Current Realities and
    Future Prospects*. Hillsdale, N.J.: Erlbaum.

259

HERTZ, ROSANNA (1986). *More Equal than Others: Women and Men in Dual Career Marriages*. Berkeley: University of California Press.

PLECK, JOSEPH H. (1985). *Working Wives/Working Husbands*. Beverly Hills, Calif.: Sage.

OTHER RELEVANT ISSUES

General Books and Articles

BANE, MARY JO (1980). *Here to Stay*. New York: Basic Books.

BELLE, DEBORAH (1990). "Poverty and Women's Mental Health. *American Psychologist* 45, 385–89.

————. (1982). *Lives in Stress*. Beverly Hills, Calif.: Sage.

BERGMANN, BARBARA (1986). *The Economic Emergence of Women*. New York: Basic Books.

BRAZELTON, T. BERRY (1985). *Working and Caring*. Reading, Mass.: Addison-Wesley.

EPSTEIN, CYNTHIA (1988). *Deceptive Distinctions: Sex, Gender, and the Social Order*. New Haven, Conn.: Yale University Press.

HEWLETT, SYLVIA A. (1986). *A Lesser Life. The Myth of Women's Liberation in America*. New York: William Morrow.

HOFFMAN, LOIS WLADIS (1980). "Effects of Maternal Employment in the Two Parent Family," *American Psychologist* 44, 283–92.

LEWIS, ROBERT A., and ROBERT E. SALT, eds. (1986). *Men in Families*. Beverly Hills, Calif.: Sage.

OAKLEY, ANN (1974). *Woman's Work. The Housewife, Past and Present*. New York: Random House Vintage Books.

SCARR, SANDRA (1984). *Mother Care/Other Care*. New York: Basic Books.

STACK, CAROL B. (1974). *All Our Kin. Strategies for Survival in a Black Community*. New York: Harper and Row Torchbooks.

STRICKLAND, BONNIE (1988). "Sex-Related Differences in Health and Illness. *Psychology of Women Quarterly* 12, 381–99.

WEISS, ROBERT S. (1990). *Staying the Course: The Emotional and Social Lives of Men Who Do Well at Work*. New York: Free Press.

ZIGLER, EDWARD F., and MERYL FRANK, eds. (1988). *The Parental Leave Crisis. Toward a National Policy*. New Haven, Conn.: Yale University Press.

ZIGLER, EDWARD F., and MARY E. LANG (1991). *Child Care Choices: Balancing the Needs of Children, Families, and Society*. New York: Free Press.

Research-Oriented Books and Articles

BARNETT, ROSALIND C., LOIS BIENER, and GRACE K. BARUCH, eds. *Gender and Stress*. New York: Free Press.

COLBY, ANNE, and WILLIAM DAMON (1983). "Listening to a Different Voice." *Merrill-Palmer Quarterly* 29, 473–81.

COVERMAN, SHELLEY, and JOSEPH F. SHELEY (1986). "Change in Men's Housework and Child-Care Time, 1965–1975. *Journal of Marriage and the Family* 48, 413–22.

CRAWFORD, MARY, and MARGARET GENTRY, EDS. (1989). *Gender and Thought*. New York: Springer-Verlag.

EAGLY, ALICE (1987). *Sex Differences in Social Behavior: A Social-Role Interpretation.* Hillsdale, N.J.: Erlbaum.

HARE-MUSTIN, RACHEL T., and JEANNE MARACEK (1988). "The Meaning of Difference. Gender Theory, Postmodernism, and Psychology." *American Psychologist* 43, 455–64.

HARE-MUSTIN, RACHEL T., and JEANNE MARACEK, eds. (1990). *Making a Difference. Psychology and the Construction of Gender.* New Haven, Conn.: Yale University Press.

KAMERMAN, SHEILA B., AND ALFRED J. KAHN (1987). *The Responsive Workplace: Employers and a Changing Labor Force.* New York: Columbia University Press.

KESSLER, RONALD C., and JAMES A. McRAE, Jr. (1982). "The Effect of Wives' Employment on the Mental Health of Married Men and Women." *American Sociological Review* 47, 216–27.

KIMMEL, MICHAEL S., ed. (1987), *Changing Men: New Directions in Research on Men and Masculinity.* Newbury Park, Calif.: Sage.

MACCOBY, ELEANOR (1990). "Gender and Relationships: A Developmental Account." *American Psychologist* 45, 513–20.

MACCOBY, ELEANOR E., and CAROL N. JACKLIN (1974). *The Psychology of Sex Differences.* Stanford, Calif.: Stanford University Press.

NOLAN-HOEKSAMA, SUSAN (1990). *Sex Differences in Depression.* Stanford, Calif.: Stanford University Press.

REPETTI, RENA (1987). "Individual and Common Components of the Social Environment at Work and Psychological Well-Being." *Journal of Personality and Social Psychology* 52, 710–20.

✦ INDEX ✦

263